BIG WINNERS
AND
BIG LOSERS

BIG WINNERS
AND
BIG LOSERS

THE 4 SECRETS OF LONG-TERM BUSINESS SUCCESS AND FAILURE

Alfred A. Marcus

Ideas. Action. Impact.
Wharton School Publishing

Library of Congress Cataloging-in-Publication Data

Marcus, Alfred Allen, 1950-
  Big winners and big losers : the 4 secrets of long-term business success and failure /
Alfred A. Marcus.
    p. cm.
  ISBN 0-13-145132-4
  1. Success in business--Case studies. 2. Industrial management--Case studies. 3.
Corporations--Case studies. 4. Business failures. 5. Strategic planning. 6.
Management. I. Title.
  HF5386.M3089 2006
  658.4'09--dc22
                                        2005016645

Vice President, Editor-in-Chief: Tim Moore
Wharton Editor: Yoram (Jerry) Wind
Executive Editor: Jim Boyd
Editorial Assistant: Susie Abraham
Development Editor: Russ Hall
Director of Marketing: John Pierce
International Marketing Manager: Tim Galligan
Cover Designer: Chuti Prasertsith
Managing Editor: Gina Kanouse
Project Editor: Rebecca Storbeck
Copy Editor: Karen Gill
Indexer: Lisa Stumpf
Compositor: Major Productions, Inc.
Manufacturing Buyer: Dan Uhrig

 Ideas. Action. Impact.
Wharton School
Publishing

© 2006 by Pearson Education, Inc.
Publishing as Wharton School Publishing
Upper Saddle River, New Jersey 07458

Wharton School Publishing offers excellent discounts on this book when ordered
in quantity for bulk purchases or special sales. For more information, please contact U.S. Corporate and Government Sales, 1-800-382-3419, corpsales@pearson-
techgroup.com. For sales outside the U.S., please contact International Sales at
international@pearsoned.com.

Printed in the United States of America

First Printing, October 2005

ISBN 0-13-145132-4

Pearson Education LTD.
Pearson Education Australia PTY, Limited.
Pearson Education Singapore, Pte. Ltd.
Pearson Education North Asia, Ltd.
Pearson Education Canada, Ltd.
Pearson Educatión de Mexico, S.A. de C.V.
Pearson Education—Japan
Pearson Education Malaysia, Pte. Ltd.

Receive Special Benefits by Registering This Book

Register this book today and receive exclusive benefits that you can't obtain anywhere else, including

- Access to updated lists of "big winners and big losers," explanations of how they were chosen, and feature articles about some of them to explain how they exhibit the 4 success secrets discussed in the book.

- A coupon to be used on your next purchase.

To register this book, use the following special code when you visit your My Account page on Whartonsp.com.

Special Code: fredsers1324

Note that the benefits for registering may vary from book to book. To see the benefits associated with a particular book, you must be a member and submit the book's ISBN (the ISBN is the number on the back of this book that starts with 0-13-) on the registration page.

113048

11304k

Ideas. Action. Impact.
**Wharton School
Publishing**

Baumohl, *THE SECRETS OF ECONOMIC INDICATORS*

Billingsley, *UNDERSTANDING ARBITRAGE*

Chatterjee, *FAILSAFE STRATEGIES*

Davila/Epstein/Shelton, *MAKING INNOVATION WORK*

Gupta/Lehmann, *MANAGING CUSTOMERS AS INVESTMENTS*

Hart, *CAPITALISM AT THE CROSSROADS*

Hrebiniak, *MAKING STRATEGY WORK*

Huntsman, *WINNERS NEVER CHEAT*

Kelly, *POWERFUL TIMES*

Lennick/Kiel, *MORAL INTELLIGENCE*

Mahajan/Banga, *THE 86 PERCENT SOLUTION*

Marcus, *BIG WINNERS AND BIG LOSERS*

Mittelstaedt, *WILL YOUR NEXT MISTAKE BE FATAL?*

Navarro, *THE WELL-TIMED STRATEGY*

Ohmae, *THE NEXT GLOBAL STAGE*

Pandya/Shell/Warner/Junnarkar/Brown, *NIGHTLY BUSINESS REPORT PRESENTS LASTING LEADERSHIP*

Prahalad, *THE FORTUNE AT THE BOTTOM OF THE PYRAMID*

Roberto, *WHY GREAT LEADERS DON'T TAKE YES FOR AN ANSWER*

Shane, *FINDING FERTILE GROUND*

Shenkar, *THE CHINESE CENTURY*

Sirota/Mischkind/Meltzer, *THE ENTHUSIASTIC EMPLOYEE*

Stallkamp, *SCORE!*

Urban, *DON'T JUST RELATE — ADVOCATE!*

Vogel/Cagan/Boatwright, *THE DESIGN OF THINGS TO COME*

Wind/Crook/Gunther, *THE POWER OF IMPOSSIBLE THINKING*

To my mother's family, the Freeds; to my grandfather, who came to the U.S. in 1913 at the age of 36 looking for opportunity; to my mother who came to the U.S. in 1924 at the age of 14 and escaped the inferno that engulfed relatives, known and unknown, in Europe; to my Aunt Kate and Uncle Milton, to their children and grandchildren and to my children, all of them winners in very different ways.

CONTENTS

Part 2: Winners   29

3

COMPANIES THAT KEEP WINNING   31

4

SWEET SPOTS   51

5

AGILITY   79

6

DISCIPLINE 113

Acknowledgments 339

Sources 345

Endnotes 371

Index 381

PREFACE

Companies that keep winning are rare. What maintains their momentum and accounts for their ongoing success? This book compares firms that have achieved long-term success with firms that have experienced persistent failure. It provides four secrets that explain why the winning firms have done so well. From the history of the winners, I extract the critical attributes that contributed to their performance. Each firm had a distinct pattern. Being a big winner means carrying out (i) a well-executed niche strategy that achieves a balance between (ii) agility, (iii) discipline, and (iv) focus.

Managing the tension among such attributes is not easy. Big winners bring together opposing traits. Other firms can imitate the individual traits of winning companies, but they cannot match the overall pattern. Similarly, big losers do not fail because of one or two bad qualities. Their poor performance is a consequence of a combination of many bad attributes.

Each trait that this book brings to light provides a valuable lesson in itself. Practicing managers have much to learn from this breakdown of the qualities that contribute to the creation of long-term advantage and disadvantage. The main challenge that they face, however, is in managing the tension between contrasting traits—a sweet spot and agility on the one hand, and discipline and focus on the other. The degree to which you can manage this tension influences the extent to which you can achieve long-term success.

Being a long-term winner—a dynasty rather than a mere one-time victor—is hard. From 1992 to 2002, few firms hit this mark. Only about 3 percent of the 1,000 largest U.S. corporations outperformed their industry's average market performance. About 6 percent underperformed this average. More firms performed consistently poorly than consistently well. Companies that are big winners generally operate under the radar. They are relatively unknown. They include such firms as Amphenol, Ball, Family Dollar, Brown & Brown, Activision, Dreyer's,

Forest Labs, and Fiserv. Their story has yet to be told. In comparison, companies that suffer from sustained competitive disadvantage are better known. They include such familiar names as Goodyear, the Gap, Safeco, Hasbro, and Campbell Soup.

This book reveals the secrets of the long-term better-than-industry performance of the winners. It shows distinct patterns in the 1992 to 2002 results. The differences in outcome are not random or a matter of mere chance. The circumstances that the big winners and big losers faced were similar. What explains the differences in performance is that the winners pursued and executed different strategies than the losers. In this book, I reveal how the traits of the big winners came together into larger patterns made up of a sweet spot, agility, discipline, and focus. Firms that achieved advantage wove together these elements into larger wholes. The positive aspects of the separate components supported and reinforced each other. Similarly, the negative traits of the losing firms supported and reinforced each other.

The takeaway for managers is to build your advantage one by one in a planned and logical way in which you start by understanding your company's existing traits. But you cannot stop there. You must continue with an awareness of how these separate traits fit together in broader and more comprehensive patterns. Do not lose sight of the fact that the more comprehensive patterns that create advantage and disadvantage bring together contradictory elements. You have to combine a sweet spot, agility, discipline, and focus, and you must avoid a sour spot, rigidity, ineptness, and diffuseness. This book highlights these patterns—on the one hand, a pattern of advantage that consists of a well-defined market niche achieved through agility, discipline, and focus; and, on the other hand, a pattern of disadvantage that rests on a poorly defined market niche sustained by rigidity, ineptness, and diffuseness.

How This Book Was Written

I enlisted the support of more than 500 practicing managers to write this book. They worked for such well-known multinational companies as Target, Best Buy, Guidant, Cargill, General Mills, Medtronic, Wells

Fargo, American Express, 3M, Ecolab, Boston Scientific, Honeywell, U.S. Bancorp, Piper Jaffray, Carlson Companies, West Group, Northwest Airlines, St. Paul Companies, Seagate, ADC, Intel, United Defense, Johnson Controls, Deloitte Touche, Supervalue, Polaris, Rosemount, Eaton, RBC Dain Rauscher, Unisys, Home Depot, Allina, Toro, United Health, Thrivent, Donaldson, and Ernst and Young.[1] The managers had more than seven years of work experience. Teams of five to six managers wrote reports on two firms. They compared characteristics of companies that achieved long-term success and companies that endured long-term failure. One of the companies substantially outperformed the average stock market performance of its industry for 10 years, and the other underperformed the average stock market performance of its industry for the same period. (See below for a list of these firms.)

Sector	Winner	Loser
Technology	Amphenol	LSI Logic
Manufacturing/appliance	SPX	Snap-On
Software	FiServ	Parametric
Food	Dreyer's	Campbell Soup
Drugs/chemicals	Forest Labs	IMC Global
Manufacturing/industrial	Ball	Goodyear
Financial	Brown & Brown	Safeco
Retail	Family Dollar	Gap
Entertainment/toys	Activision	Hasbro

The managers explained the reasons for the former company's sustained success and the latter company's sustained failure. To explain this difference, they examined the evolution of the companies' strategies. They obtained information from annual reports—in particular, the first section where executives discuss their strategy—and consulted other sources. A list of the sources on which they drew is found at the end of this book.

Five groups of managers were assigned to each of the nine company pairs. They addressed the following questions:

- What were the external challenges the companies faced?
- What were the internal strengths and weaknesses the companies had to meet these challenges?
- What moves did the companies make?
- Why were the moves of one of the companies more successful than the moves of the other?

The managers prepared 42 reports of about 30 pages each on nine company pairs. Following is an outline of a typical report.

Typical Report Outline

Explaining Sustained Competitive Advantage and Disadvantage: Strategies for Prolonged Business Success

- The Executive Summary states what you found. What distinguishes the companies? Why has one done so much better than the other?
- The Introduction should include a brief description of the companies, including details about their history, mission, goals, objectives, location, number of people employed, and main products and markets.
- Relevant performance statistics should be provided. Relevant is the important word.
- Identify the critical competitive challenges that the companies faced. How do the challenges differ?
- Identify the key internal strengths and weaknesses the companies had. How do these differ?
- Summarize the main moves the companies made. How did the companies choose to respond to the challenges they faced and why?
- Do an analysis of why, based on the strategies carried out, one company performed so much better than the other.
- Conclude and speculate on what you think will happen in the future.
- A reference page is required.
- Appendixes are permitted.

The managers made oral presentations based on initial drafts of their reports. During these sessions, they were subject to criticism. They were challenged to sharpen their conclusions about the traits that contributed to sustained competitive advantage and disadvantage.[2] Their

---

reports were supposed to be analytical, not descriptive. The aim was to develop a theory of why some multinationals thrived in the long term, whereas others did not.

This project started in the fall of 2002. By the spring of 2003, I had listened to three rounds of oral reports and felt I was hearing similar themes—that the big winners did much better than the big losers because (i) they occupied sweet spots, (ii) they had the agility to move into these spots, (iii) they had the discipline to protect these spots, and (iv) they had the focus to exploit and extend these spots. The big losers had the opposite characteristics. (i) They were in sour spots, (ii) they were too rigid to move out of these spots, (iii) they were inept at defending positions in which they found themselves, and (iv) they were not able to extend and exploit positions they occupied. I asked the last two groups of managers for challenges to this theory so that I could fine-tune and improve it.

The reports the managers wrote were the raw material I used to write this book. I carefully read the reports again and again and searched for consensus views. Recall that for each company pair, I had five reports.[3] I considered the reports the managers wrote to be reliable because they were written by competent practitioners who had been trained in the concepts and methods of strategic management. As a check on the findings, I did not accept information from a single report as valid unless I had additional confirmation. Through these means, I tried to eliminate errors of fact or interpretation.

Most of the insights in this book derive from the reports that the managers wrote. Their names and the companies they analyzed are listed in the Acknowledgments. The reports pointed me in certain directions, but I take full responsibility for where I ended up. The conclusions are my own. I presented the results and obtained feedback at a number of venues: Business Policy division sessions at the Academy of Management and seminars at the University of Minnesota, Arizona State University, Hong Kong Technical University, Hebrew University, the Technion, and Tel Aviv University. Both Prentice Hall and Wharton provided detailed critiques of early drafts of this book, to which I responded with substantial rewrites.[4]

This book is organized as follows. The first chapter explains why some firms continuously win and others regularly lose. Chapter 2 gives details on how the winning and losing companies were chosen. Chapters 3 through 7 provide an in-depth analysis of the winners—the sweet spots they occupied and the ways in which they exhibited agility, discipline, and focus. Chapters 8 through 12 are a parallel analysis of the losers—the sour spots they found themselves in and how they showed rigidity, ineptness, and diffuseness. Chapter 13 summarizes the main lessons. It is a code of best practices. Chapter 14 is essential reading if you want to achieve a turnaround. It tells you what to do to start a take-off and avoid a nosedive.

All along, lessons are learned and specific advice is given on what a company can do to become a big winner and avoid being a big loser. This advice is concrete, specific, and actionable. It is among the most important takeaways you will get from this book.

ABOUT THE AUTHOR

Alfred A. Marcus is currently the Edson Spencer chair of strategic management and technological leadership at the University of Minnesota, Carlson School of Management, where he has been on the faculty since 1984. From 1995 to 2001, he was the chair of the strategic management and organization department. He is the author or coeditor of 12 books and numerous articles in journals like the *Strategic Management Journal, Academy of Management Journal, Academy of Management Review, Organization Science,* and *California Management Review.* Professor Marcus received his Ph.D. from Harvard and undergraduate and graduate degrees from the University of Chicago. He has consulted or worked with many major corporations including 3M, Corning, Excel Energy, General Mills, Medtronic, and IBM.

INTRODUCTION

1

PERSISTENT WINNING AND LOSING

Many companies perform better than their competitors for short periods of time, but few are able to sustain competitive advantage over a long period.[1] Saks, for instance, provided investors with a return of 28 percent in 2003, but its average annual return over 1993 to 2003 was just 3 percent. Similarly, Supervalu's stock rocketed up 78 percent in 2003, but over 1993 to 2003, it earned just 8 percent per year.

Natural parity is the condition that prevails in most industries. Dow Chemical, Du Pont, and Rohm & Haas, for example, delivered virtually the same average annual return to investors—between 10 and 12 percent—from 1993 to 2003. Kroger's 14 percent average annual return to investors from 1993 to 2003 was little different from Safeway's 15 percent.

Dominant winners and losers are rare. Companies that consistently achieve sustained competitive advantage and disadvantage are outliers. Any firm can have a few good years, but for it to continue in its winning ways is difficult.

Hitting the mark means being a dynasty, not just having a few good years. Sustained competitive advantage (SCA) is "long-term profitability" or "above average performance in the long run."[2] It is long-term return on invested capital better than your competitors. In contrast, sustained competitive disadvantage (SCD) is long-term return on invested capital that is poorer than your competitors.

From 1992 to 2002, only about 3 percent of the 1,000 largest U.S. corporations consistently and significantly outperformed their industry's average stock market performance, and about 6 percent did the opposite. Table 1.1 lists companies that meet these criteria. Figure 1.1 shows how an investor would have fared had the investor put money into firms that hit the mark as opposed to those that missed it. (Chapter 2, "Companies That Hit and Missed the Mark," explains in more detail how these companies were chosen.) Surprisingly, the high performers were not regularly cited in popular business books or the media as exemplars. They often operated under the radar, and their stories have not been told until now.

In this book, I take a close look at these companies. I examine what they did to be big winners and losers. I compare the big winners and big losers and uncover the traits that led to their success and failure.

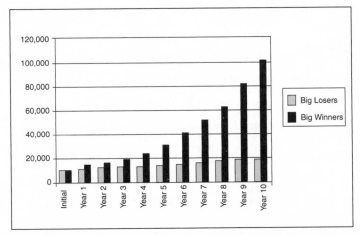

Figure 1.1 1992 to 2002 average earnings from investing in big winners as opposed to investing in big losers, assuming an initial investment of $10,000.

Table 1.1 Sustained Competitive Advantage and Disadvantage, 1992 to 20026*

9 Comparisons	18 Companies	5-Year Average Annual Market Return (%)	Sectors
Advantage	Amphenol	34.0	Technology
Disadvantage	LSI Logic	3.4	
Advantage	SPX	28.8	Manufacturing/appliance
Disadvantage	Snap-On	1.7	
Advantage	FiServ	31.2	Software
Disadvantage	Parametric	−21.2	
Advantage	Dreyers	22.4	Food
Disadvantage	Campbell Soup	−2.8	
Advantage	Forest Labs	58.5	Drugs/chemicals
Disadvantage	IMC Global	−18.7	
Advantage	Ball	23.9	Manufacturing/industrial
Disadvantage	Goodyear	−11.5	
Advantage	Brown & Brown	48.7	Financial
Disadvantage	Safeco	−1.0	
Advantage	Family Dollar	36.1	Retail
Disadvantage	Gap	9.8	
Advantage	Activision	24.1	Entertainment/toys
Disadvantage	Hasbro	−0.1	

A Sweet Spot

Winners had four qualities that led to their success. First, they were in a "sweet spot." This is a position that is so unique that they had virtually no competition.[3] Winners occupied a space that few other firms occupy. If you are in this position, you are better able to control the classic five industry forces—suppliers, competitors, customers, new entrants, and substitutes—that impact the success of your business.[4] If your company is in such a position, it is essentially a category of one, or nearly so. If your company remains as such for a considerable period, it is better able to achieve sustained competitive advantage. It offers customers something rare, hard to imitate, valuable, and nonsubstitutable.[5] It gives them something of great value that few other firms provide.

The claim that is sometimes made is that just four good spots are worth occupying. (See Figure 1.2.) A company can be a (i) narrow or (ii) broad cost leader or a (iii) narrow or (iv) broad differentiator. The conventional wisdom has been to occupy one of these four positions and avoid the middle. The middle is supposed to be a compromised position, where a firm's products or services are in no way distinct.

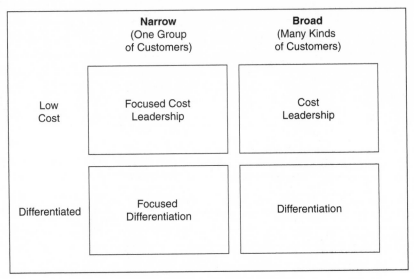

Figure 1.2 Four generic strategies.

But many companies today have moved to the middle. The position they occupy is one of best value. They combine low cost and differentiation in attractive, value-for-the-money packages. Among the examples of firms that have moved in this direction, Toyota is still one of the best. It sells inexpensive cars like the Corolla that don't have the maintenance and safety problems of earlier U.S. counterparts, such as the Corvair and Pinto. Along with other Japanese manufacturers, Toyota has demonstrated that inexpensive cars can be built well, be safe to drive, and last for years. Similarly IKEA, the Swedish retailer, has a business model based on the concept of "democratic design"—furniture that is not only inexpensive but also attractive, high quality, and extremely functional.

Agile, Disciplined, and Focused

Finding and exploiting a sweet spot means combining low cost and differentiation in striking packages that bring together exceptional value. But companies that achieve sustained competitive advantage do not just occupy sweet spots. Three other attributes are necessary for companies to be long-term winners. They must be agile, disciplined, and focused. They combine position, movement, hard-to-imitate capabilities, and concentration in hard-to-imitate packages. Agility brings these companies to sweet spots, discipline allows them to protect and defend these spots, and focus enables them to exploit the spots.

The companies that miss the mark, in contrast, migrate to or are stuck in contested or sour spots. These companies are rigid about not abandoning these spots, inept in defending and protecting them, and too diffuse to fully exploit them (see Table 1.2).

Table 1.2 The Four Secrets of Long-Term Business Success and Failure

Attribute	Advantage	Disadvantage
1. Position	Sweet spot—Being in an uncontested space	Sour spot—Being in a contested space
2. Movement	Agility—Getting to an uncontested space	Rigidity—Not getting to an uncontested space
3. Hard-to-imitate capabilities	Discipline—Protecting an uncontested space	Ineptness—Inability to protect an uncontested space
4. Concentration	Focus—Exploiting an uncontested space	Diffuseness—Inability to exploit an uncontested space

Sweet spots attract swarms of competitors. Other firms quickly move in and try to occupy the same ground. If you are in such a position, you have to have the discipline to protect it.

You must be agile to compete, but agility by itself is not enough. You must be in a position you can defend. Andy Grove recommends that companies must be "agile giants."[7] They have to have the agility to move quickly to new competitive ground, but once they occupy that ground, they must be giants who are capable of defending it. They must be able to take on all comers. A classic example of a firm unable to protect the position it occupied was Netscape.[8] In 1997, at the height of the browser wars, this company had close to 90 percent of the market. One year later, its market share was down to less than 50 percent. At first, Microsoft more or less ignored Netscape. But in December 1995, Bill Gates proclaimed that Microsoft was going to be "hard core" about the Internet. Gates was determined to break Netscape. Netscape's executives taunted Microsoft and were not prepared for Microsoft's resolve. They moved into a sweet spot but could not defend it.

Successful firms not only have an uncanny ability to move into attractive spaces, but also the discipline to protect these spots. As Porter has written, "The corporate strategist's goal is to find a position in the industry where his or her company can best defend itself."[9] Without an adequate defense, occupying a position does you little good. Movement for movement's sake gets you anywhere. You have to move to a spot you can defend.

Winning is not about achieving one-time gains. It is too demanding and difficult for this. It also does not involve digging in and defending a position against all odds. A stagnant and defensive stance where your sole aim is to protect the spot you occupy also has its limits. After you have identified, occupied, and fortified a position, you must take full advantage of it. You have to really focus on it. Of course, that takes discipline, but it is about more than discipline. You have to reap all the benefits that the spot you occupy has to offer. Focus is the ability to extend the scope and breadth of a sweet spot and reap all the benefits it has to offer. Winning companies are uniquely focused in comparison to losers. Losers never seem to find something upon which to center their attention.

This book shows you that the way to be a big winner is to identify a sweet spot with value to customers that no one else exactly provides, to move into it (be agile), to protect it (be disciplined), and to extend it (be focused).

A firm must possess all these qualities. (See Figure 1.3.) It must be *agile*—not entirely bound by the past, but free to reinvent itself for an uncertain future by moving into new territory. It must have the *discipline* to cultivate the strengths and competencies it needs to protect the space it occupies. Also, it must have the *focus* to define and expand that space. To achieve sustained competitive advantage, you must be more than agile. You have to have momentum to keep moving, and you must defend where you are at. You also must be expansive and be able to deepen and expand the space you inhabit.

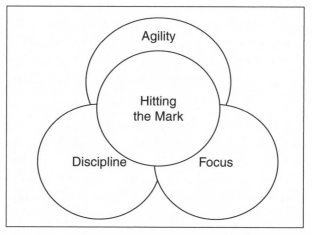

Figure 1.3 Big winners hit the mark.

To be a big winner, you must understand what you stand for; otherwise, you'll fall for everything. Say yes to some possibilities and no to others. Winning firms do not deviate from what they do best. They choose an area where they have comparative advantage and stick to it. They take full advantage of it. They have the agility to find a sweet spot, the discipline to protect it, and the focus to exploit it. Losing firms have the opposite characteristics—rigidity that leaves them in a contested or "sour spot," ineptness, and diffuseness.

These traits are complicated to develop in a single company. They contradict one another. They must be woven into patterns that are hard to copy and especially valuable because they are complex and distinctive. The characteristic patterns of the winners and losers are explored in subsequent chapters. Appendix D, "Patterns of Winning and Losing Companies," is a summary of these distinctive patterns. This book will help you understand how your company measures up. What are its strengths and weaknesses? Is it in a sweet spot? Does it have agility, discipline, and focus? If it is in a sour spot and is rigid, inept, or diffuse, what can it do to improve?

Managing the Tension

There is built-in tension to hitting the mark. **Agility** means maintaining the flexibility to change direction quickly, whereas **discipline** and **focus** imply the opposite—digging in, reinforcing, and securing a space, and refusing to budge or give it up until all the benefits have been reaped. The tension between agility on the one hand and discipline and focus on the other has to be managed creatively.[10] If managed well, you have realized one of the rarest, most valuable, and hardest-to-reproduce capabilities that your firm can possess. (See Table 1.3.)[11]

If the tension among agility, discipline, and focus is not managed well, you might have a disaster on your hands. An example of a company that did not manage this tension well was Xerox. The personal computer (PC) revolution came about because of innovations made in the 1980s at Xerox's Menlo Park research division.[12] Prior to the 1980s, its research division pioneered in almost all the building blocks that went into the PC, from the mouse to the printer. Years after Xerox played a substantial role in inventing these devices, it still was in the copying business. It saw no profits from these efforts. It did not have the agility to move to a new position.

When you find a sweet spot, you cannot let internal politics keep you from taking advantage of it. You must move into the space and occupy it. If you know about a sweet spot and do nothing, what good have you done?

Managing the tension among agility, focus, and discipline is paradoxical. To be successful, you have to explore for new territory, but you also have to exploit the ground you currently hold.[13] You have to prospect for new businesses while defending the positions you presently occupy.[14] You have to be a constant analyzer on the lookout for new ground to occupy, while protecting the spaces you currently hold. Doing all of this well and at the same time is a formidable undertaking that strains even the best management teams.

It is rare for a company to be able to do all of this simultaneously. Thus, it is rare for companies to persist in their winning ways for long.

Keep in mind that your firm is always operating in a state of tension between what it is now and what it is trying to become. Thus, you must have a mission that expresses pride in what your firm has been good at in the past and a vision that serves as a roadmap for where you would like to go in the future. You are constantly tugged and pulled apart by the poles of what you have been, what you are good at and what got you to where you are today, and what you would like to be.

Future conditions are unclear, and you need to have options for whatever contingency arises. If you want to achieve sustained competitive advantage, you must keep at least three horizons in the forefront simultaneously. You have to defend your core business, build emerging businesses, and create real options for future growth. [15]

Table 1.3 Big Winners Manage the Tension Among Agility, Discipline, and Focus

A Sweet Spot	Agility (Move)	Discipline (Protect)	Focus (Extend)
Goal	Achieve growth	Enhance profits	Realize profits and grow
	Innovation	Efficiency	Reform and refinement
	Reinvention	Operational excellence	Fine-tuning
Actions	Explore	Exploit	Explore and exploit
	Prospect	Defend	Analyze
Strategies	Vision	Mission	Mission-vision
Conditions	Disequilibrium	Equilibrium	Equilibrium-disequilibrium
Technologies	Disruptive	Sustaining	Sustaining-disruptive
Industries	Dynamic	Static	Dynamic-static
Image of the Future	Unpredictable	Like today	Gradually evolving
People	Revolutionaries	Controllers	Improvers
	Break rules	*Enforce rules*	*Fix rules*

Creating future options is where agility plays its primary role. It means building emerging businesses. Discipline means sharpening what you currently do best, while focus means reaping the full benefits of the activities in which you are currently involved. An example comes from the automotive industry. A company today must concentrate on the internal combustion engine and its associated technologies to meet current profitability goals. It has to have the discipline to do so efficiently and effectively. The competition in today's markets is brutal. But an automotive company must go beyond today's technologies and start to market hybrids that combine current technology with lighter and more aerodynamic materials, electric engines, and regenerative braking. And even this is not enough. A company must look further into the future and be open to a different tomorrow by undertaking research and development on hydrogen-based fuel and fuel cell technologies. An automotive company must consider these three horizons simultaneously and manage them concurrently, but concurrent management is not easy.

Concurrent management is a juggling act of immense proportions that helps to explain why being a big winner is so hard. You want to thrive today and plan for tomorrow and for the day after.

Winning companies put together the attributes of agility, discipline, and focus into larger wholes that allow them to function well today and to plan for tomorrow and the day after. Losing companies combine rigidity, ineptness, and diffuseness, which make it impossible for them to do well today, tomorrow, or the next day.

Real Trade-Offs

Winning firms face real trade-offs. For example, if a firm is agile, it must be constantly ready to move. It has to be able and willing to abandon the space it currently inhabits for something better. If it is disciplined, on the other hand, it foregoes the capacity to rapidly morph into something else. If it is focused, it deepens its commitment to the space it currently occupies.

Of the 1,000 largest U.S. firms from 1992 to 2002 (see Chapter 2), only about 3 percent were big winners. Another 6 percent did the exact opposite—they endured the pain of regularly losing. The ability to manage the tension of moving, protecting, and extending a sweet spot is hard. If it were easy, everyone would do it, and it would be of little value. The fact that it is so hard to do is the best indication of the contribution it makes to the creation of enduring advantage. Because enduring advantage is so uncommon, it is very difficult to do.

The problem has been that until now, gurus of one sort or another have put too much emphasis on just some of these qualities—either agility or discipline and focus. (See Appendix A, "Best Sellers Compared.") Yet the truth of the matter is that you must do it all. Excessive movement and excessive staying put are not the way to stand out. Too much agility would be just as problematic as too much discipline and focus. Distinction comes from achieving the right balance. It derives from properly managing this tension.

Winners achieve sustained competitive advantage a step at a time by cultivating qualities that capture aspects of agility, discipline, and focus. They fashion unique patterns of these attributes. Losers, on the other hand, engage in the opposite process. One by one, they accumulate the negative qualities that lead to their demise.

In Summary

Achieving sustained competitive advantage is not easy. You cannot dismiss any element. A sweet spot, agility, discipline, and focus are essential. Although managers might be able to identify future opportunities, few have the agility to move into them, the discipline to protect them, and the focus to take full advantage of them.

The firms that hit the mark showed an uncanny ability to do all this. One by one, they built an ensemble of positive traits. When the traits came together, they had a powerful force. Similarly, the losing firms took individual steps that fused together patterns of rigidity, ineptness, and diffuseness that were a deadly combination.

The next chapter describes how the big winners and losers that were analyzed were selected. The four factors that led to their success are discussed in Chapters 3 through 7. Then I turn my attention to the losers. The traits that led to their undoing are described in Chapters 8 through 12. The conclusions in Chapter 13 are based on a comparison of the successful and unsuccessful firms. This chapter is a coda of best practices for hitting the mark. You can use it to assess your own firm (or perhaps use it to choose a portfolio of firms in which you want to invest). The final chapter touches on turnarounds—sweet and sour companies that changed course. It explains what you have to do to start a take-off and avoid a nosedive.

2

COMPANIES THAT HIT AND MISSED THE MARK

To choose the companies that were big winners and big losers, I used the stock market as an indicator of performance (See Appendix B, "Using the Stock Market as an Indicator of Performance," for my reasons).[1] For a company to be a big winner, its ten-, three-, and one-year average annual market return had to exceed the average of its industry, and its five-year average annual return had to be more than double the industry's average.[2] Companies that missed the mark had the opposite characteristics. Their ten-, three-, and one-year average annual market returns were below their industry's average, and their five-year average annual return was less than half the industry average.

Using these criteria, neither being a big winner nor being a big loser was common. Missing the mark was easier than hitting it.

The winning and losing companies are listed in Tables 2.1 and 2.2. Of the 1,000 companies in the Wall Street Journal Shareholder *Scorecard, only 32 were big winners. The losers had double the number of firms (64) as the winners. That means that 3.2 percent of the firms listed on the Wall Street Journal Scorecard achieved sustained competitive advantage (SCA), and 6.4 percent endured the opposite. Most companies fell in the middle. Their prior five-year average annual returns were neither outstanding nor terrible.*

Table 2.1 Winning Companies: 1992 to 2002

Firm	5-Year Average Return(%)	Industry	5-Year Average Return(%)	Firm	5-Year Average Return(%)	Industry	5-Year Average Return(%)
1. Titan	49.2	Aerospace	10.7	17. Concord EFS	39.2	Industrial service	14.3
2. Alliant Tech	25.9	Aerospace	10.7	18. Fiserv	31.2	Industrial service	14.3
3. Skywest	49.8	Airlines	10.9	19. Lincoln National	16.3	Insurance life	6.1
4. Southwest	33.7	Airlines	10.9	20. Brown & Brown	45.7	Insurance property and casualty	14.7
5. Gentex	21.6	Auto parts	4.7	21. Gallagher	38.5	Insurance property and casualty	14.7
6. Johnson Controls	16.4	Auto parts	4.7	22. White Mountain	30.5	Insurance property and casualty	14.7
7. Commerce Banc	32.0	Banks	14.1	23. Murphy Oil	14.2	Oil secondary	5.8
8. IDEC	77.1	Biotech	37	24. Forest Labs	58.5	Pharmaceutical	27.9
9. Int Game Tech	30.5	Casinos	10.5	25. Donaldson	19.6	Pollution control	9.5
10. Cabot	21.7	Chemicals specialty	6.3	26. Harley-Davidson	36.3	Recreational	7.9
11. Amphenol	34.0	Communication technology	14.0	27. Family Dollar	36.1	Retail, broad line	12.3
12. Ball	23.9	Containers and packaging	3.7	28. Best Buy	94.8	Retail, specialty	23.0
13. Bemis	8.5	Containers and packaging	3.7	29. Activision	24.8	Toys	12.2
14. SPX	28.8	Electronic components	14.2	30. Semtech	75.5	Semiconductor	25.4
15. Dreyer's	22.4	Food products	8.8	31. RGS Energy	22.1	Utility electric	10.4
16. Stanley Works	14.5	House products durable	5.9	32. Equitable Resources.	21.9	Utility gas	10.4

Table 2.2 Losing Companies: 1992 to 2002

Firm	5-Year Average Return (%)	Industry	5-Year Average Return (%)	Firm	5-Year Average Return (%)	Industry	5-Year Average Return (%)
1. Goodrich	−5.1	Aerospace	10.7	33. FMC	−3.2	Industrial diversified	10.2
2. Raytheon	−5.5	Aerospace	10.7	34. Conseco	−31.7	Insurance life	6.1
3. AMR	3	Airlines	10.9	35. Safeco	−1.0	Insurance, property, and casualty	14.7
4. Delta	−3.6	Airlines	10.9	36. CNA Financial	−3.9	Insurance, property, and casualty	14.7
5. TRW	−3.1	Auto and parts	4.7	37. American Financial Group	−5.2	Insurance, property, and casualty	14.7
6. Goodyear	−11.5	Auto and parts	4.7	38. Bausch & Lomb	3.8	Medical supplies	17.8
7. Dana	−12.5	Auto and parts	4.7	39. Amerada Hess	2.7	Oil secondary	5.8
8. Old National	6.6	Banks	14.1	40. Kerr-McGee	−2.1	Oil secondary	5.8
9. Bank One	3.3	Banks	14.1	41. Forest Oil	−4.4	Oil secondary	5.8
10. KeyCorp	3.2	Banks	14.1	42. Burlington Resources	−4.4	Oil secondary	5.8
11. Alkermes	17.8	Biotech	37	43. Halliburton	−14.2	Oil drilling	4.8
12. VerTex	4.1	Biotech	37	44. Merck	10	Pharmaceutical	27.9
13. Disney	−1.5	Broadcasting	32.3	45. Pharmacia	4.4	Pharmaceutical	27.9
14. Mandalay Resort	−9.0	Casinos	10.5	46. Waste Management	0.1	Pollution control	9.5
15. IMC Global	−18.7	Chemical specialty	6.3	47. Belo	2.8	Publishing	11.5

Table 2.2 Losing Companies: 1992 to 2002

16. Broadwing	-4.7	Communications fixed	8.9	48. Reader's Digest	-8.8	Publishing	11.5
17. Compaq	-7.7	Computers	16.6	49. Eastman Kodak	-15.7	Recreational	7.9
18. Franklin Res, Inc.	9.8	Diversified financials	26.2	50. Wendy's	8.5	Restaurants	20.1
19. Country Wide	8.5	Diversified financials	26.2	51. McDonald's	3.8	Restaurants	20.1
20. Cooper Industries	-0.7	Electronic components	14.2	52. Gap	9.8	Retail apparel	23.7
21. Conagra	2.1	Food product	8.8	53. Nordstrom	4.1	Retail apparel	23.7
22. ADM	-2.3	Food product	8.8	54. Saks	-12.7	Retail apparel	23.7
23. Campbell Soup	-2.8	Food product	8.8	55. Kmart	-12.0	Retail broadline	12.1
24. Tyson	-11.9	Food product	8.8	56. T. Rowe Price	11.3	Securities	26.3
25. Winn-Dixie	-11.7	Food retail	15.1	57. Coca-Cola Co.	-1.1	Soft drinks	4.3
26. Georgia Pacific	3.5	Forest product	7.2	58. Novell	-13.5	Software	18.4
27. HealthSouth	-5.2	Healthcare	13.1	59. Parametric	-21.2	Software	18.4
28. Humana	-9.1	Healthcare	13.1	60. Hasbro	-0.1	Toys	12.2
29. Snap-On	1.7	House products durable	5.9	61. Mattel	-8.0	Toys	12.2
30. Newell Rubber	-0.3	House products durable	5.9	62. LSI Logic	3.4	Semiconductors	25.4
31. Honeywell	1.7	Industrial diversified	10.2	63. Constellation Energy	4.6	Utilities electricity	10.4
32. Textron	0.6	Industrial diversified	10.2	64. CMS Energy	-2.4	Utilities electricity	10.4

Characteristics of Winners and Losers

The big winners and the big losers that I found in this way were a surprising lot. Many of the companies that I identified as big winners are not well known. The most recognizable are Southwest Airlines, Harley-Davidson, and Best Buy, but they also include Brown & Brown, IDEC, and Family Dollar. In contrast, the big losers are more well known. They include such familiar names as Disney, Bank One, Halliburton, Merck, Kodak, McDonald's, Nordstrom, and Coca-Cola.

Following are some findings about the winning and losing firms:

- Big winners and big losers are found in 41 industries. In another 37 industries, no firm stands out as being especially better or worse than the pack. (See Appendix C, "Additional Data on the Companies.")

- Industries that have companies that are big winners or big losers are larger than those that do not have them. The industries that had big winners or big losers had on average 19.4 companies compared to 6.2 companies in industries that did not have big winners or big losers. In large industries, there is more room to find sweet spots. There is more empty space for differentiation and the creation of special industry subcategories and niches where the competition is less stiff. In large industries, it is also easier to hide under the radar.

- Big winners were smaller than big losers (about a third the size). They employed an average of 14,496 people compared to 48,032 persons in big losers. Their average revenue was $3.49 billion compared to $10.66 billion in the losing companies. Being small makes it easier for a firm to escape detection and avoid competitive retaliation. Smaller firms are more agile.

- The industries that had big winners and big losers had higher average market returns than the industries that did not have these firms—15.1 percent in industries with big winners or losers compared to 12.7 percent in industries without these companies. Thus, the potential for profit and loss was somewhat greater in the arenas in which the big winners and losers were competing.

Overall, large industries with small firms and more risk—more potential for profit and loss—were more likely to have highly successful and unsuccessful firms. Small industries with large firms had less potential for profit and loss and were less likely to have big winners or big losers.[3] Indeed, 17 industries had no big winners, just losers.[4] Five industries had the opposite characteristics.[5] They only had big winners. Eight industries were evenly divided with one big winner and one big loser.[6]

Time and Industry as Reference Points

The reference points I used in selecting the big winners and big losers were time (1992 to 2002) and the *Wall Street Journal* Scorecard designation of industry.[7] But the selection of 1992 to 2002 as the time period and the use of the *Wall Street Journal's* classifications are somewhat arbitrary.[8] Many anomalies exist. Is Eastman Kodak in the recreational business, with its competitors being Harley-Davidson and Polaris, in accord with the *WSJ* classification?

Tables C.4 and C.5 in Appendix C rely on *Fortune's* classification rather than the *WSJ*. The time period is 1993 to 2003, not 1992 to 2002. *Fortune* has 71 industry groups as opposed to the *WSJ's* 78. Not all the big winners or the big losers in the *WSJ Scorecard* are large enough to make the *Fortune*1000. To be included, revenues have to exceed $1.1 billion. Because the big winners are smaller than the big losers, 14 winning companies are not on the *Fortune* list, and six losing firms are missing. In addition, some firms such as Compaq, which merged with HP in 2002, and IDEC, which merged with Biogen, are not on the *Fortune* list.

Nonetheless, when relying on the *Fortune* list, nearly 90 percent of the big winners and the big losers I chose continued to outperform or underperform their industry averages. There were three ties—on the winning side, Lincoln National, and on the losing side, AMR and Conagra.[9] These results suggest that hitting and missing the mark are rare no matter how performance is measured, and performance is fairly persistent regardless of the classification scheme or the period considered.

Continued Outstanding Performance

To determine whether a company should be subjected to further analysis in the chapters that follow, I applied another test. Did the performance differences observed from 1992 to 2002 persist after that point? The companies analyzed in subsequent chapters had to outperform or underperform their industries in the six months following January 1, 2002.

This test was stringent because the market declined sharply from January 1 to June 1. The performance of most companies dropped off, including that of the big winners. They were not immune to the bust in the stock market. Johnson Controls and Harley-Davidson, for instance, did not survive this test of continued sustained competitive advantage. However, Amphenol and Family Dollar did. Of the 32 firms in Table 2.1, more than half (18) dropped out due to the application of this criterion.

Nine big winners that survived this test are the subject of further analysis in this book. (See Table 2.3.) Big losers had opposite characteristics. (See Table 2.4.) Big winners consistently beat their industry averages, and big losers consistently lagged behind not only in the ten-year period but in the immediate six months following it. With regard to five-year returns, the superiority of the big winners was most marked, double that of their industry, as was the weakness of the big losers, which was just half that of their industry.

Keep in mind that big winners and big losers were not necessarily best or worst performers overall. They exceeded or fell behind an industry target at one-, three-, five-, and ten-year intervals. Nonetheless, in comparison to all companies, some big winners subject to further analysis in this book did do extremely well. The three best in terms of overall performance were Activision, Forest Labs, and Brown & Brown.

- Among all companies on the *Wall Street Journal* Scoreboard, Activision had the second best 10-year average return (63.7 percent) and the ninth best 1-year (158 percent) average return.

- Forest Labs had the twenty-first best 5-year average return (58.5 percent).

- Brown & Brown had the forty-fifth best 10-year average return (31.9 percent) and the forty-sixth best 5-year average return (45.7 percent).
- In comparison to industry averages, Ball had the best 5-year mark. The average return in the packaging and container industry was 3.7 percent, but Ball scored an average return of 23.9 percent.

Big losers were among the poorest performing firms.

- Among all companies on the *Wall Street Journal* Scoreboard, Parametric had the fourth worst 5-year average return (–21.2 percent) and the thirty-fifth worst 3-year average return (–21.7 percent).
- IMC had the fifth worst 10-year (–6.4 percent) average return and the sixth worst 5-year average return (–18.7 percent).
- The Gap (–65.2 percent) had the twenty-third worst 3-year average return.
- Goodyear (–18.9 percent) had the forty-eighth worst 3-year average return.

Note the well-known names among big losers—Campbell, Goodyear, Safeco, and the Gap—and the absence of well-known names among big winners. The winning firms were more likely to fly under the radar than the losers.

Table 2.3 Winning Companies Used in the Analysis: 1992 to 2002 Performance

Company	Industry	Sector	One-Year Return (%)	3-Year Average Return (%)	5-Year Average Return (%)	10-Year Average Return (%)	Continues to Beat Industry Average (January Through June 2002)
1. Amphenol	Communications technology	Technology	22.6	47.1	34.0	26.7	Yes
	Industry Average		−40.1	5.1	14.0	26.0	
2. SPX	Electronics components	Manufacturing/appliance	26.5	26.9	28.8	27.9	Yes
	Industry Average		2.6	9.3	14.2	13.8	
3. Fiserv	Industrial services	Software	33.8	22.8	31.2	23.9	Yes
	Industry Average		12.3	8.3	14.3	18.0	
4. Dreyer's	Food products	Food	20.4	37.5	22.4	9.2	Yes
	Industry Average		15.2	3.8	8.8	8.4	
5. Forest Labs	Pharmaceuticals	Drugs/chemicals	23.3	45.5	58.5	23.0	Yes
	Industry Average		−5.7	21.1	27.9	17.4	
6. Ball	Packaging and containers	Manufacturing/industrial	55.3	17.3	23.9	10.2	Yes
	Industry Average		37.6	−1.1	3.7	7.6	
7. Brown & Brown	Property and casualty insurance	Financial	57.1	47.8	45.7	31.9	Yes
	Industry Average		1.8	11.9	14.7	16.7	
8. Family Dollar	Retailers, broadline	Retail	41.1	12.0	36.1	20.0	Yes
	Industry Average		29.2	1.5	12.1	11.1	
9. Activision	Toys	Entertainment/toys	158.0	51.9	24.8	63.7	Yes
	Industry Average		68.0	15.2	12.2	25.5	

Table 2.4 Losing Companies Used in the Analysis: 1992 to 2002 Performance

Company	Industry	Sector	One-Year Return (%)	3-Year Average Return (%)	5-Year Average Return (%)	10-Year Average Return (%)	Continues to Lag Industry Average (January Through June 2002)
1. LSI Logic	Semiconductors	Technology	-7.7	25.1	3.4	22.8	Yes
	Industry Average		7.5	28.4	25.4	29.3	
2. Snap-On	Durable household products	Manufacturing/appliance	24.9	2.1	1.7	7.6	Yes
	Industry Average		27.2	2.8	5.9	8.1	
3. Parametric Technology	Software	Software	-41.9	-21.7	-21.2	7.6	Yes
	Industry Average		-5.5	15.3	18.4	16.9	
4. Campbell Soup	Food products	Food	-11.3	-16.3	-2.8	6.3	Yes
	Industry Average		15.2	3.8	8.8	8.4	
5. IMC Global	Chemicals, specialty	Drugs/chemicals	-15.9	-13.9	-18.7	-6.4	Yes
	Industry Average		21.2	6.7	6.3	10.3	
6. Goodyear	Automobiles and parts	Manufacturing/industrial	8.0	-18.9	-11.5	1.3	Yes
	Industry Average		26.2	-4.7	4.7	12.9	
7. Safeco	Property and casualty insurance	Financial	-2.3	-6.1	-1.0	6.1	Yes
	Industry Average		1.8	11.9	14.7	16.7	
8. Gap	Retailers, apparel	Retail	-45.1	-65.2	9.8	6.6	Yes
	Industry Average		20.2	3.9	23.7	11.6	
9. Hasbro	Toys	Entertainment/toys	54.1	-11.2	-0.1	4.1	Yes
	Industry Average		68.0	15.2	12.2	25.5	

How Market Leaders Create Shareholder Value

As argued in Chapter 1, "Persistent Winning and Losing," being in a sweet spot means that you can carve out a niche that is nearly uninhabited.[10] The big winners showed investors that they had the agility to move to a sweet spot, the discipline to protect it, and the focus to exploit it. (See Figure 2.1)

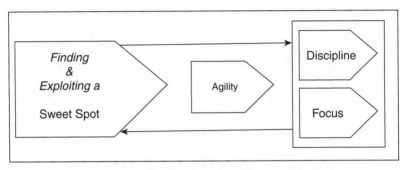

Figure 2.1 Showing investors that you are in a
sweet spot and that your firm has agility, discipline, and focus.

Performance reflects investors' understanding of your accomplishments and what you intend to do. Although based on fact, it is a socially constructed reality. To be successful in influencing the perceptions of investors, you must define a competitive space into which you move and show how you can protect and achieve dominance within it. If you can convey what you are trying to do and manage the performance expectations of analysts, you can build confidence that translates into ongoing success.[11] This type of confidence depends on these factors:

- **Strategic intent**—Strategic intent is what you would like others to think your company is doing. It is expressed in public documents like annual reports, especially in the company's 10K, and in other pronouncements that come from you and your top management teams.

- **Evidence of feedback and reconsideration**—You must show that you have a good grasp of what your company has done and the results it has achieved. Do your explanations suggest that you really know what you are doing?

You have to be a credible communicator. Do you possess the qualities shown in Figure 2.1 and the evidence to back it up? That is your challenge.

In Summary

This chapter has shown that firms that are big winners and firms that are big losers are hard to find. Being a big winner is harder than being a big loser. Some industries have no firms that are big winners or big losers. Firms that are big winners are concentrated in large industries; in large industries, there is more open space for finding a sweet spot. Big winners are smaller than big losers. Small firms are more agile than large firms. Their smallness makes it easier for them to escape detection. They are more likely to avoid competitive retaliation. Big winners and big losers are in industries with higher market returns. The potential profits are greater. There is more risk and more opportunity.

The next chapter examines big winners that have been selected for further analysis. (See Table 2.3.) Chapters 4 through 7 show how executives in these firms demonstrated that their companies were in sweet spots and had agility, discipline, and focus. These firms built up patterns of effective managerial traits, each by itself of some value, but when combined of infinitely greater worth. The combined traits of the sustained competitive disadvantage firms, on the other hand, were evidence of their being in sour spots and their being rigid, inept, and diffuse (Chapters 9 through 12).

WINNERS

3

COMPANIES THAT
KEEP WINNING

This chapter describes nine big winners. (See Table 2.3 in Chapter 2, "Companies That Hit and Missed the Mark.") Their strategies will be analyzed in depth in chapters 4-7. These firms were selected based on the following criteria:

- *As of January 1, 2002, the big winners' ten-year, five-year, three-year, and one-year average annual market returns exceeded that of their industry.*

- *Their five-year average annual market return was double or more than double their industry average.*

- *Their six-month average return, January 1 to June 1 of 2002, was greater than that of their industry.*

I provide information about the industries in which these companies competed, the products they sold, and their competitors. The sweet spots they occupied and the traits of agility, discipline, and focus they exhibited are analyzed in more detail in later chapters.

Amphenol

Amphenol, according to the *Wall Street Journal* Scoreboard, is in the telecommunications technology industry. This industry is large—it was composed of 31 companies—and it had fairly good returns. In this way, Amphenol is a typical big winner.

Average annual returns in the telecommunications technology industry from 1997 to 2002 were 14 percent. Amphenol was the only big winner in the telecommunications technology industry. Its 1997 to 2002 average annual returns were 34 percent.

Amphenol makes high-performance application-specific connectors, interconnect systems, and cable. These products have many uses, including wireless, Internet networking, mobile phones, modems, cable TV, servers, data storage devices, PCs, peripheral equipment, and integrated circuit boards. Amphenol's sales have encompassed not only telecommunications technology, which made up about 50 percent of its revenues in 2002, but also the industrial and aerospace markets, which made up another 50 percent of its revenues. (See Table 3.1.)

Of the 31 companies in the telecommunications technology industry, only Corning and Andrew were direct competitors. (See Table 3.2.) Commscope, Molex, and Tyco competed with Amphenol in the electronic instruments and controls sector. (See Table 3.3.) Other companies that competed with it in some of the diverse sectors in which Amphenol operated were Alcatel, Pirelli, Sumitumo (see Table 3.4), and Tyco. All of these are larger firms than Amphenol.

Table 3.1 Amphenol's Primary Markets

Type of Markets	Telecommunications Technology	Industrial/Automotive: Electronic Instruments and Controls	Commercial and Military Aerospace: Electronic Instruments and Controls
Sales % in 2002	52%	23%	25%
Primary end applications	Wireless handsets and personal communication devices Base stations and wireless and telecommunications infrastructure Video, cable television networks, and set converters Cable modems, servers, and storage systems Computers, PCs, and related peripherals Data networking	Factory automation Instrumentation and medical systems Automobile safety systems and other on-board electronics Mass transportation Oil exploration Off-road construction	Military and commercial aircraft: • Avionics • Engine controls • Flight controls • Passenger-related systems Missile systems Battlefield communications Satellite and space station programs

Table 3.2 Telecommunications Technology Industry

Company Name	One-Year Return (%)	Three-Year Average Return (%)	Five-Year Average Return (%)	Ten-Year Average Return (%)
Amphenol	22.6	47.1	34.0	26.7
Corning	−83.0	−15.4	−6.1	−0.3
Andrew	0.6	9.9	−9.2	20.6
Industry Group Average	−20.1	5.1	14.0	26.0

Table 3.3 Competitors of Amphenol

	Amphenol	Commscope	Molex	Tyco
Employees	13,900	4,500	17,275	258,600
Revenue ($)	1.32B*	678.95M**	2.09B	38.81B
Operating margins	16.74%	−4.50%	7.18%	9.98%

As of June 2003
* B=billion
** M=million

Table 3.4 Other Competitors of Amphenol (Identified in the Company's 2002 Annual Report)

Company	Fiscal 2002 Revenues	Products/Services
Alcatel (France)	E16.5 billion*	Terrestrial and submarine optical networks, public switching, and GSM portable phones
Pirelli S.P.A. (Italy)	E16.5 billion	Tire, wire, and cable
Sumitumo (Japan)	$11.98 billion	Electric wires and cables
Smiths Group PLC (UK)	E4.9 billion	Aerospace, medical, sealing solutions, and industrial markets
Wesco International, Inc. (U.S.)	$3,325 million	Distributor of electrical supplies and services
Thomas & Betts Corp. (U.S.)	$1,345 million	Electrical and electronic connectors and components
Cable Design Technologies Corp (U.S.)	$553.8 million	Copper cables, fiber optic, structured wiring systems, and cable management solutions
Aeroflex Inc. (U.S.)	$202.6 million	Microelectronic module, integrated circuits, interconnect and testing solutions

*E=Euro

SPX

SPX, according to the *Wall Street Journal* Scoreboard, is in the electric components and equipment industry, which is a relatively small industry. In 1992, the electric components and equipment industry had 14 companies. Returns in this industry were similar to those in other industries with big winners or losers. SPX, with average annual returns of 28.8 percent, was the only big winner in the electric components and equipment industry.

SPX had its start in specialty tools (this is similar to Snap-On; see Chapter 8, "Companies That Keep Losing"), but it moved rapidly from sole reliance on specialty tools to engineering and systems design. It competed in four areas of engineering and design. The first was industrial products (32 percent of its revenues in 2002). This segment included power systems and compaction equipment. The second was flow technology (27 percent of revenues in 2002). This segment included cooling technology and fluid power systems. The third segment was technical products (27 percent of revenues in 2002). It included lab, life sciences, security and safety systems, broadcast and communication systems, and electrical test and measurement products. The final segment in which SPX competed was specialty tools (14 percent of revenues in 2002). The company was broadly diversified, but even after its diversification, it continued to do business in specialty tools.

SPX sold to many industries, including chemical processing, pharmaceutical, mineral processing, petrochemical, telecom, financial services, transportation, and power generation. Somewhat similar firms in the miscellaneous capital goods sector (see Table 3.5) included United Technology, ABB, and Bosch. All of them were considerably larger than SPX.

Table 3.5 Competitors of SPX

	SPX	ABB	Robert Bosch Corporation (Privately Held)	United Technologies Corp
Employees	22,200	116,000	25,000[1]	203,300
Revenue ($)	5.27B*	18.80B	5.59B[2]	32.98B
Operating margins	10.08%	3.49%	N/A	10.92%

[1] = As of 2002
[2] = As of 2003
*B=billion

Fiserv

Fiserv is in the industrial services industry, an industry that had 36 companies. Industrial services was almost twice as large as other industries with big winners or losers. The mean annual returns in the industry, 14.3 percent from 1997 to 2002, were about the same as other industries with this type of company. Mean annual returns in industrial services also were similar to those in telecommunications technology and electric components and equipment, the industries in which Amphenol and SPX competed.

Fiserv had three competitors in the industrial services industry. One of them, Concord EFS, also achieved sustained competitive advantage. (See Table 3.6.) However, from January 1 to June 1 of 2002, Concord

EFS did not continue to outperform its industry. Therefore, it was excluded from further analysis. Fiserv's average annual returns from 1997 to 2002 were 31.2 percent, which is significantly better than the industry average of 14.3 percent.

Table 3.6 Industrial Services Industry

Company Name	One-Year Return (%)	Three-Year Average Return (%)	Five-Year Average Return (%)	Ten-Year Average Return (%)
Concord EFS	49.2	32.4	39.2	40.3
Fiserv	33.8	22.8	31.2	23.9
Equifax	43.2	7.3	9.4	21.1
Convergys	−17.3	18.8	N/A	N/A
Industry Group Average	12.3	8.3	14.3	18.0

Fiserv offered financial institutions outsourcing and back office systems, services, and support. It had data processing solutions for transactions, checks, securities clearing, and other activities in which its customers were engaged. Its specialized systems for the development, enhancement, and maintenance of applications software were sold to banks, security brokers, insurance companies, investment advisers, mutual funds, underwriters, and bond dealers. A breakdown of Fiserv's revenues by customer category is found in Figure 3.1.

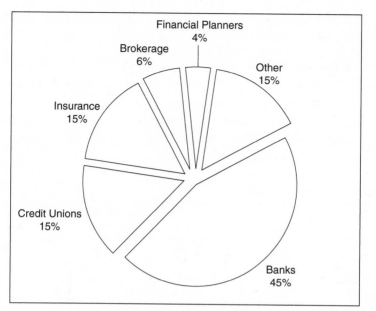

Figure 3.1 Fiserv's revenues by customer category.

Some of Fiserv's competitors are found in Table 3.7.

Table 3.7 Competitors of Fiserv

	Fiserv	BISYS Group	Metavante Corporation (Private Firm Subsidiary)	Total System Services, Inc.
Employees	21,700	4,900	N/A	5,185
Revenue ($)	3.28B*	998.68M**	662.30M[1]	1.09B
Operating margins	17.18%	16.80%	N/A	17.62%

[1]=As of 2002
* B=billion
** M=million

Dreyer's

Dreyer's is in the food products industry. This industry had 18 companies, which is close to the average of industries with big winners or losers. The food products industry had average annual 1997 to 2002 returns of 8.8 percent, below that of other industries with big winners or losers. Dreyer's was the only company in food products that was a big winner. Its average annual returns during from 1997 to 2002 were 22.4 percent.

Dreyer's manufactured and distributed ice cream and frozen deserts, including its two well-known brands, Dreyer's and Edy's. It also distributed competitors' products, including those of Haagen Dazs and Ben and Jerry's. A direct competitor, Conagra (see Table 3.8), was much larger than Dreyer's. Table 3.9 has a list of competitors other than Conagra.

Table 3.8 Food Products Industry

Company Name	One-Year Return (%)	Three-Year Average Return (%)	Five-Year Average Return (%)	Ten-Year Average Return (%)
Dreyer's Grand Ice Cream	20.4	37.5	22.4	9.2
Conagra	−4.8	−5.6	2.1	5.7
Industry Group Average	15.2	3.8	8.8	8.4

Table 3.9 Competitors of Dreyer's

	Dreyer's	Blue Bell Creameries (Privately Held)	Nestlé	Unilever
Employees	6,100	N/A	230,000	247,000
Revenue ($)	1.41B*	280.00M**	67.5B	82.8B

As of 2003
* B=billion
** M=million

In the U.S. ice cream market in 2002, Dreyer's had a 28.3 percent share. (See Table 3.10.) With the exception of Blue Bell, other companies in this market, such as Nestlé (which owns Breyers and Haagen-Dazs) and Unilever (which owns Ben and Jerry's and Good Humor), were considerably larger than Dreyer's. In 2002, Unilever had $82.8 billion in sales and 247,000 employees, and Nestlé had $67.5 billion in sales and 230,000 employees.

Dreyer's market can be broken down into premium and super-premium segments. In the premium segment, Dreyer's and Breyers were running about neck and neck in market share. (See Figure 3.2.) In the super-premium segment, Dreyer's trailed Haagen-Dazs and Ben and Jerry's. (See Figure 3.3.) What Dreyer's dominated was distribution. In distribution, it had no significant competitors. In 2002, it had about 90 percent market share.

Table 3.10 2002 Shares of the U.S. Ice Cream Market

	% of Market	Sales $
Total ice cream industry	100%	$5,021.00
Dreyer's (Dreyer's)	20.5%	$1,029.31
Breyers (Nestlé)	7.8%	$ 391.64
Edy's (Dreyer's)	7.8%	$ 391.64
Haagen Dazs (Nestlé)	4.4%	$ 220.92
Ben & Jerry's (Unilever)	3.2%	$ 160.67
Blue Bell (Independent)	2.5%	$ 125.53
TOTAL DREYER'S	28.3%	$1,420.94

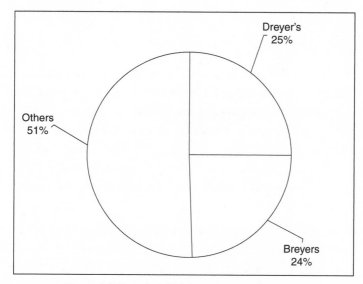

Figure 3.2 Premium U.S. ice cream market 2002.

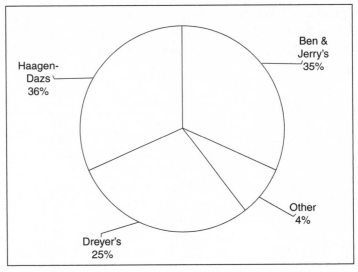

Figure 3.3 Super-premium U.S. ice cream market 2002.

Forest Labs

Forest Labs is in the pharmaceutical industry. Pharmaceuticals had 20 firms, which is about average for an industry with big winners or losers. The pharmaceutical industry had mean annual returns of 27.9 percent from 1997 to 2002, which is high for an industry with winning or losing companies. Forest Labs, with average annual returns of 58.9 percent, was the only winner in the pharmaceutical industry. Among big winners I analyze in this book, Forest Labs had the highest average 1997 to 2002 annual returns.

Forest Labs can be compared to firms such as Andrx, King, Pfizer, Lilly, and King. (See Table 3.11.) It was a niche-oriented pharmaceutical company that sold branded, generic prescription drugs in addition to over-the-counter (OTC) medications. Andrx and King also were niche players, but they did not share Forest's business model. Andrx developed and acquired a limited assortment of products that could use its proprietary drug delivery technologies, and King acquired lesser-performing prescription pharmaceuticals that large global companies divested. Andrx's returns also were stellar, but it did not have a full ten-year history to analyze, so it did not qualify for additional analysis in this book.

Lilly, GlaxoSmithKline PLC, and Pfizer were much larger companies than Forest Labs. (See Table 3.12.) They had broader portfolios of drugs. Forest Labs' main drug product, which constituted more than 65 percent of its revenues, was Celexa. Celexa was a selective serotonin reuptake inhibitor (SSRI) used to treat depression. It was developed abroad and brought to the U.S. by Forest Labs. Sales of Celexa grew from $92 million in 1999 to $1.5 billion in 2003 boosted by its efficacy, fast onset of action, and reduced side effects and drug interactions in comparison to older antidepressants Prozac (Eli Lilly & Co.), Zoloft (Pfizer), and Paxil (GlaxoSmithKline). Forest Labs licensed Celexa from H. Lundbeck A/S, a privately held drug company in Copenhagen, Denmark. Along with an enhanced version of Celexa called Lexapro, which was launched in 2002, Celexa and Lexapro accounted for about 15.6 percent of the U.S. market for antidepressant prescriptions in 2003.

Forest's other products included Tiazac for treatment of hypertension ($200 million sales in 2003); Aerobid for the treatment of asthma; Lorcet, an analgesic; and a number of drugs used for treatment of respiratory and urinary tract disorders. A Forest Labs subsidiary, Inwood Laboratory, sold generic drug products specializing in controlled release pharmaceuticals. Forest Labs also had a pipeline of drugs that included treatments for Alzheimer's, central nervous disorders, irritable bowel syndrome, and other conditions.

Table 3.11 The Pharmaceuticals Industry

Company Name	One-Year Return (%)	Three-Year Average Return (%)	Five-Year Average Return (%)	Ten-Year Average Return (%)
Andrx Group	21.7	76.5	77.2	N/A
Forest Laboratories	23.3	45.5	58.5	23.0
Pfizer	−12.5	−0.6	24.7	20.9
Lilly (Eli)	−14.4	−2.7	18.1	17.0
King Pharmaceuticals	8.7	68.6	N/A	N/A
Industry Group Average	−5.7	21.1	27.9	17.4

Table 3.12 Competitors of Forest Labs

	Forest Labs	Eli Lilly and Co.	GlaxoSmith Kline PLC	Pfizer Inc.
Employees	4,240	46,100	106,166	122,000
Revenue ($)	2.58B*	13.07B	39.31B	49.15B
Operating Margins	38.44%	25.89%	29.81%	6.45%

[1] = As of 2003
* B=billion

Ball

Ball is in the containers and packaging industry, an industry that had eight firms, which is considerably fewer than the average for an industry with big winners or losers. The containers and packaging industry had average annual returns of 3.7 percent from 1997 to 2002, which was low for an industry with big winners or losers. Ball's average annual returns in those years were 23.9.

Ball occupied a unique position in its industry. It defined itself as a company that discovered "packaging solutions" for its customers. This meant that it met its customers' needs regardless of the kind of packaging they wanted. This definition was different from other players in the industry who focused on a particular kind of packaging.

Ball's net sales by segment can be found in Figure 3.4. Owen Illinois (see Table 3.13) provided plastic (PET) packaging, which was about 10 percent of Ball's revenues. Alcan, Alcoa, and Rexam (see Table 3.14) sold metal beverage cans, which were about 60 percent of Ball's revenues. Crown Cork and Seal sold food containers cans. None of these companies was in each of the segments that Ball was in simultaneously. Another difference between Ball and the other firms was that Ball had an aerospace business, which made up about 12 percent of its revenues. Other aerospace firms—Boeing, Lockheed Martin, Honeywell, and Northrup Grumman—tended to be much larger and less specialized than Ball. In each segment in which Ball competed, its rivals were larger than it was. Like Amphenol, SPX, Dreyer's, and Forest Labs, Ball was small compared to its competitors.

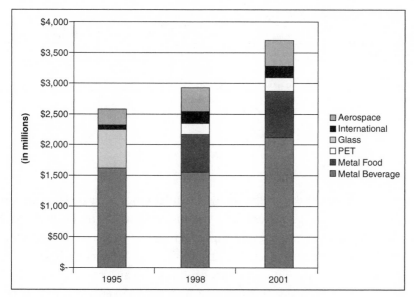

Figure 3.4 Ball's net sales by segment.

Table 3.13 Plastic Container Industry

Company Name	One-Year Return (%)	Three-Year Average Return (%)	Five-Year Average Return (%)	Ten-Year Average Return (%)
Ball	55.3	17.3	23.9	10.2
Owens-Illinois	75.6	−31.2	−15.2	−1.8
Industry Group Average	37.6	−1.1	3.7	7.6

As of 2003

Table 3.14 Competitors of Ball

	Ball	Alcan	Alcoa	Rexam
Employees	12,700	52,000	120,000	21,800
Revenue ($)	5.14B*	16.65B	22.06B	5.71B
Operating Margins	9.01%	3.77%	8.44%	3.54%

As of 2003
*   B=billion

Brown & Brown

Brown & Brown (B&B) is the smallest firm among those analyzed in this book. In 2002, its sales were $572 million. B&B is in the property and casualty insurance industry. This industry had 32 firms, which was considerably higher than other industries with big winners or losers. The 1997 to 2002 average annual returns in property and casualty were 14.7 percent. B&B's average annual returns were 45.7 percent. In the property and casualty insurance industry, Gallagher also did very well, but it could not maintain its industry beating performance in the first six months of 2002; therefore, it has not been analyzed further. (See Table 3.15.)

Table 3.15 Property and Casualty Insurance Industry

Company Name	One-Year Return (%)	Three-Year Average Return (%)	Five-Year Average Return (%)	Ten-Year Average Return (%)
Brown & Brown	57.1	47.8	45.7	31.9
Gallagher (Arthur J.)	10.3	49.6	38.5	23.2
Progressive	44.4	−3.9	17.6	24.1
St. Paul	−16.9	11.2	11.5	12.6
Allstate	−21.1	−2.3	4.9	N/A
Safeco	−2.3	−6.1	−1.0	6.1
Industry Group Average	1.8	11.9	14.7	16.7

A group of miscellaneous insurance companies that are somewhat similar to B&B are found in Table 3.16. Some are much larger than B&B, such as Metlife, Inc. and the Hartford Financial Services Group. These firms do not compete with B&B in every market, but they have some overlapping businesses. Although small overall, B&B is a substantial player in specific niches. In the Southeast, it has achieved regional dominance. Overall, B&B was the sixth largest independent insurance company in intermediary insurance and reinsurance products.

Like other winning companies, small size did not mean that B&B was unable to find good niches in which to compete. The company offered professional liability insurance for specific classes of persons, industries, trade groups, and other targeted niches. The services it offered included third-party administration of employee benefit and managed health care plans. The company did risk management consulting. It competed in the worker's compensation and employee benefit self-insurance markets. It was a broker for excess commercial insurance and reinsurance. In addition, B&B was a distribution channel for larger carriers that underwrote the policies it sold. It sold to commercial, governmental, professional, and individual clients. Retail commissions and fees provided 76 percent of its 2002 revenues, with the rest coming from the programs it ran and the services it provided.

Table 3.16 Competitors of Brown & Brown

	Brown & Brown	Aon	Gallagher	Marsh & McLennan
Employees	3,517	54,000	7,359	60,500
Revenue ($)	571.87M*	10.01B**	1.35B	11.95B
Operating Margins	32.67%	12.47%	16.74%	21.36%

As of 2003
*   M=million
** B=billion

Family Dollar

Family Dollar is in the retail broadline industry, one that had 12 firms, which was below the average for industries with big winners or losers. From 1997 to 2002, the retail broadline industry had average annual returns of 12.1 percent, which was also under the mean for industries with big winners or losers. Family Dollar's five-year average annual market return was 36.1 percent. It was the only big winner in its industry.

Although many firms might be considered Family Dollar's competitors, few were quite like it. (See Tables 3.17 and 3.18.) The company that was most similar was Dollar General. Most of the company's other competitors were larger, had broader product lines, and more customers.

Like other big winners, Family Dollar had to contend with industry giants. It had to meet challenges posed by Wal-Mart, Kmart (now Sears), and Target. Its story has some parallels with that of Wal-Mart. It started in Charlotte, North Carolina, as a self-service retailer. Its focus was on low-income customers. However, unlike Wal-Mart, Family Dollar offers its customers a convenient location to buy everyday necessities. The company has many small stores (7,500 to 9,500 square feet) in rural areas, small towns, and poor neighborhoods. In 2003, 40 percent of its new store openings were in poor urban areas. About a quarter of all of its stores were in inner-city locations. Unlike Wal-Mart, Kmart, and Target, Family Dollar was not vertically integrated. It ran a very simple business. It was a back-to-basics throwback to an earlier era in retailing. Unlike Wal-Mart, Family Dollar had about 1,800 suppliers to handle its distribution, trucking operations, and merchandising operations.

Table 3.17 Broadline Retail Industry

Company Name	One-Year Return (%)	Three-Year Average Return (%)	Five-Year Average Return (%)	Ten-Year Average Return (%)
Wal-Mart	8.9	12.8	39.1	15.3
Family Dollar	41.1	12.0	36.1	20.0
Target	28.0	15.5	34.2	24.9
Costco Wholesale	11.1	7.1	28.7	14.2
Dollar General	−20.4	0.2	12.9	25.4
Penney (J.C.)	154.6	−12.9	−7.2	3.9
Kmart	2.8	−29.1	−12.0	−12.1
Industry Group Average	29.2	1.5	12.1	11.1

Table 3.18 Competitors of Family Dollar

	Family Dollar	Dollar General	Kmart	Wal-Mart
Employees	21,000	57,800	212,000	1,500,000
Revenue ($)	5.03B*	7.05B	30.76B	266.90B
Operating Margins	8.24%	7.42%	N/A	5.51%

As of 2003
* B=billion

Activision

Activision is in the toys industry, which had few players compared to other industries with big winners or losers. Average annual 1997 to 2002 returns in this industry, 12.2 percent, were below the average of industries with big winners or losers. (See Table 3.19.) Activision's average annual returns were 24.8 percent.

The company developed, published, and distributed interactive entertainment and leisure games. These games covered action, adventure, sports, racing, role playing, simulation, and strategy. The games that Activision made worked on many consoles and systems, including PlayStation, Xbox, Nintendo, and Game Boy. In the niche it occupied, Activision had few direct competitors. The company developed, marketed, and sold its games mainly to young males either directly or via license. It had third-party development agreements with many software companies. A significant portion of its revenue came from a small number of popular games. In its dependence on a few hits for most of its revenues, it resembled Forest Labs, which was heavily dependent on Celexa and Lexapro.

Nearly all of Activision's competitors were larger than it was. Privately held Infogames was an exception. (See Table 3.20.) Activision's small size in comparison to its competitors was a trait it shared with other winning companies.

Activision's largest customer was Wal-Mart; this is similar to Dreyer's. Wal-Mart accounted for 15 percent of Activision's revenue in 2002. The big losers—Campbell Soup and Hasbro—also had Wal-Mart as their main customer (see Chapters 8 through 12), but whereas Activision and Dreyer's successfully dealt with this challenge, Campbell Soup and Hasbro were not able to do so.

Table 3.19 The Toy Industry

Company Name	One-Year Return (%)	Three-Year Average Return (%)	Five-Year Average Return (%)	Ten-Year Average Return (%)
Electronic Arts	40.6	28.8	32.0	28.8
Activision	158.0	51.9	24.8	63.7
Hasbro	54.1	–11.2	–0.1	4.1
Mattel	19.4	–8.5	–8.0	5.4
Industry Group Average	68.0	15.2	12.2	25.5

Table 3.20 Competitors of Activision

	Activision	Electronic Arts	Infogames Entertainment (Privately Held)	Sony
Employees	1,214	4,000	1,846[1]	167,500
Revenue ($)	947.66M*	2.96B**	713.30M[1]	67.83B
Operating Margins	11.59%	26.23%	N/A	1.10%

As of 2003
* M=million
** B=billion

In Summary

This chapter has described the nine big winners that are the subject of further analysis in this book. Several points stand out. (See Table 3.21.) The nine winning companies succeeded despite being in small industries that did not have good returns. These industries were not ones where they could easily find sweet spots no other firms occupied. The big winners succeeded despite low overall returns in the industries in which they competed. These firms were survivors of a poor overall stock market in the first six months of 2002. The fact that their sales tended to be spread out helped them do well in this period. When the tech market collapsed, they had alternative customers to which they could turn

These firms had few direct competitors that competed head to head with them in all the markets in which they participated. They picked niches, or specialty markets that other firms tended to ignore or avoid. They also were generally smaller than their competitors. This meant that they could escape easy detection by their rivals. They had the agility to move to a sweet spot, the discipline to protect it, and the focus to exploit it, as the next chapters show.

Table 3.21 The Nine Companies That Hit the Mark in Relation to Their Industries and Their Competitors

	Large Industry	Good Returns in the Industry	Sales Spread Out	Few Direct Competitors	Smaller Than Most Competitors
Amphenol	*	*	*	*	*
SPX			*	*	*
Fiserv	*		*	*	
Dreyer's				*	*
Forest Labs		*			*
Ball			*	*	*
Brown & Brown			*	*	*
Family Dollar					*
Activision				*	*

4

SWEET SPOTS

One of the main reasons that the big winners did so well is that they were in sweet spots. By a sweet spot, I mean that these companies picked a special niche in which to compete. They chose a specialty that other firms tended to ignore or avoid. By choosing this niche, they had fewer competitors with which to contend. Within this niche, they provided the best value for the money.

This chapter explores what it means to be in a sweet spot. A major requirement of being in such a position is to achieve closeness with your customers. Now, being close to your customers might be considered a cliché. All firms have to be close to customers. But what I am referring to is not mere normal closeness, but a special closeness that the big winners achieved. They did the following for their customers:

- *Co-designed products and services with their customers*

- *Embedded themselves in their customers' infrastructure*

- *Were brokers between their customers' needs and the satisfaction of these needs*

These patterns involve significant alignment with customers. In contrast, the patterns that prevailed among sour spot companies involved significant misalignment. (See Chapter 9, "Sour Spots.")

This chapter elaborates on these points. It provides three examples of big winners that co-designed with their customers, three examples of big winners that embedded themselves in their customers' infrastructure, and three examples of big winners that were brokers.

Each example of alignment is based on a number of traits that the winning firms exhibited. (See Table 4.1.) What made their positions so unassailable was the way they combined these traits into larger patterns. The combining of traits into larger patterns is set out in Appendix D.

Each way of achieving closeness with customers—co-designing, embedding, and being a broker—has implications. If you are trying to co-design, embed, or be a broker, you can do the following:

- Co-design
    - Try to co-design products and services with your customer, because it saves on research and development (R&D) costs and raises customers' switching costs.
    - Customize your products and services to meet your customer's specific needs.

- Embed
    - Try to make your closeness to your customer physical and tangible.
    - Try to establish an onsite presence with your customer.

- Be a broker
    - Stay connected as an intermediary between producers and consumers.
    - Understand where your products fit into the value chain.

Table 4.1 Traits That Create Closeness to Customers

Sweet Spot	Company	Traits That Create Closeness to Customers
Co-design	Amphenol	Niche marketing Leverage with suppliers Full integration
	SPX	Providing solutions Multiple growth platforms
	Ball	Help with brand differentiation Meeting changing needs Price, service, quality, and performance
Embed	Fiserv	Seamless integration Comprehensive bundling Outsourcing Independence
	Dreyer's	Mastering a challenging niche Distribution Total immersion Brand building
	Family Dollar	Underserved customers Old-fashioned neighborhood experience Simplicity
Broker	Forest Labs	Licensing Proven products from abroad Targeted sales force
	Brown & Brown	Retail outlet Small and focused The best deal
	Activision	Rapport with prime audience Hub in spoke of a wheel

Co-Design

In this section, I show how three companies—Amphenol, SPX, and Ball—co-designed products and services with their customers. I describe the traits of co-designing that they exhibited. These created a special closeness with their customers.

Example 1: Amphenol

Amphenol manufactures high-performance, application-specific products. It develops these high-margin, high-growth, application-specific products in a variety of niches. Depending on the product and market, the products compete as either low-cost or differentiated alternatives, and they provide very good value for the money. Amphenol has exhibited three co-design traits—niche marketing, leverage, and full integration.

NICHE MARKETING

Niche marketing with customers allows the company to avoid direct competition with larger companies. The firm's global market share is estimated to be just 5 percent, but it is successful because of the niches it occupies. The company competes with both large diversified manufacturers and small firms. The industry segments where it competes are highly fragmented. The range of competitors and markets is broad, and Amphenol's sales are spread out. More than 2,000 participants globally can provide connectors, interconnect systems, or cables. Ten firms hold 50 percent of worldwide market share based on revenue. Amphenol stands out in several niches. The niches in which it competes are not susceptible to significant price pressures. It is the largest supplier of high-performance (military spec) connectors, for instance. These high-performance connectors are used in sophisticated aerospace, commercial, and industrial equipment. They withstand extreme stress in hostile environments. They have to be error-free; they cannot be just a little better than those of the competitors. To win military and security contracts, they have to be far superior. Because Amphenol products met the specialized needs of such markets, it was able to experience profitable growth after 9/11.

LEVERAGE

Figure 4.1 summarizes the leverage Amphenol has over suppliers, customers, and competitors. It has low reliance on suppliers because there are many sources for its raw materials—steel, aluminum, copper, gold, silver, brass, plastic, plating, and molding. The company locates its facilities near markets. It is close to original equipment manufacturers (OEMs) to whom it sells. This enables it to design its products with its customers. It can focus on design because it outsources much of the manufacturing. The company was able to increase the ratio of new product introduction to sales to 20 percent without increasing R&D spending. And its close ties to its customers have meant that it has been able to forecast customer needs and provide products just in time, which is something that its customers greatly value.

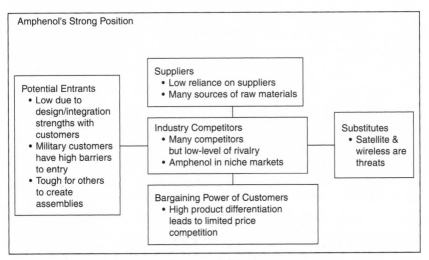

Figure 4.1 Leverage.

FULL INTEGRATION

Amphenol's customers are looking for a fully integrated supplier. They want a single source to meet their needs. With consolidation of the industry, the company's customers do not want to go shopping in many different places for products they use. The firm's customers have been moving toward creating lists of qualified suppliers, which has worked to the company's advantage because Amphenol offers a large variety of products and services for specific niche markets. The company can be the single source that meets nearly all of a customer's needs.

Example 2: SPX

SPX has been trying to become a specialty engineering and systems design firm. It wants to be a company that offers complete solutions across a range of engineering disciplines. It hopes to bring together high-performing teams from the company's divisions to co-create unique and proprietary product/service combinations with its customers. SPX's two co-design traits are discussed next.

PROVIDING SOLUTIONS

The company aims to sell in profitable business niches in a variety of industries with growth potential. Its goal is to be a complete solutions provider in these niches. It has sought multiple growth platforms in the following areas: industrial products, flow technology, technical products, and specialty tools. It has carefully targeted high-margin businesses in these industries. Through aggressive acquisitions, it has moved into a number of these profitable niches with growth potential. Almost all the niches have high market share. SPX has been looking for firms in the top three market rankings in their industries as targets for its acquisitions. These firms must have better growth potential and operating margins than SPX's prior automotive product lines. Figure 4.2 shows the alignment of SPX's businesses prior to implementing this acquisition strategy and the alignment after the strategy was implemented. As is apparent, the company has more growth platforms than previously. Many of its businesses now are stars, whereas previously they were cash cows.

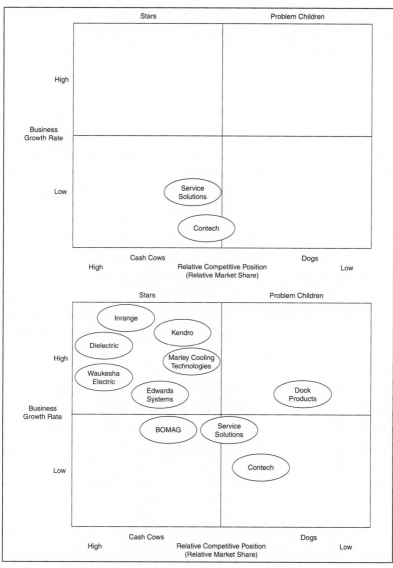

Figure 4.2 The alignment of SPX's businesses in 1995 and 2001.

MULTIPLE GROWTH PLATFORMS

By having multiple growth platforms in many niches, SPX is trying to be less dependent on a single customer or industry. It is more able to weather economic storms regardless of origin. With the diverse niches in which it competes, the company's strengths in one area compensate for weaknesses in another. After 9/11, for instance, SPX's strength in security and building safety systems made up for problems in the electric power business.

Example 3: Ball

Ball co-designs its products with its customers. It is not tied to specific products. But what it is tied to is a process of working with customers to best supply their packaging needs. It tries to accommodate their needs for uniquely shaped and featured specialty packaging. Its co-design characteristics are described below.

HELPING WITH BRAND DIFFERENTIATION

Aware that packaging might be a critical differentiator in its customers' markets, Ball works with its customers to produce unique packaging to meet its customer needs. The specialty packaging it designs with customers helps customers with brand differentiation and loyalty. The unique packaging solutions are developed in anticipation of new markets. Ball serves its customers by making their brands stand out. It does this by staying at the forefront of change. The company succeeds despite the fact that the market for beverage cans is mature, and there is excess capacity and a saturated carbonated drink market in North America. The demand for carbonated drinks has leveled off as alternative beverages have gained in popularity, but Ball has taken advantage of this trend. Its specialty bottles have grown in importance with the surging demand for sports and nutrition drinks and bottled water.

MEETING CHANGING NEEDS

Ball has repeatedly changed its focus with the evolution of packaging requirements. It has abandoned business niches that no longer have good growth prospects, even if there are sentimental reasons for holding on to them. For instance, it spun off its original glass container product line when profits and growth declined. The company has been at the forefront of the shift from glass to metals to plastic. Plastic is appealing because of lower costs and the ability to mold plastic into different shapes, making it easier to differentiate products. Ball was one of the first firms that entered this market. It has altered its product offerings to meet new types of demand, such as the demand for tall thin cans for performance drinks and for 8.4-ounce cans targeted to the growing energy drink market.

PRICE, SERVICE, QUALITY, AND PERFORMANCE

Among customers, Ball is known for its outstanding R&D. Its products therefore score very high on price, service, quality, and performance. The company's R&D has focused on the needs of customers for lighter, stronger, customizable containers. Ball started doing R&D on plastics and plastic manufacturing in the late 1970s and sold its glass production capabilities in 1995. Ball also is known for the alliances it has forged with other companies. For example, it has forged an exclusive agreement with Daiwa to be the distributor of a recloseable metal beverage container. These alliances have enhanced the company's reputation for price, quality, and performance.

Embed

This section shows how three companies—Fiserv, Dreyer's, and Family Dollar—embedded themselves into the infrastructure of their customers and brought themselves in close touch with their customers' core needs, thus enhancing customer loyalty and greatly increasing switching costs. I describe the traits associated with the embeddedness upon which these companies relied.

Example 1: Fiserv

Fiserv's embeddedness is based on a mentality of service that succeeds in creating direct, intimate ties with customers. Being embedded in customers' infrastructure forestalls customer defection. Fiserv's business (80 to 85 percent) rests on long-term contracts with its customers, which adds to the difficulty of customers switching.

Fiserv does not preserve and enhance its ties to customers by means of patents as does some of its competitors, but by means of its intimate knowledge of what its customers want. This intimate knowledge is based on a near-total immersion in its customers' businesses. The company does well because its employees are able to work with customers as if they were a part of the customers' business. Employees seamlessly integrate with customers to the point where it is hard to tell for whom they are working. Through this mechanism, the company develops a close understanding of customer needs and is able to create customized solutions for unique customer problems. Fiserv thus occupies a space that no other firm can easily occupy, a space based on ongoing and continuous customer contact. The company is very committed to being close to its customers, aligning its business to what customers need and being intensely focused on customer relationships. After a customer signs up to work with Fiserv, it becomes difficult to switch to another company. A customer is not going to risk the disruption associated with hiring a new data services provider.

COMPREHENSIVE BUNDLING

A breadth of niche offerings, built on intimate customer ties, has insulated Fiserv from downturns. More profitable niche areas pick up for those experiencing slower growth. The company provides a full array of systems, services, and support solutions. Broad, integrated offerings of related products and services save customers money, allow them to operate more efficiently, and permit them to concentrate on their core banking, brokerage, and insurance business. The comprehensive bundle of products and services that Fiserv provides does not consist of just sophisticated products. These products and services involve many support functions. Fiserv, for instance, is known for its training, consulting, and implementation as well as for its products. The focus on training, consulting, and implementation arises out of a "customer-centric" approach. The company's emphasis is on a package of solutions designed to meet all of a customer's needs. Fiserv thrives on this capacity to understand and manage the full array of customer needs. It aims to support a customer's entire enterprise and not just a customer's technical people. Fiserv has been one of a few firms that has been able to provide a comprehensive bundle of niche products and services to its customers, not just sophisticated software. The many related products and services that Fiserv provides save its customers money. The company also is perceived as selling best-in-class services as well as customizable offerings at a low price. The low cost derives from economies of scale. Because Fiserv's overhead is fixed, the company has a need for volume, which it has built successfully.

Outsourcing

Fiserv has taken advantage of the growth in demand for outsourcing that developed as a result of the 1999 passage of the Gramm Leach Bliley Act. Gramm Leach Bliley repealed Glass Steagall. This act allowed banks, brokerages, and insurance companies to provide common services and thereby compete with each other. Financial institutions thus had large infrastructure needs to support the increase in transactions. The market for data processing and information management systems outsourcing took off. Fiserv's customers were looking for vendors to outsource noncore processes like transaction processing and payments and provide the integrated solutions that Fiserv was selling.

Independence

Hardware vendors encouraged Fiserv's customers to build and maintain their own data processing systems. If customers developed a competence in data processing, they could sell this service to other companies. However, firms that bought data processing services from a competitor were in a compromised position. Fiserv took advantage of this factor. It made the case to customers that it was better to deal with Fiserv than with its competitors. Customer satisfaction was based on the company's independence. Though the company had to fend off an ability of some customers to vertically integrate, Fiserv has been able to claim that it offers unbiased solutions unlike its vertically integrated competitors. Thus, Fiserv has a unique value proposition that has made it a big winner, a value proposition based on a its independence.

Example 2: Dreyer's

Dreyer's embeddedness arises from the fact that the company has faced huge challenges. It has had to convince people who consume ice cream that better quality deserves a premium price. It has had to deal with the challenge of finding ways to differentiate its products to increase brand and customer loyalty. These challenges have been hard ones to cope with in the premium and super-premium ice cream categories.

Mastering A Challenging Niche

Being in a sweet spot has not been easy for Dreyer's. It is not in an especially attractive industry niche. The margins are low; over time, they have averaged just 1 percent. Almost everything in the premium ice cream business is difficult. First, the competition is intense. Low-priced ice creams compete with premium and super-premium brands. The low-priced brands are supplied by national and regional manufacturers, full-line dairies, and independent processors. They often have a grocer's private label attached to them. Production costs are low, and in the competition for shelf space, the private label brands often obtain preferential space allocation treatment. Low-priced brands, moreover, have the potential to move into the turf of the high-quality ice creams. They are potential competitors. Another factor that makes competing in the premium and super-premium ice cream business difficult is that customers have huge choices; they can substitute any dessert, cake, cookie, and confection for ice cream. And most importantly, there is the obesity issue that limits growth. Many people are trying to skip sweets altogether. Still another factor that makes competing in this business difficult is that supply costs are high and hard to predict. No substitutes exist for the dairy products and sugar that constitute the main raw materials, and Dreyer's has to be concerned that suppliers of dairy goods and sugar might integrate forward and become competitors. Another issue is energy costs—gasoline needed to deliver the ice cream and the electricity for freezers is highly unpredictable. But there is a positive aspect to the challenges Dreyer's faces—because the niche is so difficult to compete in, it has deterred competition.

In this challenging niche, it is hard to win over people with innovation in image, quality, taste, packaging, advertising, and breadth of selection. It is also difficult to beat competitors by expanding the business across more and different channels. Dreyer's competes in these areas and does so competently, but these factors do not account for it being a big winner. What accounts for Dreyer's being a big winner, is that it dominates elsewhere than in just the product realm.

Where Dreyer's really dominates is in distribution. Its direct store delivery system has been the key to its success. This is a key to the company's success because running the freezer space for customers is so difficult. Dreyer's has mastered this function; it has become a super-efficient distributor. The company is in total charge of the freezer space in most retail grocery chains and convenience stores in the United States. It entirely manages this function; it has little real competition in this area. It is the ultimate solution provider for grocery chains and convenience stores, giving the companies it services the right product at the right place at the right time, which is a very difficult task to accomplish because of ice cream's perishable nature and the eating public's fickle tastes. The company improves the productivity of the stores it services by reducing the total costs of delivered goods. It has a lock on this function. Indeed, its main competitors—Haagen Dazs and Ben and Jerry's—have depended on Dreyer's distribution system to get their products to market. The company has become the master of ensuring not only the freshness and quality of its own products but that of its competitors. In addition, it has taken away the burden of inventory management from its customers, which find the management of this part of their business challenging.

Dreyer's does more than just product delivery; it provides an array of full-fledged service solutions, including merchandising displays and assistance with in-store promotions. By managing this function in its entirety for its customers, it has gained intimate knowledge of end consumers' preferences. Its closeness to the consuming public has enabled it to be first or nearly first to the market with a series of innovations such as whole fruit bars, a variety of new flavors, and light and low-fat yogurts and ice creams. From Dreyer's embeddedness in the store freezer department has arisen an unparalleled customer intimacy.

TOTAL IMMERSION

This system of total immersion in the stores that the company serves yields an intimacy with customers that is hard to beat. The foundation of the company's success is that it is not just Dreyer's that benefits from this system. Retailers too benefit from the distribution system that Dreyer's runs for them. The retailers have eliminated backroom space. They are hard pressed to manage the supply of premium and super-premium ice cream, one of the most perishable items in their stores, themselves. They have shown virtually no resistance in delegating this task to Dreyer's. Dreyer's has a consignment arrangement with most stores it serves whereby it restocks, rearranges, and takes ownership of the store's inventory. This system means that Dreyer's not only maintains, but that it owns the products at each store and has the burden of keeping track of them. Dreyer's bills retailers solely based on the goods they sell, not on the basis of products on the shelf. This arrangement also is advantageous to the retailers since it takes away their risk of holding the inventory. Dreyer's representatives have handheld computers that they bring into stores from which they feed detailed data to headquarters on what is selling and what is not. The data gives Dreyer's an intimate knowledge of customer preferences that its competitors do not have.

BRAND-BUILDING

Building a leading high-margin brand across the premium and super-premium end of the ice cream category has not been easy. The knowledge Dreyer's has gained from its distribution system has allowed it to take many steps to build its brand that its competitors could match only later, if at all:

- In 1995, Dreyer's had more than 125 flavors. By 2002, it had more than 150.

- Dreyer's expanded delivery across many different channels. Its channels now extend from grocers, convenience stores, club stores, and mass merchandisers to such outlets as restaurants, ice cream parlors, stadiums, and other commercial and institutional establishments. In 2002, it served 59,000 retail stores in 48 states and reached approximately 90 percent of the places where Americans shopped for ice cream (up from 70 percent in 1994). The sales of partner brands through its distribution network averaged about 40 percent of its net sales from 2000 to 2002.

- To distinguish itself from the competition, the company made a promise to end consumers to include only the highest-quality ingredients in its ice cream products. These ingredients had to be 100 percent pure. Unlike competitors, Dreyer's did not make compromises by reducing costs with imitation flavorings, like imitation vanilla, upon which competitors relied.

- Dreyer's managed the costs of its raw materials very well. It relied on the futures market (Chicago Mercantile Exchange) for butter and milk purchases. It bought early in the season when demand was low and supply high to hedge against the risk of fluctuating prices. It had to have a competence in futures trading as well as distribution because the market for cream was volatile, and if price increases were passed on to customers, they would dampen sales. Competitors that aggressively discounted would be able to take market share.

Example 3: Family Dollar

Family Dollar's embeddedness is a bit different than that of Fiserv or Dreyer's. The company is not so much embedded in its commercial customers' businesses as it is embedded in the neighborhoods of its customers. Its embeddedness is a function of the location of its stores. Its small stores (7,500 to 9,500 square feet) are in rural areas, small towns, and poor neighborhoods, and are very accessible to customers. The company offers its low-income customers a convenient location to buy everyday necessities.

Family Dollar does so well because other retailers have more or less abandoned the commercial spaces it occupies. They do not see the attractiveness of the business model or the customer base. The underserved demography of people (combined family income of $25,000 to $32,000) that Family Dollar serves is very price sensitive. This demographic does not have the same mobility as other shoppers. It cannot hop into the family pickup and make the trek on a superhighway to a Wal-Mart. Because there are few good alternatives, people in this group have no real choice but to shop at a local store. Other retailers have not paid attention to such people in these locales—declining rural areas, out-of-the-way small towns, and poor urban neighborhoods. Located far from big box stores, like Wal-Mart, people in these areas find the trip to the big chains inconvenient and too complicated. Family Dollar has opened its stores near its customers and has captured a space the giant retailers like Wal-Mart have not taken seriously. It has moved into the tight spots that big boxes cannot fill; the firm's stores have been squeezed into locations that are near to customers where the big boxes cannot go.

OLD-FASHIONED NEIGHBORHOOD EXPERIENCE

As Wal-Mart has become upscale and more mainstream, Family Dollar has secured an opening in landscapes where the big retailers do not operate. Family Dollar has made its smallness into an asset and transformed the big retailers' strengths into a weakness. By being close to its customers, it understands its markets very well. Although not precisely an old-fashioned neighborhood shopping experience, the company has endeavored to move in this direction. Its stores provide a less overwhelming shopping experience than Wal-Mart. They are more convenient and friendly. Family Dollar has more locations than the big chains, and its stores are easier to navigate. In areas where they are located, the property values are cheap. These places will never show up on best places to live, but they are where the firm's customers are mostly found. The low-income households that the company serves include small-town, low-income people especially in the South, African Americans, Hispanics, retirees, and dual-income families. Tiny stores in areas generally not considered desirable thrive under the Family Dollar format.

Other companies like Dollar General and Dollar Tree have battled with Family Dollar for the loyalty of its customers. Family Dollar also competes against department stores, discount stores, variety stores, discount clothing stores, drug stores, grocery stores, convenience stores, outlet stores, and warehouse stores. The products it sells are undifferentiated, and the competition is stiff and largely based on price. Family Dollar, moreover, always has to be apprehensive that a Wal-Mart, Costco, or Target might enter this niche. Wal-Mart, indeed, has tested the concept, but to the relief of Family Dollar, until now it decided it had better opportunities elsewhere. Family Dollar thrives against so many tough competitors because everything in its stores is simple. The stores carry a very narrow selection of mostly standard brand-name essentials at a very low price. Every store has the same product mix, arrangement, presentation, and identical margins that are super thin. To establish a low overhead environment and simplify management, Family Dollar has the same general floor plan in each store. The stable product mix also minimizes customer guesswork. It gives the firm's customers assurance that they can find what they want quickly. Family Dollar thrives on this type of predictability, which helps both in managing its stores and in its customer relations. The system works because it is simple; and because it is simple, it is easy to expand and grow the number of stores it has and the number of customers it serves.

Broker

This final section of the chapter shows how three companies (Forest Labs, Brown & Brown, and Activision) acted as brokers between producers of products and services and ultimate end users. They knew their customers well and they understood how to get their customers what they wanted. I describe the traits associated with the brokerage role that these companies played.

Example 1: Forest Labs

Forest Labs is mainly an intermediary between drug producers and consumers, getting consumers the pharmaceutical products they need even though it does not develop all of these products itself. Its superior performance is based on its being connected to drug developers and at the same being in touch with those who need the drugs.

LICENSING

The pharmaceutical industry in which Forest Labs competes is not as attractive as it once was. Regulations governing drug development and the expiration of patents depress profits. Medicare and Medicaid reimbursement guidelines require substitutes for brand-name prescriptions when the substitutes are less expensive. Generic drugs pose a huge threat. They rapidly erode the market share and profitability of patented medicines. Prozac, for instance, which competes with Forest Lab's Celexa in the anti-depressant market, went from a 29 percent market share to 6 percent market share in just three months after its patent expired. Healthcare costs continue to be a significant issue in the United States, with health maintenance organizations (HMOs) and pharmacy benefit managers (PBMs) under tremendous pressure to engage in cost containment. Forest Labs navigates well in this turbulent environment by meeting its biggest challenge, the competition for licensing opportunities. It follows what the drug developers are doing and is keenly aware of how their products can satisfy patient needs. It has the capacity to select the right drugs for the market and has proven to be efficient and effective in obtaining approval to sell and distribute these drugs. Its main strength has been in commercializing foreign drugs in the United States. Its biggest hit, the antidepressant Celexa, was licensed from H. Lundbeck, a privately held drug company in Copenhagen, Denmark. The management at Forest Labs recognized that this medication provided distinct advantages, including reduction in dosage and fewer side effects. Howard Solomon, Forest Labs' chairman and CEO, actively sought the licensing agreement for Celexa because his son, Andrew, suffered from acute depression.[1] The company's niche commercialization strategy has been based on the licensing of foreign drugs and its aptitude for customer relationship management in the United States, a market in which its foreign drug developers have little experience.

The United States is the world's largest market for prescription drugs. In 2000, the United States constituted more than 48 percent of the market. Access to this market has made Forest Labs an especially attractive partner for foreign drug developers. Relying on these foreign drug developers has been an especially good strategy for Forest Labs to follow because by licensing drugs developed and used abroad, it has not had to invest as heavily in R&D as its competitors.[2] As a result, it also does not have to bear as much risk. Instead, Forest Labs invests heavily in gaining approval for use of the drugs in the United States, in market development, and in its sales force. The strategy has paid off, because the company's gross profit margins have averaged 76 percent in comparison to the 48 percent average among other pharmaceutical companies from 1997 to 2002.

For foreign firms, Forest Labs has become a uniquely desirable partner. It has built its business on the strategic alliances it has established with foreign drug manufacturers. It has identified drugs and other focused therapies used in other countries and successfully marketed them to targeted groups in the United States.

Like other pharmaceuticals, the company has to avoid too much reliance on a few top-selling medications. It has tried to avoid being a one-hit wonder. To get beyond its reliance on Celexa, it has had many other drugs in the pipeline, many of them originating in the alliances it has with foreign firms, including a copromotion agreement with Biovail to share in the marketing and selling of Tiazac and with Sankyo Pharma to share in the marketing and selling of Benicar. These drugs, used for treatment of a disease of considerable concern to the elderly, hypertension, have had great promise. For this strategy to be successful, the company has to be good at product selection, at choosing the right medication with a good chance of success in the United States. This requires an intimate understanding of customer needs. Forest Labs use of key strategic alliances to bring products developed, tested, and proved in other countries to market provides it with a unique role of brokering the transfer of promising medicines from producers to consumers.

How does Forest Labs win the competition to market foreign drugs? Five U.S. firms, for instance, competed for the licensing rights to Celexa. After FDA approval in 1998, the medication was to be marketed by Warner-Lambert in partnership with Forest Labs. However, Warner-Lambert was acquired by Pfizer, which had its own antidepressant, Paxil. This gave Forest Labs the opportunity to buy its way out of the deal and to grow its own sales force.

The company's rapid expansion of its sales forces—by more than 50 percent—has made it a uniquely desirable partner for small foreign firms hoping to get products off the ground in the United States. A willingness to deploy its large sales force made Forest Labs such an attractive partner. The sales force constituted 2,100 of the company's 3,731 employees in 2002. The sales force grew from 638 persons before Forest Labs started to market Celexa to 850 in 2000 to 2,300 in 2003. (See Figure 4.3.) Forest Labs has targeted its marketing to focused therapies. It mainly emphasized diseases that affect the elderly—such disorders as

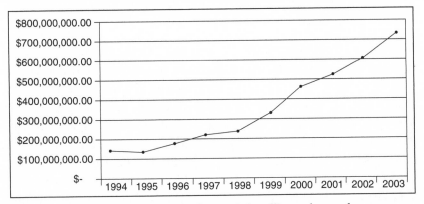

Figure 4.3 The growth of Forest Labs selling and general administrative expenses.

depression, hypertension, respiratory disease, gastrointestinal disease, and neuropathic pain. This niche strategy has allowed its sales force to maximize their efforts, unlike other drug company representatives that have a broader portfolio of drugs to sell.

Example 2: Brown & Brown (B&B)

The brokerage role B&B serves is as an insurance broker. It services targeted niches and acts as a distribution channel for products that other companies originate. As a broker and agent, its role is similar to that played by Forest Labs; it does not assume the risk of product origination, and it has access to products from a number of providers. (See Figure 4.4.)

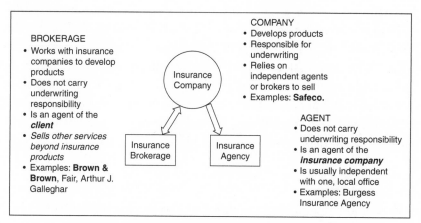

Figure 4.4 Insurance brokerages, companies, and agents

RETAIL OUTLET

B&B is a retail sales outlet for many different insurance companies' products. There are many advantages to B&B not being an underwriter but being a broker for policies that other underwriters provide. Underwriters have to pay defined benefits to policyholders should certain circumstances come into being. The benefits are a payment usually in the form of cash for the loss of property or assets. By not being an underwriter, B&B does not have to involve itself in the complex variables and assumptions upon which underwriting is based.

These variables include such factors as judicial changes, legislative enactments, and economic trends that are inherent in the estimation process. B&B does not require sophisticated actuarial models to figure out how much it should charge for the policies it sells. Being an underwriter is a risky business. Being an intermediary reduces the overall risk. The intermediary role also allows for customization and flexibility in meeting specific client needs. The challenge that B&B faces is to understand what customers want and to know how to get it. The company does not depend on a single underwriter as a source of its products. Because B&B can choose from so many underwriters, it can readily enter and exit different markets, chasing opportunities when they occur and abandoning them when they no longer are profitable. B&B provides the various underwriters who supply it with insurance policies with a continuous flow of information about customers. In turn, B&B gets tailored policies at good prices in niches for customer categories that otherwise might be hard to insure. B&B is compensated both from the commission paid by insurance underwriters and the fees paid by clients. The commission typically is a percentage of the premium price paid by the insured depending on the type of product. This income is completely independent of the claims made on the policy that the underwriter must bear. Being a specialist in niche products thus provides access to higher premiums and margins.

SMALL AND FOCUSED

B&B is good at analyzing the needs of clients for underutilized products and services where there is less competition. It is a specialist in niche products that it designs with its clients. These niche products also help boost its margins. They enable it to escape detection from bigger competitors, who tend not to be that interested in these specialized markets. The markets that B&B serves generally are small and focused. These unique markets have few substitutes. For instance, there is a low level of competition in markets for cargo haulers insurance, railroad insurance, and professional insurance for such groups as CEOs, CFOs, COOs, dentists, lawyers, optometrists, and specialty products for manufacturers, wholesalers, and distributors. Customers therefore command less bargaining power. B&B switches from underwriter to underwriter based on what the supplier is offering to satisfy customers' unique needs. It looks for the best value package, which it determines by three main criteria: price, quality, and innovation. Its culture is focused, responsive, and oriented to the individual customer. Its success is based on knowing customer needs and understanding how to satisfy these needs.

THE BEST DEAL

B&B promises customers it will get the best deal for them no matter who provides it or how. It shops for underwriters who make the best deals available. B&B gets the best price for customers because suppliers compete for its business. B&B also does risk management surveys, analyses, and insurance consultation for its clients. Thus, it provides services and expertise as well as products. For example, for companies that want to do self-insurance, it provides management services. The services and expertise complement its main product offerings. It is mainly by being a distributor of other companies' policies and a distributor of other companies' policies that it is able to mitigate risks and maximize returns. Its closeness to customers makes it especially valuable to insurance originators. As a small company, B&B is able to quickly chase down new opportunities in specific niche markets. It tailors the products to meet the needs of individual customers and works closely with its clients to develop products that meet their specific requirements.

Example 3: Activision

The brokerage role that Activision plays is an intermediary between the creators of hit computer games and the games' main audience, mostly young males. In its intermediary role, Activision is similar in many ways to B&B and to Forest Labs.

RAPPORT WITH PRIME AUDIENCE

Activision has a long history of rapport with its prime audience; it was the first independent developer and distributor of entertainment software with its 1980 introduction of the *Pitfall!* game for Atari Home entertainment. In 2002, it was second in computer game market share to Entertainment Arts. It has grown because it has been able to win control over successful software titles in a clearly defined niche. (Its prime audience is the 12- to 28-year-old male market.) In this niche, Activision is perceived as an innovator. A few of its titles have nearly a cult following. People in its demographic keep coming back again and again for sequels of the same genre. *Tony Hawk Pro Skater Series* is Activision's Celexa. In 2001, about 25 percent of Activision's revenues came from its 16 *Tony Hawk* titles. Superhero games like *Tony Hawk* and *Spider Man* are the mainstay of its business. Activision has been able to maintain the loyalty of its prime audience despite challenges from Sony and other relatively large competitors like Infrogames. Activision's rivals compete for the same product development talent. They try to lure the third-party developers with high-priced licensing and development fees. They use aggressive pricing to increase their retail shelf space. The software game industry is turbulent. One new game console with improved graphics has been introduced after another. Activision has grown at a phenomenal pace even though the industry in which it competes is extremely competitive, because it has such good rapport with its prime audience.

Hub in the Spoke of a Wheel

Activision's brokerage role may be understood as follows. The company is a hub in the spoke of a wheel that consists of software developers, console makers, retail outlets, and game players. It has relationships with talented programmers and game designers. With many software companies, it has third-party development agreements. To reduce the risk of product development, Activision contracts out much of game development to independent producers and production companies that work under contract. Therefore, it does not have to incur the fixed overhead obligations of having large numbers of these people as permanent staff. Neither does it have to pay nor manage them. It develops, markets, and sells games via license as much as it does directly. In this way, Activision is like Forest Labs and B&B in that it has been outsourcing much of its product development costs to lower its business risk.

Activision's largest customer in 2002 was Wal-Mart, which accounted for 15 percent of its revenue. Other customers included Best Buy, Blockbuster, Circuit City, and Target. As a hedge against powerful retailers, the company purchased distribution arms including CentreSoft Ltd. and NBG Distribution. The company has increased the space it has at major retail outlets and also has expanded its direct retail distribution network. In addition, it has been moving toward offering games directly on the Internet.

But to remain viable, the company needs additional hits. It is always looking for new titles within the action/adventure genre and trying to diversify into other product categories and genres. Where can it locate the next big hit? Many of Activision's games are based on motion pictures and sports figures. It has development deals with Marvel Comics, Disney, Dreamworks, LucasArts Entertainment, and Columbia Pictures and with vertical ramp biking champion Condor Hoffman and snowboarder Shaun Palmer. It would like its appeal to extend more broadly to families and children. Activision is a hit maker—the hub in the spoke of a wheel—in a risky and rapidly changing business. The main challenge it confronts is to create new games and sequels to replace the old. Thus, it is always on the lookout for other product categories and genres to diversify. Being at the center of this wheel puts Activision in a uniquely advantageous position to do so.

In Summary

This chapter has provided examples of the sweet spots that the big winners occupied. These sweet spots depend on gaining control over the classical five forces in strategy starting with customers. Big winners gained control of the five forces through the following measures: (1) co-designing products and services with their customers, (2) embedding themselves in their customers' central processes and infrastructure, and (3) being a broker between themselves, their customers, and their suppliers. The sweet spots that the big winners occupied increased their alignment with their customers. They raised their customers' switching costs. They made it less likely that their customers would abandon them. Big winners solidified their relationships with their customers and increased the number, amount, and quality of goods and services they sold them. This special affinity they had with customers—which was above and beyond that of a typical firm—rested on the key traits the big winners cultivated (see Table 4.1). These traits created customer closeness. None by itself might be enough to achieve a superior position but taken together they had a powerful impact.

A firm need not engage in all of them, but to succeed, it is likely that the firm will be the master of more than one of them. If you only possess one key trait, it can be too easily reproduced by your competitors. More than one key trait is harder to replicate. A combination of traits that interact with each other is extremely tough to copy.

From this analysis emerges the following series of actions that you can take to occupy a sweet spot:

- Engage in niche marketing.

- Achieve leverage with suppliers and customers.

- Be a fully integrated supplier.

- Aim for niches that have high growth potential and good margins.

- Have multiple growth platforms.

- Design unique products that help customers with brand differentiation.

- Alter products to meet customers' changing needs.

- Gain recognition for price, service, quality, and performance.

- Seamlessly integrate with your customers.

- Provide a broad array of systems, services, and support solutions.

- Take advantage of outsourcing.

- Build customer advantage based on your independence.

- Pick a challenging niche.

- Dominate distribution.

- Achieve total immersion.

- Take numerous steps to build your brand.

- Choose a market that others have not served well.

- Secure an opening in which other companies cannot operate.

- Thrive on simplicity and predictability.

- Introduce a new business model into an industry whose attractiveness is waning.

- Reduce risk by bringing products that have been sold successfully abroad to the U.S. market.

- Build capabilities for winning the competition to market foreign products.

- Be a retail outlet for other companies' products.

- Understand customers' needs for products and services, where there is less competition.

- Get customers the best deal.

- Gain control over a defined niche.

- Be the hub in the spoke of a wheel.

You should strive to cultivate a number of these traits in combination. You need not master them all, as singly they may not yield the sustained advantage you seek, but in combination, they are more powerful.

Combine them in packages that achieve overall sweet spots, unassailable positions such as those co-designing, embeddedness, and being a broker establish. The next chapter provides a better understanding of the mobility you need to get to these sweet spots.

5

AGILITY

Big winners knew where to go. They understood where they had to head. (See Table 5.1.) Their movement was based on knowledge of their customers. It was driven by markets, as opposed to technology or products.

Big winners moved toward markets where they could be more fully aligned with their customers. They wanted to provide their customers with the best value for the money.

Big winners not only understood where to go. They also understood how to get there. Their movement was based both on mergers and acquisitions and on internal growth. As well as adding businesses that had more promise, they divested themselves of businesses that had little promise. Not bound by the past, they regularly reinvented themselves.

Table 5.1 Traits of Agility

Company	Movement
Amphenol	Works closely with customers
	Goes toward specialty markets
	Becomes a consolidator
	Diversifies into new markets
SPX	Collaborates with customers
	Finds new industries
	Purchases diverse firms
	Acquires varied products
Ball	Responds rapidly to changes in market demand
	Develops customer intimacy
	Creates new concepts
	Purchases competitors
	Diversifies into new technology
Fiserv	Responds quickly to industry consolidation
	Grows by integrating with customer infrastructure
	Moves to back office
	Buys best of breed companies
	Diversifies into related products
Dreyer's	Responds quickly to innovation
	Responds flexibly
	Grows by controlling distribution
Family Dollar	Operates under radar
	Moves with low-income customers
Forest Labs	Engages in new product development without expensive R&D
	Grows with innovative products
	Moves to alternative markets and suppliers
	Diversifies into generic products
Brown & Brown	Responds quickly to threat of large companies
	Develops customized products and services
	Moves to underserved niches
	Broadens geographic scope
	Diversifies into small niches
Activision	Responds quickly to powerful industrial players
	Leverages outsiders
	Makes alliances
	Relies on creative people
	Buys additional talent and efficiencies
	Diversifies into multiple platforms

Figure 5.1 summarizes the lessons that have been learned from an analysis of the moves of the big winners. It shows how these companies rapidly responded to change. They went into new and promising markets and quickly achieved diversification. They cultivated the traits of agility needed to support sweet spots they occupied. For each lesson in Figure 5.1, I provide examples of agile traits (Table 5.1) that the big winners exhibited.

1. Respond swiftly to threats and opportunities.
2. Don't get too big—with smaller size comes greater flexibility.
3. Grow your business in accord with your customers' changing needs.
4. Move toward new and promising markets where customers have specialized needs that only you can meet.
5. Be an aggressive acquirer, taking advantage of the opportunities to broaden and enhance your product offerings.
6. Be sufficiently diversified so that you can compensate for a decline in one segment with strengths in another.

Figure 5.1 Lessons about agility.

Respond Swiftly to Threats and Opportunities

Big winners respond quickly. This lesson is illustrated by five agile traits of the big winners. They respond quickly to (i) overcapacity and changes in market demand, (ii) the threat of large companies, (iii) powerful industry players, (iv) industry consolidation, and (v) innovation. Ball, Brown & Brown, Activision, Fiserv, and Dreyer's provide examples of this rapid response.

Respond Quickly to Overcapacity and to Changes in Market Demand

The food and beverage container industry was mature. It had low profit margins and overcapacity. Production in North America was greater than demand, which created a highly competitive environment, but Ball was at the forefront of change. It responded quickly to these challenges. It detected and accurately predicted shifting consumer preferences. It exited its noncore businesses, sold its glass manufacturing line, and moved from glass, tin, and aluminum to plastics. It applied its formidable research and development powers to meet customers' desires for lighter, stronger containers. The company acted in anticipation of trends that other firms missed, all the while striving to be at the vanguard of industry developments.

Respond Quickly to the Threat of Large Companies

Before the passage of the 1999 Gramm-Leach-Bliley Act (GLB) that repealed restrictions on banks affiliating with securities firms to provide lower prices and one-stop shopping, there were predictions that independent insurance companies, which controlled about a third of the market, would lose virtually all their business. GLB gave incentives to large financial companies to merge and acquire other firms and offer diversified products and services that competed with the insurance products that Brown & Brown (B&B) sold. One-stop shopping was a powerful marketing tool for consumers seeking convenience and simplicity that B&B could not match. B&B responded to this threat by rapidly growing and expanding its business and taking it in new directions. It put a new emphasis on niche markets that large companies were not able to serve well.

Respond Quickly to Powerful Industry Players

The environment in which Activision operated was a difficult one because the company competed with the two large and powerful industry players, Sony and Microsoft. Sony and Microsoft were hardware manufacturers. They had their own platforms for which they developed their own software. The Sony platform was the PlayStation, and the Microsoft platform was Xbox. Activision could ill afford to alienate either of these companies, yet it was regularly in competition with them for talented software developers. It had to retain the talented software developers that might defect to Sony or Microsoft. Activision also had the challenge of maintaining good relationships with such large and powerful retailers as Wal-Mart and Best Buy. There was fierce competition from other game developers for shelf space in these companies' stores. Activision promptly met the threats posed by these large and powerful industry players. Every time a more advanced gaming system was introduced, the company rapidly replaced its older games with ones that worked on the newer systems. The company learned this lesson because in 1991, it had to declare Chapter 11 bankruptcy when it did not adapt quickly enough to a change in platform. To avoid such a situation from recurring, Activision put great emphasis on quick response.

Respond Quickly to Industry Consolidation

Financial institutions were consolidating to generate synergies in increasingly commoditized markets. New alternative lending and investment products were rapidly being introduced, with emphasis on transaction-oriented, fee-based services that required large data processing capabilities that were costly to maintain within the financial institutions. Fiserv rapidly moved from its original market to this broader segment. It shifted from its original target customer, small community banks and thrifts, toward consolidating mega-banks, insurance companies, brokerages, and firms that were international in scope. As the market changed, it predicted the direction that the market would take. It understood its external environment and adapted quickly. It initiated a growth strategy to establish itself as an industry leader with new clients and broad service offerings.

Respond Quickly to Innovation

When T. Gary Rogers and William F. Cronk purchased Dreyer's from one of the original owners in 1977, they moved quickly from being a specialty ice cream firm, whose products were sold mainly in San Francisco area grocery and ice cream stores, to a company with a broad line of products sold throughout the United States and the world. Dreyer's went public in 1981, and by 1994, it had gained the U.S. market's leading position in premium ice cream and a top three slot in the super-premium category. In that year, it formulated a strategy for continued growth. Dreyer's net sales rose from $407 million in 1993 to $1.3 billion in 2002. It consistently realized strong growth in sales by means of innovation. Dreyer's was the first ice cream maker on the West Coast to offer round containers with window lids. It was one of the first to offer a "healthier" ice cream product, Grand Light. It introduced new products, opened new manufacturing and warehouse facilities, acquired regional distribution companies, and invested heavily in information technology. Dreyer's distributed its own products and that of its main competitors, including Haagen Dazs and Ben & Jerry's, through the direct-store-delivery (DSD) system it put in place. It expanded the number of flavors it sold to 150. The company had the widest variety of ice cream flavors of any national brand. The Dreyer's line of products was available in western states and Far Eastern and South American markets, and the Edy's line was sold in the remaining U.S. states, the Caribbean, and Europe. Dreyer's responded quickly to the threats it faced by means of rapid innovation.

Don't Get Too Big—With Smaller Size Comes Greater Flexibility

Five agile traits illustrate this lesson. First, big winners aim to be the best, not the biggest. Second, they save money on new product development and R&D by working with other firms. Third, they are good networkers—they function by means of strategic alliances and partnerships. Fourth, they operate under the radar of large firms and hence often escape competitive retaliation. Fifth, they keep their options open. The lesson to learn from the big winners is to control your growth. Do not grow for the sake of growing. Be aware that there are liabilities in being too large. Ball, Forest Labs, Activision, Family Dollar, and Dreyer's provide good examples of this lesson.

Be the Best, Not the Biggest

Ball's aim was not to be the biggest beverage can company, but to be the "best." With about 13,000 employees and $3.86 billion in annual sales, it was a small player in an industry dominated by such giants as Alcoa, which had more than 127,000 employees and $20 billion in sales, and Alcan, which had more than 48,000 employees and $14 billion in sales. Ball made acquisitions, but only those that fit its mission. Its aim was profitable growth, not growth at any cost. Thus, it shed assets after each acquisition to keep its size manageable and to ensure profitability. Its purchase of Reynolds greatly increased its size and debt load, but the company acted quickly (within 18 months) to prevent itself from being burdened with excessive debt. To keep itself lean, it quickly identified $70 million in inefficiencies and shut down two former Reynolds plants. From 1999 to 2002, Ball's sales declined, but it remained profitable relying not on bulk but on its abilities.

Enjoy New Product Development Without Expensive R&D

Forest Labs competed against the pharmaceutical giants Merck, Pfizer, Eli Lilly, and GlaxoSmithKline. All of them were larger than Forest Labs and had better research capabilities. To surmount this obstacle,

Forest Labs had strategic alliances with less well-known firms. These firms had promising drugs they could not effectively commercialize in the U.S. market. By making alliances with these firms, Forest was able to take on the giant pharmaceutical firms. Its agreements with these firms allowed Forest to compete with the pharmaceutical giants without being exposed to the risks of expensive research and development. Investments in licensing and copromotion agreements with these firms, instead of outright acquisition, enabled Forest to bring high-potential products to the market without incurring a great deal of risk. The company relied on agreements with foreign pharmaceutical companies for the exclusive rights to develop and market products in the United States. Forest's best-selling drug, Celexa, was licensed for sale in the United States from the Danish firm, H. Lundbeck. H. Lundbeck developed Celexa's successor, Lexapro. Forest Labs had strategic alliances with the Danish company for exclusive marketing rights to three other central nervous system drugs. The company also had a copromotion agreement with the Japanese firm Sankyo Pharma to share the marketing and selling of Benicar. Forest found these undervalued drugs that the foreign firms had successfully marketed in their own countries. By licensing and copromoting these drugs with its foreign partners, Forest avoided incurring the high development costs itself. This strategy permitted it to move quickly and focus on especially attractive and proven new products.

Leverage Outsiders

Activision also kept itself small on purpose, preferring to leverage help from outsiders rather than doing everything itself. It contracted out software development to small firms. It licensed and marketed games that independent companies created. Another example is the decision that Activision made not to create its own Internet gaming site. It viewed the Internet as another gaming platform like PlayStation and the Xbox, which was best provided by a third party. Rather than investing in this channel directly, Activision outsourced the function to Gamespy.com, a company that provided access to a multitude of games. Gamespy.com had to get access to the big-name games, so it had to accommodate what Activision wanted.

Operate Under the Radar of Large Firms

As a small player in a highly competitive industry that included such retail giants as Wal-Mart and Target, Family Dollar responded quickly and flexibly without capturing the attention of these giants. It appealed to customers who were seeking the convenience of small stores located closer to where they lived. Its aim was to be better, not necessarily bigger. Its management met the challenge of growth by closing, renovating, and remodeling, besides opening stores. In 2000, Family Dollar opened 91 new stores, closed 41, relocated 72, and renovated 122 stores.

Be Flexible

Dreyer's faced competition in the premium and novelty ice cream business from competitors that were much larger than it in overall size. ConAgra (Healthy Choice Ice Cream) had $27.6 billion in net sales and 63,000 employees, Nestlé (Haagen-Dazs and Nestlé's products) had $67.5 billion in net sales and 230,000 employees, and Unilever (Good Humor and Ben & Jerry's) had $82.8 billion in net sales and 247,000 employees. Because it faced these giants, Dreyer's had little room for error. To compete, it had to make constant improvements. By being flexible, Dreyer's outperformed its competitors.

Grow Your Business in Accord with Your Customers' Changing Needs

Big winners growth is in accord with their customers' changing needs. There are eight traits to illustrate this lesson. Big winners work with their customers on (i) product design and delivery, (ii) special projects, (iii) joint ventures and long-term contracts, (iv) innovative products, (v) customized products, (vi) alliances, (vii) infrastructure integration, and (viii) distribution. The lesson to grow in accord with your customer's changing needs is illustrated with examples that come from Amphenol, SPX, Ball, Forest Labs, B&B, Activision, Fiserv, and Dreyer's. These companies collaborated with their customers in many important ways. Their growth was not random but it was well coordinated with what customers wanted.

Work Closely with Customers on Product Design and Delivery

Amphenol got to know and understand its customers through a global sales force and through independent manufacturers' representatives who were located in 60 countries. In many instances, Amphenol had approved vendor status with its customers, and product design teams that had collaborative arrangements with customers. The design teams made specialized products to meet specific needs. For instance, Amphenol jointly developed a reliable coaxial cable with the cable companies. The coaxial cable delivered signals at 1.0-gigahertz speed, which permitted cable companies to offer more channels. The Amphenol brand resonated strongly with its customers because the company worked so hard on product design and delivery. It owned many patents, and they were valuable assets, but not as valuable as its close ties to customers. The main goal of Amphenol's account managers—emphasized again and again in company documents—was to meet customers' needs.

Collaborate Closely with Customers on Special Projects

SPX wanted to be valued for its technological leadership. Especially profitable were specialty-engineering ventures with customers. SPX bundled together engineering products and services. With the General Signal and UDI acquisitions, it was able to create integrated flow solutions. In the mixer-valve-pump arena, it had top market share in a number of areas. The acquisition of General Signal brought on board Lightnin, a manufacturer of industrial valves and controls, and Dezurik, a leading producer of industrial process equipment. The UDI acquisition added the valve and control companies Mueller Steam and CMB Industries and the air filtration and dehydration business of Flair. Customers could bring together products and services from SPX's divisions. Business-to-business e-commerce allowed SPX to introduce collaboration to the built-to-order industrial mixer and agitator market.

Buyers were able to talk directly to SPX representatives and generate their own blueprints rather than working with third-party representatives. This system was faster and less prone to the specification errors made by third-party representatives. Internal costs and cycle times went down by more than 50 percent. SPX retreated from selling individual products and services and started to offer full-package solutions, a pattern it tried to repeat in the many markets it served. In the automotive sector, it switched from selling mechanical tools, a commodity business, to full-service offerings. Differentiation came from online technical information and training, rather than just products.

Develop Intimacy with Customers Through Joint Ventures and Long-Term Contracts

Ball also partnered with its major customers. It had a joint venture with ConAgra (Ball Western Can Company) to make use of ConAgra's packaging materials and a joint venture with Coors to manufacture most of Coors' cans. Rocky Mountain Metal Container was owned half by Ball and half by Coors. It had one of the largest can production facilities in the world. Ball also had long-term contracts with other major customers such as Pepsi, Coke, and Miller Brewing Company. These relationships created a level of customer intimacy that allowed Ball to respond quickly to changes in customer needs. They were critical to ensuring long-term demand for Ball's products.

Grow Your Business with Innovative Products

Forest Labs had to be concerned about the expiration of patents on its major products. The expiration of the Celexa patent forced it to confront the future. The lucrative nature of the drug allowed Forest Labs to invest heavily and develop Lexapro to take Celexa's place. The company ended promotions for Celexa and started to focus on marketing Lexapro. It touted Lexapro as the most effective depression treatment ever and maintained that the drug was the most rapid acting and the best-tolerated antidepressant. The challenge that Forest Labs faced was to increase the speed by which it brought new products like Lexapro to the market. Its aim was to expand the size and scope of its pharmaceutical offerings with innovative therapies that focused on such conditions as hypertension, central nervous system disorders, and the pain associated with arthritis, asthma, and gastrointestinal problems. (See the list below.) Forest's pipeline of drugs included Benicar for hypertension, Namenda for Alzheimer's, and Acamprosate for alcohol addiction. In 2002, the company launched Benicar, and it was relying on Namenda to be its next big success. Benicar and Namenda treated the growing needs of an aging population. Namenda, which was intended for moderate to severe Alzheimer's patients, slowed the pace of deterioration rather than offering total relief and reversal of effects. Because of the cash flow generated by Celexa, Forest was able to invest in these products and expand its portfolio to create a pipeline of innovative drugs it hoped to commercialize in the future. The company did not stop with a single hit but continued to search for new products to replace those whose patents were expiring.

Forest Labs products include:

- **Tiazac**—An antihypertensive, cardiac, blood pressure control, calcium channel blocker.
- **Celexa**—An antidepressant from the family of drugs known as selective serotonin reuptake inhibitors, or SSRIs.
- **Lexapro**—Another SSRI for the treatment of depression.
- **Benicar**—A drug for the treatment of hypertension.
- **Namenda**—A drug that reduces Alzheimer's symptoms.
- **Acamprosate**—A drug for alcohol addiction.
- **Lorcet**—A prescription pain reliever.
- **Aerobid**—An anti-inflammatory steroid.
- **Armour Thyroid**—A natural replacement for thyroid hormone.
- **Thyrolar and Levothroid**—Synthetic products for hypothyroidism.
- **Aerospan**—An inhaled corticosteroid for the treatment of asthma.
- **Aero Chamber Plus**—A product that maximizes delivery of inhaler medications to patients' lungs.

- **Infasurf**—A lung surfactant that aids in respiratory capacity in infants.

- **Cervidil**—A product that allows for controlled drug release.

Grow with Customized Products and Services

B&B successfully developed customized insurance policies by working directly with its customers to understand their current and future needs. The policies it developed locked the customers into working with B&B because it would be difficult for them to repeat the process that they engaged in with B&B with another firm. The addition of customized policies to B&B's portfolio created high switching costs for B&B's customers. The company also differentiated itself with its experienced sales force, which a new entrant would have difficulty matching. The services that the B&B provided included risk management surveys and analysis, insurance consultation, and claims adjustment. The mergers and acquisitions in which it engaged increased its size and allowed it to offer these services at less cost. The cost reduction came from economies of scale. B&B was determined to continuously expand the services it offered. Through a partner (Afni Insurance Services), it was relying on the Internet to make it easier for customers to review information about their policies. B&B provided the service 24 hours a day. This information enabled customers to make better decisions. As B&B added customized offerings and services in collaboration with its customers, its pretax margins improved. It gained new business growth and operating efficiencies.

Grow Via Alliances

Activision had many alliances and partnerships that helped it grow. These alliances and partnerships gave it the rights to various properties its customers valued. Thanks to agreements that Activision had with such companies as Marvel Enterprises, Disney, and LucasArts, it became the number-two video game publisher in the United States behind Electronic Arts. (See the next list.) Activision had the rights to publish products based on Marvel Comics' super heroes, including

Spider-Man, X-Men, Iron Man, and the Fantastic Four. It had the rights to popular animation hits such as DreamWorks SKG's *Shrek 2*. It had a relationship with the publisher of the best-selling children's book, *A Series of Unfortunate Events*. These relationships enabled Activision to achieve a better match between the technology it created and market the readiness. A lesson management learned from its 1991 Chapter 11 bankruptcy was not to depend on just a few titles for most of its earnings. The company had to have a pipeline of products ready for falloff in popularity of its hits. By 2001, it had restored its pipeline, and more than 75 percent of its revenues came from titles other than the 16 *Tony Hawk* action adventures.

Activision's major licensing agreements include:

- Marvel—*X-Men, Blade, Fantastic Four,* and *Iron Man*
- Disney Interactive
- Viacom—*Star Trek*
- Tony Hawk—*Skateboard*
- Matt "Condor" Hoffman—Vertical ramp biking id Software—Wolfenstein sequel
- Shaun Palmer—*Snowboarder*
- Columbia Pictures *Spider-Man*
- BBC Multimedia—*Weakest Link* game show
- Shaun Murray—*Wakeboarder*
- Sony Pictures Family Entertainment—*Jackie Chan Adventures*
- Steven Spielberg's *Minority Report*
- Revolution Studios' *XXX*
- LucasArts Entertainment's *Star Wars*
- *Lemony Snicket's A Series of Unfortunate Events*
- DreamWorks SKG—*Sharkslayer, Madagascar,* and *Over the Hedge*

Grow by Means of Integration with Your Customers' Infrastructure

Fiserv's reputation was built on a "hands on" philosophy with customers; it partnered with customers "anywhere, anytime, anyway." The company used its size and depth to provide solutions that customers wanted. A combined customer-Fiserv team selected software, hardware, personnel, and location of facilities. For some customers, Fiserv provided the software or the hardware and let the customer manage the data center. For others, it provided personnel to run a client-owned and client-managed facility. For still other customers, Fiserv processed transactions offsite at its own data processing centers. The close integration with a customers' infrastructure served as a barrier to entry. Even if a competitor could offer the same service, it could not obtain a customer's business, because it was not similarly embedded. Data processing, which was a significant portion of what Fiserv provided, was relatively undifferentiated. Fiserv amalgamated products and services around a philosophy of the customer coming first. For its customers, the company provided a vast array of services along with ongoing support. By developing long-term relationships and striving to be an integral part of customers' business, Fiserv enjoyed recurring revenues and relative security from termination. If a customer switched, it would incur high risks and costs. The integration of Fiserv's products and services into customers' infrastructure forestalled the possibility of customers abandoning the company. The most important benefit that Fiserv achieved from this integration was the ability to further implant its services in its customers' business processes. Its strategy of developing highly specialized services using proprietary products and product enhancements created captive customers to whom Fiserv sold related additional products and services. The benefit for customers was that they could focus on their core business, which was not data processing. By using Fiserv's products and services, customers saved money and were able to do what they did best.

Grow by Controlling Distribution

Dreyer's had control over the grocery store freezer space for premium ice cream, distributing not only its own products but almost all the products of its major competitors including Nestlé (Haagen Dazs), Unilever (Ben & Jerry's), and ConAgra (Healthy Choice). Its superior distribution network allowed it to turn over its inventory at a high rate. Dreyer's had no real competitors in this side of the business. Almost half of its revenue came from distribution. Of the nearly $1.35 billion in net sales for fiscal year 2002, partner brand sales were valued at almost $600 million and accounted for 44 percent of the firm's net sales. From 1998 to 1999, Ben and Jerry's transferred approximately one-half of its distribution business from Dreyer's to another distributor, but under a new agreement in 2000, Ben & Jerry's returned all of its distribution business to Dreyer's. Ben and Jerry's came to understand that Dreyer's was indispensable to its success. By virtue of its control over distribution, Dreyer's was able to precisely know inventory levels at each retailer. The company gained intimate knowledge of customer preferences and was able to deliver products on time when they were needed. Dreyer's billed retailers solely based on product sold rather than inventory on the shelf. The retailer did not have to pay for product left on the shelf. To keep track of inventory, the company had a system that worked with scanners that retailers used. The retail grocers processed paperless orders with handheld computers, a feature that was attractive to the chains that Dreyer's served. Kroger Co., Safeway, Inc., and Albertson's, Inc., which constituted more than 30 percent of Dreyer's annual sales in 2001, liked that Dreyer's also had innovative promotions such as movie tie-ins with *Toy Story*, *Scooby-Doo*, and *101 Dalmatians* and that it offered both television and print advertising. The advertising created brand awareness and the point of sale displays induced impulse purchases.

Move Toward New and Promising Markets Where Customers Have Specialized Needs Only You Can Meet

Big winners moved toward new and promising markets where customers had specialized needs only they could meet. Eight traits illustrate this lesson. Big winners moved to (i) specialty markets, (ii) new industries, (iii) new concepts, (iv) alternative markets and suppliers, (v) underserved niches, (vi) creative people, (vii) the back office, and (viii) low-income consumers. Movement toward new and promising markets where customers have specialized needs is illustrated with examples from Amphenol, SPX, Ball, Forest Labs, B&B, Activision, Fiserv, and Family Dollar. These companies knew how to develop specialized niches.

Move to Specialty Markets

Amphenol migrated to industry niches and sectors where the competition was less intense. Its focus was on special classes of connectors that it designed with its customers. These products required superior performance and reliability under conditions of stress in hostile environments. The company started in 1932 as American Phenolic, a manufacturer of artificial fibers. Its product line changed many times from production of artificial fibers in the 1930s, to plastic insulation materials over the next several decades, to being a leading producer of interconnect products. A high proportion of its 2001 sales (38 percent) were in the troubled telecommunications and communications sector; sales of these products declined 10.2 percent in that year. The decrease in telecom sales, however, was offset by a 24-percent growth in military/aerospace sales. Amphenol benefited from the post 9/11 state of affairs. Its connectors were found in a diverse array of products from the Boeing 777 to the international space station. Complex computer flight control systems were attached with its connectors. The joint strike fighter used its connectors for weapons and guidance systems. For Amphenol's customers, it was hard to find substitutes for the firm's high-performance, specialized products.

Move to New Industries

To combat the cyclical nature of its business and low profit margins, SPX searched for specialized customers in new industries. These industries included chemical processing, pharmaceuticals, infrastructure, mineral processing, petrochemical, telecommunications, financial services, transportation, and power generation. The board of directors recognized the need to move toward customers in these new industries. It hired a new CEO in 1995, John Blystone, a 17-year GE veteran who had been a high-level manufacturing executive at the company. Under Blystone's leadership, SPX tried to make a turnaround, acquiring new technologies, increasing its geographical reach, and penetrating new markets, where it met specialized customer needs. In 1995, SPX had been a 90-year-old, undermanaged, auto tool and parts manufacturer. It designed and made specialty tools, diagnostic systems, and service equipment that franchised vehicle dealers and independent repair facilities used. This business had numerous competitors and low operating margins. GM, Ford, and Chrysler constituted 37 percent of SPX's revenues. By 2002, auto tools, parts, and equipment constituted less than 20 percent of the company's revenues. Blystone had moved the firm into new industries.

Move to New Concepts

Ball positioned itself as developer of new concepts that worked with customers to bring these concepts to fruition. Its goal was to meet customers' needs for customizable products that enhanced their brands. The company was once best known for producing glass canning jars, the Mason jars found in many American homes. Before that, it had been in the business of making paint containers. In 1969, it entered the metal beverage container business. In 1988, it went into food canning, and in 1994, it entered the plastic (PET) bottle business. PET appealed to Ball's customers because the costs of the plastic were low compared to the costs of metal. For Ball's customers, the ability to mold the plastic into different shapes was an advantage because it allowed them to differentiate the look of their products from those of their competitors. Fueled by growing demand for bottled water, the plastic bottles that

Ball codesigned with its customers were its fastest-growing segment, expanding by 21 percent in 2002. Plastic bottle demand was rising at a pace of about 7 percent annually, whereas demand for soft drink containers as a whole was shrinking because consumption of soft drinks was leveling off. Ball had an 8-percent market share in the plastic container industry. The dominant producer had a 17 percent market share. But Ball did not just provide the bottles. It introduced new concepts to the industry, such as the 8.4-ounce can that targeted the growing energy drink market and the recloseable aluminum bottle (Daiwa's "new bottle can") that it was selling in the United States.

Move to Alternative Markets and Suppliers

Through reaching out to new markets and new sources of supply, Forest Labs' sales tripled and its profits swelled from $37 million in 1998 to $338 million in 2002. The company was organized in 1956 in New York with the initial mission of selling vitamins and candy products. It went public in 1967. Howard Solomon became CEO in 1977 after serving as the company's outside counsel. His first move as CEO was to leave vitamins and candy and find new markets. First, he entered the generic drug business. Then he looked for new suppliers. He acquired drugs from other companies and improved them with Forest Labs' proprietary drug-delivery system. Under Solomon's direction, the company continued the search for new markets and sources of supply. It made an angina medication and sold it overseas. But not every endeavor the company undertook was successful. In 1991, it discontinued an incontinence treatment (Micturin) that had dangerous side effects. In 1996, Forest Labs reached a licensing agreement with Biovail Corporation to introduce Tiazac, a treatment for hypertension and angina. Tiazac accounted for 23.7 percent of the company's total revenues in 1999. Solomon's son Andrew suffered from severe depression. Unhappy with the treatments he was getting, he came upon Cipramil, a European product with high efficacy and low side effects. Cipramil had captured more than 50 percent of the Swedish market. Forest Labs saw this drug as a huge opportunity. It came to an agreement with the drug's Danish producer, H. Lundbeck, to gain FDA approval and market this drug in the United States under the name Celexa. Following its

1998 approval, Celexa achieved phenomenal success, snapping up market share from competitors like Zoloft, Paxil, and Prozac. Sales of Celexa reached $1.1 billion in 2002. It had a market share of 17 percent, as the antidepressant category as a whole expanded by more than 15 percent. In 2002, Celexa accounted for 69.4 percent of Forest Labs' sales. The company rode the wave of Celexa's success. It grew to more than 3,700 employees. It had a sales force of more than 2,100 and revenues of more than $1.5 billion.

Move to Underserved Niches

Brown & Brown (B&B) worked with its customers and suppliers to design and sell insurance policies for underserved niches. It served markets as different as railroads and cargo haulers and CEOs, COOs, and CFOs. The unique markets into which it moved gave it access to high premiums and margins that were the primary sources of its growth. Although some of the markets into which B&B moved were small and thus neglected by the large players in the industry, the rewards were ample because it managed the business lines well. B&B developed the slogan that it had to be "as agile as the cheetah." Despite the fact that it could not compete with the breadth of products offered by larger firms like Marsh & McLennan, Aon, and Gallagher, it survived by its agility. The company's strength was its ties to its customers and to the sources that underwrote policies.

Move to Creative People

Activision's founders were looking for talented and creative people who understood the audience for the software games they were making. This market was composed mainly of young adolescent and post-adolescent men. Activision's founders, a group of former Atari employees and a music industry executive, tried to build their company around creative people. They were pioneers in the industry who were not afraid to take risks. They started the company on the principle of innovation and entrepreneurship. Their firm was the first independent entertainment software developer. They succeeded in their aim of attracting creative people. Not all these people were Activision employees; some were in independent clusters of closely allied and affiliated companies upon which Activision relied. The first game that Activision produced was called Dragster. It was released in 1980, and along with Pitfall, another early game from Activision, it was a huge success. The company released 52 games in its first eight years. Asteroids, its first arcade game release, dominated the market in the early and mid 1980s. The *Tony Hawk Pro Skater* series, first released in 1998, became Activision's biggest hit in the 1990s. By means of the creative people it attracted, *Activision* knew its customers and knew where to go to get its customers what they wanted. The retail game and toys industry was extremely competitive. Many companies pursued the same leisure, spare-time dollar. Consumers could spend leisure money on many alternatives to computer games, including reading, participating in sports, going to movies, attending concerts, chatting with neighbors, taking care of a pet, and running a marathon. To succeed, Activision had to have a network of talented people who were capable of connecting to this market.

Move to the Back Office

Fiserv moved to the back office. It processed and managed a growing number of transactions for its customer because they wanted to avoid the costs of carrying out this function themselves. As distinctions among banks, thrifts, insurance, and brokerage companies narrowed the market for Fiserv's products, and services grew. There were fewer financial institutions, but they were looking for sophisticated software to support a wider range of offerings. The total number of clients was decreasing, but remaining clients wanted additional services. Their number was down, but their spending on outsourcing was growing. The continuous need for secure and accurate transactions was a major concern. Meeting this need required impeccable standards. Customers expected seamless interlinking of back-end systems. These systems had to account for many different kinds of transactions—insurance, personal checking, credit cards, mortgages, and investments. The systems had to be reliable, secure, and fast. To establish its status as the premier provider of these services, Fiserv offered customers many different options. It had a broad array of transaction-oriented and fee-based financial services that included licensing software products, processing customers' data, managing the internal data processing functions, and allowing its customers to use its own service bureaus and facilities. Fiserv had the capabilities to meet the demand for the processing of information by financial institutions.

Move to Low-Income Consumers

Family Dollar made a niche for itself among a seemingly unattractive, yet underserved demographic of low-income consumers. It moved into the so-called "extreme value sector" within discount retailing, implanting itself in the lives of cost-conscious customers who had no choice but to reduce their expenses. Family Dollar was a good fit for these customers' needs. Its stores in rural and small-town markets were 52 percent of the stores it operated in 2002. Management also had moved to the low-income consumer in urban areas. It pushed for greater penetration of large urban markets where traffic was higher than in rural areas and small towns. It pursued a strategy of rapid urban expansion, opening a large number of new stores in inner city neighborhoods. From 1999 to 2002, the company's store count grew nearly 40 percent to 4,616 stores, 66 percent of which were in inner cities. (See Table 5.2.) The company benefited from a weak economy. Its competitors also expanded at break-neck speeds in urban environments during this period. From 1999 to 2002, Dollar General opened an average of 669 stores per year, and Dollar Tree opened an average of 230 stores per year. Family Dollar was in a race to expand rapidly and gain a foothold in these markets before they were saturated by other discount retailers.

Table 5.2 Growth in the Number of Family Dollar Stores

Year	Total Number of Stores
2002	4,616
2001	4,198
2000	3,777
1999	3,371
1998	3,066
1997	2,820
1996	2,602
1995	2,451
1994	2,257

Be an Aggressive Acquirer, Taking Advantage of the Opportunities to Broaden and Enhance Your Product Offerings

Big winners were aggressive acquirers. They took advantage of opportunities to broaden and enhance their product offerings. Six traits illustrate this lesson. Big winners were (i) consolidators, (ii) diversifiers, (iii) buyers of competitors, (iv) broadeners of their geographic scope, (v) purchasers of talent and efficiency, and (vi) purchasers of best of breed companies. The lesson is illustrated with examples from Amphenol, SPX, Ball, B&B, Activision, and Fiserv. These companies were active and aggressive acquirers.

Be a Consolidator

In 1997, Amphenol merged with NXS Acquisition, a subsidiary of the investment bank, Kohlberg Kravis Roberts & Co (KKR), which was best known for its $31 billion takeover of RJR Nabisco in 1989. The capabilities KKR's management team provided additional capital. It gave Amphenol the chance to be an aggressive acquirer. The company's acquisitions broadened and enhanced its product offerings and expanded its global reach. Amphenol was a consolidator among interconnect companies. The opportunity to be a consolidator existed because the market was fragmented and declining. In 1996, the top 10 companies controlled just 32 percent of this market. By 2002, this number increased to nearly 50 percent. When feasible, Amphenol avoided paying a high price for hard assets such as buildings and equipment. It bought employees and technologies. Often the companies it purchased were ailing, and it bought them at bargain rates.[2]

Purchase Diverse Firms

SPX started as a supplier of tools to automotive mechanic shops, but it morphed into a $5 billion company by means of acquisitions in various industries including power, cooling, fluid technologies; compacting; security, building safety; electrical testing, measurement, and laboratories and life sciences. (See Figure 5.2.) Two of its acquisitions were very large. In 1998, SPX bought General Signal, an electrical and industrial control manufacturer that had $2 billion in sales. At the time, General Signal was nearly twice SPX's size. In 2001, it acquired the flow technology business of United Dominion Incorporated (UDI), a diversified manufacturer of proprietary engineered products with sales of $2.4 billion. The company aggressively pursued growth through acquisitions.

1993	Lowener Maschinen Gmbh
	Allen Testproducts
1997	A.R. Brasch Marketing, Inc.
1998	Valley Forge Group
	Tecnotest
	General Signal Corp.
	Toledo Trans-Kit
1999	North American Transformer
2000	High Voltage Supply
	Copes-Vulcan
	JEWETT, Inc.
	Ziton
	Fenner Fluid Power
2001	Central Tower & Ryan Construction
	TCI International, Inc.
	United Dominion Industries
	Plenty Group
	Kendro Laboratory Products, L.P.
	Power Systems Development, Inc.
2002	Dukane Communications Systems
	Daniel Valve Company

Figure 5.2 Key SPX acquisitions: 1993 to 2002.

Purchase Competitors

The food and beverage industry in which Ball competed was a mature one with low profit margins. Companies faced intense pricing pressures and the threat of consolidation. To achieve a strong position in this industry, Ball successfully acquired and integrated some of its major competitors. In 1998, it expanded its aluminum can business with the acquisition of Reynolds Metals. With this purchase, Ball accounted for more than 30 percent of North American aluminum can shipments. In 2002, it acquired Germany-based Schmalbach-Lubeca, the second largest beverage can manufacturer in Europe (31 percent unit market share, second to Rexam's 39 percent). Schmalbach-Lubeca had 2,500 employees, produced 12 billion aluminum and steel cans a year, and had 2002 sales exceeding $1 billion.

Broaden Geographic Scope

B&B also grew through mergers and acquisitions. Because its overhead and administrative costs were low, it could channel its capital into this activity without debt rising. B&B financed its mergers and acquisition with cash and stocks. From 1998 to 2002, its revenue increased at an average annual rate of 25 percent, and its net income grew 20 percent yearly. From 1992 to 2003, B&B acquired a total of 118 small insurance agency companies with estimated annual revenues in excess of $30 million. Table 5.3 lists the companies that it acquired or merged with in 2001 and 2002. By means of the acquisitions, the company grew from less than 500 employees in 1990 to more than 3,500 in 2002. It broadened its geographic scope to include such states as California, Connecticut, Indiana, Michigan, Minnesota, Nevada, New Jersey, New Mexico, New York, Texas, Washington, and Wyoming. B&B's aim was to acquire only small, profitable companies. Its acquisitions were carried out for two main reasons: (1) to further consolidate retail services; and (2) to branch out into underutilized, niche markets with high margins. With regard to the latter, B&B was able to increase its ability to deliver products to doctors, dentists, lawyers, and other professionals. It expanded its involvement in professional programs, and it added capabilities in consulting and plan administration.

Table 5.3 Brown & Brown's Acquisitions and Mergers: 2001 and 2002

2001	2002
Taber and Taber, Inc.	Technical Risks, LP
Robert L. Matson Insurance, Inc.	Dunn-Murphy-White Insurance Agency
Raleigh, Schwarz & Powell, Inc.	John Manner Insurance Agency, Inc.
Golden Gate Holdings, Inc.	Cooper, Brown & Currie, Inc.
McKinnon & Mooney, Inc.	Andersen Group, Ltd.
Froehlich-Paulson-Moore, Inc.	Louisiana Agencies, Inc.
Bynum, Grace & Joffrion	Pilkington Insurance Agency, Inc.
Web-Kor Insurance Agency, Inc.	Rhodes & Associates, Inc.
Henry S. Lehr and AFC Insurance	Mottner & Company, Inc.
Associated Insurance Agency	Healthcare Professionals' Insurance Services
Sanborn's Mexico Insurance	The Turner Group
Logan Insurance Agency, Inc.	Graham-Rogers, Inc.
Menk & Associates, Inc.	Standard Lines Service, LLC
The Benefit Group, Inc.	Valley General Agency
The Connelly Insurance Group, Inc.	Manhardt-DiLeo Insurance Agency, Inc.
Finwall & Associates Insurance, Inc.	Associated Insurance Services of Bristol
Insurance Professionals Inc.	Jim Wallace Agency, Inc.
CompVantage, L.L.C.	
Abrahms Group Benefits, Inc.	
Abrahms Life Services, Inc.	
Meadowbrook Villari Agency	
Layne & Associates, Ltd.	
Parcel Insurance Plan, Inc.	
The Young Agency, Inc.	
The Harris Agency, Inc.	
Spencer & Associates, Inc.	
Huval Insurance Agency, Inc.	
Sestito Insurance Agency	
LLP'S	
Mangus Insurance & Bonding, Inc.	

Purchase for Talent and Efficiencies

Activision was an aggressive acquirer of other gaming companies. It made 14 acquisitions from 1997 to 2002. These acquisitions allowed it to diversify its operations, add channels of distribution, develop new pools of talent, and expand its library of titles. The acquisitions also added to its value-chain efficiencies. Among the companies it acquired were Head Games Publishing, Expert Software, and Elsinore Multimedia. (See Figure 5.3.) These companies strengthened Activision's mass-market PC software business. To assist it in distribution in Europe, the company bought CentreSoft, Ltd. and NBG.

1997	Premier game developer Raven Software CentreSoft Ltd. and NBG Distribution
1998	Head Game Publishing CD Contact Data distributor
1999	Expert Software, a publisher and developer Elsinore Multimedia, a software company Neversoft Entertainment, a software developer
2001	Treyarch Innovation LLC, a software developer
2002	Shaba Games LLC, a software developer Z-Axis Ltd. Luxoflux Corporation, a software developer Gray Matter Interactive Studios, a software developer Distribution rights to id Software's *DOOM III*

Figure 5.3 Activision's major acquisitions: 1997 to 2002.

Purchase Best-of-Breed Companies with Proven Track Records

From 1984 to 2002, Fiserv made more than 110 acquisitions. (See Figure 5.4.) There were many small, local, and regional third-party data processors from which to choose. The large number of small players in data processing, item processing, and automated card services that the company acquired provided Fiserv with the opportunity to grow. Firms were consolidating with larger providers like Fiserv, but Fiserv did not jump into every opportunity to acquire other companies. Its acquisitions were targeted at "best-of-breed" firms with proven products and track records in promising markets. From 1992 to 1995, Fiserv's acquisitions expanded its scope in such areas as disaster recovery, asset/liability management, mortgage banking services, imaging technology, network integration, cash management, and software. From 1996 to 1999, its acquisitions added to its capabilities in securities services, automobile leasing software, insurance data processing, insurance marketing systems, and insurance software systems. The 12 acquisitions it made in 2001 added about 4,000 employees to the company. They bolstered its offerings in insurance data processing (Benefit Planners, NCSI, and Trewit Inc.), loan services (Integrated Loan Services), software and services (Catapult Technology Ltd. and FACT 400 credit card solution), insurance software systems (Facilities and Services Corp.), and automobile leasing software (Remarketing Services of America Inc.).

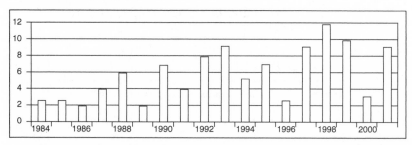

Figure 5.4 The number of Fiserv's acquisitions per year: 1984 to 2001.

Be Sufficiently Diversified So That You Can Compensate for a Decline in One Segment with Strengths in Another Segment

Big winners were sufficiently diversified so that they could compensate for a decline in one segment with strengths in another. They took advantage of opportunities to diversify their product offerings. This lesson is illustrated with examples from Amphenol, SPX, Ball, Forest Labs, B&B, Activision, and Fiserv. These companies made sure that they were sufficiently diversifed.

Diversify into New Markets

Although interconnect products were found in almost every consumer electronic product, including PCs and cellular phones, the industry as a whole was shrinking. Sales of interconnect products fell from $37 billion in 1999 to $30 billion in 2002. Interconnect products and assemblies accounted for 82 percent of Amphenol's 2002 sales. Coaxial cable, which accounted for 18 percent of 2002 sales, was used by cable networks to distribute programming and provide Internet connectivity, but sales of these products also were down. They declined by 44 percent in 2002. With its two main markets in decline, Amphenol was facing fierce price competition and thin profit margins. It adjusted to these conditions by diversifying into new markets. By virtue of the companies it acquired, it moved beyond the telecommunications business into the (i) commercial and military aerospace markets; and (ii) industrial, transportation, and other applications. In 1999, when the communications market was in high gear, 60 percent of Amphenol's sales were in telecom. By 2002, the company's sales mix had changed: just 52 percent was in telecommunications. The company sold to many different firms in the United States and abroad, none of which accounted for more than 5 percent of its total sales. Diversification gave Amphenol the flexibility to weather the economic storm in telecom and adjust to changes in market demand.

Diversify into Varied Products

SPX's original business units were tools and original equipment components that it manufactured for the automotive industry. However, the company rapidly evolved from its sole reliance on these products into other industrial and technical markets through its acquisitions, global sourcing, and partnerships. It acquired companies like General Signal and United Dominion that had little overlap with what it originally did. About 36 percent of United Dominion's sales did not share characteristics with those of SPX. The company became involved in everything from industrial construction to franchised motor vehicle dealers, the power industry, industrial manufacturing, water, the life sciences, and storage networks. Management felt that the potential rewards of diversification outweighed the risks. Growth in one area compensated for downturns in another. For example, as the power market declined, the company's road construction business picked up. A division called BOMAG, which was doing road construction in China, grew rapidly. To reduce risk, the company was involved in such diverse businesses as TV/radio broadcast antennas and towers to automated fare collection systems, high-integrity die-castings, and storage area network products.

Diversify into New Technology

Production of beverage and metal food containers exceeded demand in North America, creating a highly competitive pricing environment. There was overcapacity in the industry. Cans were a commodity, and purchasers had pricing power. Being capital-intensive, the industry was hard to exit. Raw material costs, for inputs such as aluminum, were volatile. They were hard to control, and subject to sudden spikes, as occurred in 1995 when prices jumped unexpectedly. To escape these conditions, Ball diversified. It exited the glass bottles and jars business, made and sold aluminum and metal cans, and moved into plastic bottles, but these businesses were not secure. So it also created a separate division based on an entirely different kind of technology. It set up Ball Aerospace and Technologies Corporation in 1956. This subsidiary designed and produced space and defense control and instrumentation and airborne antenna communications systems. Its products were integral components of the space shuttle. They helped various nations gather spy data using satellites. They were key components in giant telescopes. This division won accolades for helping to fix the Hubble telescope's blurry images. Ball had a product line of color and monochrome cameras for in-flight safety, security, and entertainment. It had a contract with Boeing for a device that enabled pilots to better see an aircraft's nose and main landing gear. The Aerospace and Technologies division obtained 90 percent of its revenues from government contracts and competed with other large defense companies such as Northrop Grumman, Honeywell, Boeing, and Lockheed-Martin. The customers of this division were the U.S. Department of Defense, the National Aeronautics and Space Administration, and foreign governments. The division accounted for just 10 percent of Ball's profits, but its post-9/11 growth was strong, and it was at the forefront of technological and scientific change.

Diversify into Generic Products

Forest Labs was not satisfied with a single hit (Celexa). By means of licensing agreements, it brought to market such drugs as Benicar, Lercanidipine, Acamprosate, and Aerospan in the hope that it would have additional hits, but it did not just play in the risky prescription drug market. Given that the pressure in the United States to reduce spending on prescription drugs was likely to remain intense, Forest Labs continued to market and produce generic drugs. It was eager to market such drugs when a competitor's patents expired, and it was able to be the first to market the product. Although the profit margins were lower than in prescription drugs, it tried to keep from giving wholesalers and distributors large discounts. It tried to attain economies of scale so that it could make money. If it could keep discounts low and spread overhead costs, it calculated that generics continued to be worth pursuing. They were not the company's core business, but they were also not something it should abandon completely. The company's Inwood Laboratories subsidiary continued to focus solely on the manufacturing and marketing of generic drugs. Forest Labs wanted to be able to effectively hedge the downside risk of the market in which it was competing. It prudently protected its branded prescription business by continuing to engage in the manufacture and marketing of generic drugs.

Diversify into Small Niches

B&B repeatedly demonstrated that it had the capacity to identify promising insurance niches outside the mainstream of its business and to quickly move into them. The diversification it achieved by means of movement into these niches came mainly through mergers and acquisitions. The diversification was critical because it protected the company from the market swings and the severe competition that plagued other companies. Diversification enabled B&B to move from being a low-cost insurance provider to one that provided unique products and services that carried high premiums. The specialty products it expressly designed for specific classes of customers proved be very profitable.

Diversify into Multiple Platforms

Activision became diversified to avoid dependence on a few hit titles that appealed to its mainly young male audience. The company developed and distributed products spanning a wide array of categories from action/adventure to action sports, racing, role-playing, simulation, first-person action, and strategy. It produced software for people who ranged from the cult-consumed game enthusiast to children, mass-market customers, and value buyers. It had a diversity of markets, product mixes, and platforms that it tried to serve. Its product line was varied in terms of audience, genre, and platform. By seeking to appeal to a wide audience, not just its core of young males, and maintaining a varied mix of products that operated on multiple platforms, its growth in revenues and earnings were steadier than they might have been otherwise. In 2000, faced with a sluggish video-market, Activision retooled by cutting unprofitable product lines and refocusing on games geared to the next generation of entertainment consoles. To avoid dependence on hit titles, the company produced software that operated on PlayStation, Game Cube, Xbox GBA, PCs, and many other devices.

Cross-platform products reduced the risks of single-platform dependence; it leveraged the costs of development over a larger installed base, increasing sales and enhancing profitability.

Diversify into Related Products

When Fiserv started as a company in 1984, it could have stuck to a single business focus. However, the company observed changes that were occurring and continued to develop new products while remaining within its "back-room" service competency. Diversification through opportunistic and strategic acquisition was the hallmark of its growth. This growth drastically reduced the risk involved in its business. Since its inception, Fiserv expanded by strategically acquiring other firms. The acquisitions brought new customers and considerably broadened the company's offerings. (See Figure 5.5.) Through a vast array of acquisitions, Fiserv diversified its business to respond to its customers' needs. If Fiserv determined that a demand existed for a product or service, it found a company that could meet this need, purchased it, and integrated it into its business.

1. Data Processing
2. Asset / Liability Management
3. Retirement Planning
4. Specialized Forms
5. EFT Networks
6. Item Processing
7. Automated Card Services
8. Imaging Technology
9. Network Integration
10. Cash Management
11. Software and Services
12. Laser Printing / Mailing Services
13. PC-Based Financial Systems
14. Securities Services
15. Financial Seminars and Training
16. Automobile Leasing Software
17. Insurance Data Processing

Figure 5.5 Fiserv: Services acquired: 1984 to 2001.

In Summary

This chapter has shown the moves that the big winners made. They were agile. There was no single formula they followed, but a general pattern to their agility. They responded swiftly to threats and opportunities. Their small size gave them great flexibility. They grew their business in accord with their customers' changing needs. They moved toward new and promising markets where their customers had specialized needs that only they could meet. In addition, they were aggressive acquirers, taking advantage of opportunities to broaden and enhance their product offerings. They also were sufficiently diversified so that they could compensate for a decline in one business with strengths in another. All these moves were meant to keep them in a sweet spot. Each firm had a specific pattern or approach to agility (Refer to Table 5.1.) It cultivated different aggregations of agile traits. None of the traits was remarkable in and of itself, but together the traits formed a powerful force that helped to create and sustain positions that big winners occupied. The way that the big winners protected the sweet spots they occupied is the topic I will take up in the next chapter.

6

DISCIPLINE

Big winners not only understood where to go and how to get there. They also understood how to protect the positions they occupied. Big winners created scarce and hard-to-imitate capabilities that enabled them to protect the ground they inhabited (See Table 6.1.) Their discipline was based on many different traits such as advanced manufacturing, global sourcing, acquisitions, hiring, service, distribution, technology, negotiations, project management, regulatory compliance, and sound ethics. The managerial skills to create best-value propositions allowed them to defend the positions they held.

Table 6.1 Traits of Discipline

Company	Discipline
Amphenol	Uses systems such as advanced computer-aided design and manufacturing, statistical process control, and just-in-time inventory Relies on globalization and long-term supply agreements Is adept at selecting acquisitions targets
SPX	Relies on a value improvement process (VIP), with the goal being to increase economic value added (EVA) Has a formal process for consolidating acquired businesses
Ball	Installs process controls, shares best practices, and prunes inefficient operations Carefully evaluates target companies and quickly integrates them Has selective hiring that breeds loyal employees Establishes a good environmental record
Fiserv	Develops best-in-class service paired with volume-driven efficiency Has proficiency in identifying, acquiring, and integrating new businesses
Dreyer's	Creates a direct store delivery (DSD) system Maintains systems to closely monitor sales Gives employees the opportunity to make a difference
Family Dollar	Relies on no-frills stores, innovative store designs, and neighborhood locations Establishes unique technology to keep track of merchandise
Forest Labs	Gives recognition and shows respect to employees Promotes ethics and integrity
Brown & Brown	Designs with customers and elicits competitive bids from vendors Negotiates with suppliers to get good deals for customers Screens acquisitions carefully prior to purchase Hires skilled, well-trained, energetic, and aggressive employees
Activision	Institutes a formal project review process Uses global sourcing and contacts with independent product developers Willingly complies with regulations

Figure 6.1 summarizes lessons learned about the big winners' discipline. These firms maintained ongoing, effective programs to reduce costs and raise quality, controlled distribution, smoothly managed acquisitions, had a special employee culture, and effectively managed government regulation. For each lesson in Figure 6.1, I provide examples of the traits (Table 6.1) the big winners exhibited.

1. Maintain ongoing, effective programs that reduce costs and raise quality.

2. Control distribution.

3. Make for smooth transitions in managing your acquisitions.

4. Create a special culture to get your employees involved.

5. Monitor and influence regulatory changes, and promptly comply with policies that affect the firm.

Figure 6.1 Lessons about discipline.

Maintain Ongoing, Effective Programs That Reduce Costs and Raise Quality

Big winners maintained ongoing, effective programs that reduced costs and raised quality. This lesson is illustrated by eight traits that the big winners exhibited. Big winners relied on (i) advanced manufacturing, (ii) value improvement, (iii) process controls, (iv) designing with customers, (v) formal project review, (vi) best-in-class service combined with volume-driven efficiency, (vii) direct store delivery, and (viii) innovative store designs. Amphenol, SPX, Ball, Brown & Brown, Activision, Fiserv, Dreyer's, and Family Dollar provide examples of the big winners' programs to reduce costs and raise quality.

Use Systems Such as Advanced Computer-Aided Design and Manufacturing, Statistical Process Control, and Just-in-Time Inventory

Amphenol imposed aggressive cost controls on its manufacturing and distribution functions. It had ongoing programs to rationalize its production facilities, reduce expenses, and maximize return on capital. Its efforts were concentrated on service and productivity improvements. The improvement involved advanced computer-aided design and manufacturing systems, statistical process controls, and just-in-time inventory programs. The aim was to increase product quality, shorten product delivery schedules, and reduce plant overhead. Nearly all of Amphenol's manufacturing facilities were certified to ISO 9000 quality standards. It also had a program similar to Six Sigma to raise productivity. Increases in the cost of raw materials, labor, and services were offset by productivity improvements and cost savings.

Amphenol's customers wanted more than just good products. Their vendors had to have strong process and cost controls and had to be able to deliver goods just in time. They wanted outstanding service and timely delivery. They wanted their vendors with broad product design capabilities and a worldwide presence. Being near to customers allowed

Amphenol to engage in just-in-time manufacturing. Amphenol was able to predict production requirements, which limited inventory-carrying costs and resulted in faster production cycles. It was able to more accurately forecast demand for current and future products.

Amphenol competed on the basis of product quality, service, delivery time, and price. Because it worked closely with its customers, it was able to produce quality, reliable products at competitive prices. The payoff was high operating profit margins that averaged 18 to 20 percent for interconnect products and 16 to 23 percent for coaxial cable products between 1995 and 2002.

Rely on a Value Improvement Process (VIP), with the Goal Being to Increase EVA (Economic Value Added)

SPX reduced costs and raised quality by subjecting its businesses to a "Value Improvement Process." All of its businesses went through the same process. (See Figure 6.2.) The process led to many changes. For instance, the company revamped the business model for specialty tools (its original business). The streamlining resulted in outsourcing production of one-third of the tools, reducing manufacturing facilities from six to two, and discontinuing low-value products. SPX often moved out of in-house manufacturing if it found that it was no longer profitable. Employees worked in "high-performance teams." They were rewarded for the contributions they made to long-term profitability, growth, and continuous improvement. The company's goal was to achieve EVA, defined as net operating profit after taxes minus a charge for the cost of the capital. EVA was the central component in the company's financial management and incentive compensation system. All of SPX businesses and more than 60 percent of its employees were subject to EVA-based compensation.

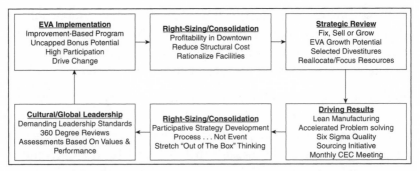

Figure 6.2 SPX's value improvement process (VIP).

Install Process Controls, Share Best Practices, and Prune Inefficient Operations

Ball continually worked to increase its manufacturing efficiency. One way was by means of process controls. Another way was by sharing best practices among plants. After an acquisition, it paired a new plant with a similar existing plant. The two plants worked together to create optimal processes. They shared training. Throughout its operations, Ball worked toward achieving optimal results with common methods. This approach applied not only to manufacturing, but also to inventory control and other functions.

Ball also pursued efficiency by pruning inefficient operations. It exited old and antiquated plants, scaled back unproductive ones, and consolidated operations. From 1999 to 2001, it closed five plants to shrink overheads.

Ball was committed to matching demand with supply and adjusting manufacturing accordingly. Due to declining demand, it phased out of three-piece steel cans. As a consequence of these efforts, it ran its plants leanly, at close to 90-percent capacity.

Ball also leveraged its high market share (above 30 percent in both the United States and Europe) to achieve economies of scale and obtain better deals when purchasing materials. The company steadily lowered unit costs and increased productivity, but it also maintained a high level of service and quality. It was able to lower unit costs and enhance quality by reducing the usage of materials while preserving structural integrity. Lighter products that performed the same functions better kept costs down and enhanced quality.

The 2001 acquisition of Wis-Pak Plastics provided key customization capabilities, allowing Ball to produce specialty bottles that helped customers with brand differentiation.

All of these actions helped the company withstand relentless pressures toward low prices in an industry that was highly competitive and had overcapacity.

Design with Customers and Elicit Competitive Bids from Vendors

To grow its customer base, B&B tried to maintain a combination of low cost and differentiation. It not only was price competitive, but it also strengthened the services it provided in a manner that would be difficult for other insurance agencies to duplicate. Customers saw many of the insurance agencies as similar in nature. Bargain shopping was common. A low-cost strategy by itself was not enough to retain customers. Some degree of differentiation was also necessary. B&B determined that three criteria drove customer choice: price, quality, and innovation. It generated a smaller quantity of policies sold, but it had higher margins on each policy because they were tailored to customer needs. It sold its insurance products and services to niche markets such as mid-size businesses and key industry professionals. Without compromising quality and innovation, it provided a competitive price for its services to these groups. It then worked closely with its individual clients to develop policies that met their individual requirements. After the company and the customer agreed upon the characteristics of the desired policy, B&B went to various suppliers to get an underwriter for the policy at the lowest price. This technique generated competition between underwriters to get B&B's business, satisfied customers, and kept prices low.

Institute a Formal Project Review Process

After Activision reached critical mass ($600 to $700 million in annual revenue), it built the necessary infrastructure, both the support services and managerial depth, to keep costs down and raise quality. It put into operation a formal control process that it used for game selection, development, and production. This system included in-depth reviews of each project at five important stages by a high-ranking team of operating managers made up of sales and marketing personnel and software development staff. Each step in the process had to be coordinated and take into account the views of those in touch with customers and those in touch with technology. It used the same reviews whether a product was internally or externally developed. The company inaugurated periodic evaluations of expected commercial success, development costs, and the expected payback. Mid-course corrections were common. Projects not heading in the right direction were discontinued. The payoff was that Activision's operating margins steadily rose. They grew from 6.5 percent in 2001 to 10.3 percent in 2002 compared to the 3.25 percent that the company had averaged in the prior five years.

Develop Best-in-Class Service Paired with Volume-Driven Efficiency

Fiserv nourished capabilities in the areas of low cost, quality, reliability, and new product introduction. These capabilities allowed it to differentiate itself by providing best-in-class services and customizable offerings in addition to price competitiveness. The principle "The Client Comes First" was the starting point in providing customizable service at low cost. The firm had an unshakeable dedication to providing ongoing client service and support. Employees were encouraged to work closely with clients to provide them with services that were tailored to their specific needs. Fiserv made use of its acquisitions to achieve economies of scale and scope so that it could deliver the array of products that its customers were seeking at a low price. With each acquisition, it made improvements in cost efficiencies and reduced expenses. Fiserv needed scale because its overhead was fixed. Some of its processes, such as the manual processing of hard copy checks, had required numerous employees and were resource intensive. The company invested in digital transaction processing technology and saw impressive gains in profit per employee. The rewards were higher margins. The company offered efficiencies and economies of scale to its client base by performing similar transaction-oriented and fee-based products and services for numerous customers. It reduced costs by maintaining the same software for these customers. With lower costs, it was able to afford a high level of services. Fiserv flourished because of a unique combination of differentiation and low cost—best-in-class service paired with volume-driven efficiency.

Create a Direct Store Delivery (DSD) System

Dreyer's had to be disciplined for many reasons:

- Building and maintaining a superior brand required orchestrating many factors, including consumer taste preferences, packaging, flavor selection, pricing, and image. Formulation complexities, flavor requirements, and seasonality issues also made ice cream manufacture a discontinuous process.

- The cost of the main raw materials was an important factor in determining profitability. The price of cream was linked to the volatile market for butter, which was traded on the Chicago Mercantile Exchange (CME).

- Barriers to entry were few. Manufacturers, dairies, major grocery chains, and independent ice cream processors could make and sell their own ice cream.

- The challenges associated with distribution included transporting a perishable frozen product, having adequate shelf space, and maintaining inventories. If the product experienced temperature variations during distribution, it developed crystals that hurt texture and flavor.

- The competition for shelf space was intense. The average supermarket had about 30,000 products and as many as 15,000 new products to select from each year. Frozen foods and snacks were among the most competitive categories. Retail stores often asked for slotting fees. Wal-Mart did not want slotting fees, but price breaks based on volume and early payment of invoices. Stores expected promotional displays to create brand awareness, advertising, and other forms of individualized attention.

- Customer loyalty was not high. If a brand was out of stock, a consumer typically bought another one.

- With the elimination of back rooms in most supermarkets, the room for error was lower. Without storage space for additional inventory, manufacturers required just-in-time (JIT) delivery.

Dreyer's met these challenges through rigorous control of costs and maintaining quality by means of its direct-store-delivery (DSD) system. The company owned eight manufacturing plants, primarily in the western United States, and had agreements with five others for the manufacture of its products. It disposed of underutilized equipment and facilities. In 1998, it reduced production in a plant in Texas that was not meeting goals. Also in 1998, it divested an unprofitable soft-serve equipment manufacturing concern. The company production plants in California, Indiana, Texas, and Utah manufactured Dreyer's own brands, and the company had agreements with five other companies to make its novelty products. It had agreements to produce products for other manufacturers (about 10 percent of its total production), and it had 30 distribution warehouses scattered throughout the United States and in 15 countries, including China, Russia, and Japan. These assets allowed the company to extend DSD throughout the United States and the world and not depend on supermarket warehouses, where ice cream was susceptible to spoilage and heat shock from loading and unloading. The DSD system ensured the quality and freshness of products delivered to the shelf. It enabled the products to be highly competitive on a range of attributes that included image, quality, breadth of flavor selection, and price.

Rely on No-Frills Stores, Innovative Store Designs, and Neighborhood Locations

Family Dollar's market segment (combined family income of less than $32,000) was extremely sensitive to price. The company competed with national, regional, and local retailing establishments, department stores, other discount stores, drug stores, grocery stores, convenience stores, outlet stores, and warehouse stores. Competitors that beat it on price could take market share. To keep costs down, the company sold basic goods for family needs in a no-frills, low-overhead environment. Most stores were open six evenings a week and on Sunday afternoons. The company did not accept credit cards or extend credit. It operated its stores on a self-service, cash-and-carry basis. To avoid debt, it funded its expansion almost entirely with cash flow. In switching to everyday low pricing (EDLP), Family Dollar drove additional costs out of the business. The company no longer had special sales to drive traffic.

Family Dollar did not hone in only on the cost dimension. With Dollar General and Dollar Tree operating similar types of stores, Family Dollar tried to distinguish itself by having nationally advertised brand-name merchandise that constituted about 33 percent of its sales. By boosting its selection of brand-name goods, it lured in buyers that the other discount chains could not attract. Family Dollar also innovated in store design. It tried to be a "compelling place to shop" by improving merchandise presentation, installing new fixtures, and widening the aisles. To generate higher sales per square foot, it executed a space reallocation program. It maximized the use of limited shelf space by removing the shoe department and some clothes to allow room for hard lines. Each store was laid out in a similar way, with similar product offerings and the same low prices. Customers liked the fact that each store was nearly the same and the products were presented similarly. Store size attracted customers who did not want to maneuver around large, discount chains. Older people especially appreciated this feature.

Control Distribution

Big winners tried to control distribution. This lesson is illustrated by five traits that the big winners exhibited. Big winners relied on (i) globalization and long-term supply agreements, (ii) negotiation with suppliers to get good deals for customers, (iii) global sourcing and contacts with independent product developers, (iv) systems designed to achieve close alignment with customers, and (v) unique technology for keeping track of merchandise. Amphenol, Brown & Brown, Activision, Dreyer's, and Family Dollar provide examples of these programs to control distribution.

Rely on Globalization and Long-Term Supply Agreements

Amphenol relied on globalization to keep its distribution costs under control. It outsourced manufacturing to low-production-cost countries. It purchased companies in developing nations that were close to its markets. It had facilities in North America, South America, Europe, Asia, and Australia. The Latin American (Mexico and Brazil), East European (Czech Republic and Estonia), and Asian (China) facilities served their respective local markets while also providing a source of low-cost manufacturing. Amphenol purchased a wide variety of raw materials for the manufacture of its products from sources all over the world. The raw materials included precious metals such as gold and silver used in plating; aluminum, brass, steel, and copper used for cable, contacts, and connector shells; and plastic materials used for cable and connector bodies and inserts. The company mitigated currency risk by manufacturing and procuring products in the same country or region in which the products were sold. Because raw materials were purchased locally from a variety of suppliers, the costs reflected local economic conditions.

The company also was not dependent upon any one source for raw materials. If it relied on a single source, it protected itself through long-term supply agreements. Further cost reductions came from bulk purchases of standard electronic components and preferential business relationships established with manufacturers. Through acquisition of companies such as Advanced Circuit Technologies, Amphenol also achieved greater control over the costs of components previously procured externally.

Negotiate with Suppliers to Get Good Deals for Customers

Some firms in the insurance industry specialized in distribution (marketing). Other firms specialized in manufacturing (underwriting). Still others, like Safeco, did some of both. B&B was exclusively a distributor of other companies' products. Thus, it had the freedom to pick and choose among these products and provide its customers with the best of the lot. Because it did not underwrite its own policies, it did not have to pay claims arising from such causes as natural disasters or terrorism. Thus, Brown & Brown was able to align itself with its customers, positioning itself as exclusively a seller of insurance services. It eliminated its underwriting business in 1982 when the company developed a strategic plan to focus on the bottom line and growth and to provide quality insurance contracts and services without assuming underwriting. In 1988, B&B made the critical move to eliminate its risk-assuming business, a component similar to underwriting. This move positioned B&B strictly as an insurance broker and isolated it from claims made on losses. B&B could offer many different brands of insurance to get the best value for its customers. By being exclusively a distributor, B&B avoided this risk of investing the premium dollars it received. Insurance companies had little power over these investments because they could not control the direction of markets. B&B eliminated activities not directly relating to negotiating good deals for customers.

Use Global Sourcing and Contacts with Independent Product Developers

Activision relied on global sourcing to keep production and distribution costs down. Its publishing arm, based in Europe, handled the development, marketing, and sale of DVDs, CDs, and cartridge entertainment software. Its distribution arm, based in the United States, handled logistical and sales services needed for its own publishing and for publishing by third-party publishers and manufacturers. To eliminate fixed costs and overheads, it allocated a portion of the development of its games to experienced independent development companies working under contract with it. Relying on these companies helped reduce fixed overhead obligations with permanently employed staff.

Maintain Systems to Closely Monitor Sales

In 1994, Dreyer's came up with a "Grand Plan" that intended to expand DSD to a national level and improve it by means of better manufacturing and sophisticated information and logistics. The undertaking was expensive. It also involved a fourfold increase in spending on consumer marketing, but Dreyer's top management believed that would eventually result in higher market share and greater earnings. To achieve the upgrade, Dreyer's management invested more than $150 million. It redesigned its delivery routes. It increased the territory that its distributors serviced, cut 42,000 "unnecessary" stops, and realized $11 million in savings.

To properly transport ice cream, Dreyer's needed trucks that were able to keep the product at a constant temperature between −10 and −20 degrees Fahrenheit. Thermo King Corporation provided the technology in the form of a fleet of trucks with these capabilities. The company mandated that independent distributors that shipped its products had to adhere to the same strict guidelines that it applied to its own trucks. The trucks' insulation was 4 inches deep as opposed to the more common 2 inches. The trucks had monitors that sounded an alarm if the temperature of the cargo fell below a desired level. The company had relationships with cold storage facilities nationwide for such emergencies to prevent loss of product. Dreyer's adapted DSS for convenience outlets, sending out trucks carrying smaller packages and more indulgent products to better serve the impulse buying of the convenience store customers. It gave drivers leeway to work with these outlets to improve or install freezer display space and to provide promotional assistance.

The company tracked product sales with the links to its store checkout scanners. It was paid on a daily basis and monitored its sales closely. Its delivery people used handheld computers to report detailed data and information back to headquarters. Each was an ice cream expert who knew about proper handling, quality control, flavor selection, and retail display. The delivery people were able to rapidly replenish hot-selling products when inventory levels were low.

Establish Unique Technology to Keep Track of Merchandise

Like all discounters, Family Dollar had to balance inventory in such a way so as not to overstock its shelves. If it was unable to control inventory levels, it would have to mark down prices to clear out items it did not sell. The way to gain this control was to achieve mastery over the distribution process. The company aimed for distribution efficiencies through investments in information technology, which kept track of inventory. These investments enabled it to squeeze costs out of the system. Family Dollar achieved higher margins than competitors, because it managed the supply chain more efficiently. The inventory management system it installed allowed it to monitor the flow of merchandise through the supply chain, from prior to placing an order to purchase from a vendor until customers bought the goods at a store.

The company was able to forecast inventory levels at stores and distribution centers, automatically replenish basic merchandise, and allocate nonbasic merchandise based on store sales and volume. Its stores had accurate in-stock positions that reduced markdowns and increased inventory turnover. Two centrally located departments managed the distribution systems: merchandise planning and inventory control. The company's leading-edge infrastructure initiatives included automating distribution centers, adopting a common layout for each one, and using point-of-sale technology for automatic store replenishment. The company opened new distribution centers to reduce transportation costs. By 2002, it had six distribution centers, with a seventh scheduled to open in 2003. These moves decreased the average distance between its stores and the centers from 409 miles in 1995 to 313 in 2003. The company redesigned the centers' layout based on the flow of goods, streamlined activities, and upgraded the software used to keep the stores at optimum in-stock levels, reduce markdowns, and improve inventory turnover.

Family Dollar carried roughly 3,200 SKUs in its stores. Its basic items (60 percent of what it sold) it tried to keep in stock 365 days per year. The remaining SKUs, or roughly 40 percent, were allocated to seasonal items. The majority of the products it had in the stores sold for less than $10. Family Dollar selected suppliers by means of a "best-of-breed" bidding process. They had to meet several requirements, including adhering to EDI (electronic data interchange). The company had about 1,800 suppliers. It had great flexibility because no single supplier accounted for more than 6 percent of sales. Family Dollar also was planning a fully integrated transportation management system (TMS) to complement the warehouse management system. It already was achieving optimal truckloads to reduce freight costs. It had its own fleet of carriers and relied on outsourced carriers. In cases where full truckloads were not cost efficient, it outsourced consolidated loads to third-party providers. The company could handle supply chain glitches well because it had many options and was able to react quickly and flexibly. Family Dollar also introduced account reconciliation software that reduced banking fees to eliminate slack and make the system seamless. The aim was to match supply and demand as closely as possible.

Make for Smooth Transitions in Managing Your Acquisitions

Big winners made smooth transitions in managing their acquisitions. This lesson is illustrated by five traits that the big winners exhibited. Big winners were adept at (i) selecting targets, (ii) consolidating acquired businesses, (iii) quickly integrating them, (iv) screening them prior to their purchase, and (v) buying them. Amphenol, SPX, Ball, B&B, and Fiserv provide examples of the big winners' proficiency in making acquisitions.

Be Adept at Selecting Targets

Amphenol's mergers and acquisitions went smoothly because it was good at selecting targets, completing the mergers and acquisitions, and integrating the acquired companies. It took advantage of Kohlberg Kravis Roberts & Co (KKR), considerable expertise in the management and evaluation of companies in a variety of industries. Since KKR's founding in 1976, it had completed more than 100 transactions involving more than $100 billion in total financing. The company did not eliminate recognized brands. It allowed the acquired business companies to operate independently, thereby maintaining their freedom to act.

Have a Formal Process for Consolidating Acquired Businesses

SPX had the discipline to consolidate businesses it acquired, cut costs, and eliminate low profit margin segments and unprofitable operations. Although diversification creates economic opportunities and buffers a firm from financial hardship, it also presents challenges. Success requires paying the right price for acquired companies and achieving synergies with them. Clashing cultures and operational blunders can prevent gains. SPX mimicked the industrial conglomerate, GE, from which its CEO came.

The segments in which SPX competed were highly cyclical. Affected by cutbacks in capital spending, over-capacity, and price-cutting, they were not recession proof. Key participants in these industries were not growing rapidly. SPX responded by taking a disciplined approach to acquisitions. First, it was looking for companies that had proprietary and unique technologies, which broadened and filled gaps in its product offerings. From the General Signal and UDI acquisitions, it obtained DeZurik, a producer of industrial valves and controls; Dielectric, which manufactures and installs TV and radio transmissions systems; and Waukesha Electric, a leading manufacturer of small and medium transformers. These companies held high market share in their industries, good operating margin, and good growth potential. Waukesha, which was purchased as part of the General Signal transaction, was the leading

U.S. supplier of power transformers. SPX completed nearly 40 acquisitions from 2000 to 2002. SPX's approach to portfolio management came from GE's playbook. It moved quickly to properly size and structure the businesses it acquired so that they would be profitable and efficient. When buying a company, SPX had methods for removing overlap and consolidation. It rapidly cut costs and closed unprofitable operations to increase margins.

Besides choosing the right businesses to buy, SPX carefully integrated these business units. It had a formal process for amalgamating them that consisted of (i) manufacturing procedure and supply chain rationalization and plant closings, (ii) elimination of redundant administrative overhead and support activities, (iii) restructuring and repositioning of sales and marketing functions to eliminate redundancies, and (iv) rapid disposition of nonperforming product lines and businesses. With this process, SPX was able to achieve economies of scale from its acquisitions and access new markets. For example, the General Signal acquisition resulted in cost savings of $100 million. The savings came from reducing headcount by 10 percent, closing 21 facilities, and replacing half of the General Signal's operating management. SPX continually reviewed its business units pursuant to a "fix, sell, or grow" strategy. If an acquisition did not pan out, SPX did not hold onto it for long. It was not reluctant to divest unprofitable enterprises.[1]

Carefully Evaluate Target Companies and Quickly Integrate Them

Ball evaluated acquisitions before they took place and promptly integrated the companies it purchased into the rest of the company. Although it engaged in numerous acquisitions, it also monitored them to make sure they were profitable. The company kept track of its acquisitions after buying them and was not hesitant to divest an acquisition that did not live up to expectations.

Screen Acquisitions Carefully Prior to Purchase

B&B had a highly selective and aggressive strategic mergers and acquisitions process. The company incorporated a thorough screening process prior to acquiring a company. It concentrated only on profitable companies in areas where it wanted to gain a foothold. To reduce the risk of this activity, B&B mainly limited itself to small companies. The reasons for concentrating on small companies was that the cost of acquiring them was less than the cost of acquiring larger companies; and the smaller companies could be more easily assimilated into existing operations. B&B evaluated potential acquisitions by reviewing what the companies offered, and it tried to assess whether the companies would continue to be profitable.

Besides searching for good market performance and a history of financial success, B&B was looking for companies that were a good fit with its overall philosophy and direction. There were two types of insurance agencies in which it was interested: freestanding and fold in. Freestanding agencies helped B&B move into uncharted territory, whereas fold-in ones were integrated into its existing profit centers. B&B targeted profitable firms between $2 and $3 million in annual revenues for the freestanding entities and firms with a minimum of $1 million for the fold-in entities. An acquisition that fell into the freestanding category was granted considerable freedom. The managers of the freestanding businesses were responsible for their own successes and were personally rewarded or penalized based on performance. CEO J. Hyatt Brown said that B&B was "not a consolidator," but an operator of separate insurance agencies. The company purchased companies similar to itself that offered opportunities for growth and consolidated its expertise with what it acquired. It had an orientation program that it rolled out after a company was acquired. It was respectful of the existing owners and managers. It minimized the ill will that typically arose with takeovers. When it acquired Riedman Corporation, it invited family members to assume key management positions.

Each of the company's 117 offices acted as a profit center, competing against its own goals and those of other offices. The offices were not geographically bound; they were empowered to seek new businesses wherever they found it. Although guided by pretax margin goals and performance expectations, the offices were free to act independently. They were empowered to generate innovative ideas and adjust their business strategies to meet changing customer and community needs. The goals were to encourage superior customer service, higher pretax margins, and improved operational efficiencies. Although the company was divided into individual profit centers, where managers had considerable freedom, there was cohesiveness in the performance standards set centrally. Every profit center had to achieve the same high levels of performance attained historically by B&B's older businesses. A lesser level of performance prompted negative feedback. Because of these practices, B&B grew its customer base rapidly and adapted quickly to clients' changing needs.

Develop Proficiency at Identifying, Acquiring, and Integrating New Businesses

With so many acquisitions completed in its history, Fiserv became proficient at the process of identifying, acquiring, and integrating new businesses.[2] It was adept at identifying companies that had the services it desired and the management and staff it needed. A major reason it was in a good position was that its acquisitions were strategically prudent and fiscally sound. Fiserv was prudent in the sense that it faced few cultural problems with its acquisitions and fiscally sound in that the company performed exceptional due diligence to avoided paying too much for its targets. Fiserv did not have to overpay for acquisitions because it could be selective, looking for fit and alignment between its business plan and that of its targets. In general, its targets had little room for further growth because they could not achieve economies of scale as standalone companies. Fiserv's acquisitions typically were financed through cash flow from operations, borrowing from its credit facilities, and occasionally through issuing securities. It had a long history of acquisitions that it had carried out to achieve related diversification and had the pertinent experience to do the acquisitions right.

Integration of any new business was challenging. It was difficult to combine cultures and ideologies of the merging companies. Because of these difficulties, Fiserv paid particular attention to maintaining the quality and stability of the culture and employee base of the companies it acquired. During the acquisition, it went out of its way to show respect for the culture of the companies it acquired and to making the transitions as smooth as possible. It strove to preserve the autonomy of acquired companies. Because these companies on the whole had been successful before they were acquired, Fiserv wanted to avoid making too many changes to ensure that they would continue to be successful. Fiserv recognized the need to acquire companies that were profitable and well run, and it worked to keep the management, employees, and the culture of the acquired companies in place. Although this acquisition strategy provided for Fiserv's rapid growth and broadened its product offerings, not all of its acquisitions were successful. When they did not achieve desired results, Fiserv was fast to react. Divestitures were costly, but usually it was able divest failed acquisitions quickly enough to keep its risks and costs to a minimum.[3]

Create a Special Culture to Get Your Employees Involved

Big winners had special cultures that got their employees involved. This lesson is illustrated by four traits that the big winners exhibited. Big winners (i) had selective hiring practices, (ii) gave recognition and showed respect to their employees, (iii) hired skilled, well-trained, and aggressive employees, and (iv) gave their employees the opportunity to make a difference. Ball, Forest Labs, B&B, and Dreyer's provide examples of the big winners' approach to employees.

Have Selective Hiring That Breeds Loyal Employees

Ball was selective in the hiring process, even at the factory level, and it invested large amounts of money in training. Its employees were extremely loyal because of this. The company's nonunionized line workers had an entrepreneurial spirit and were encouraged by management to contribute to making operations more efficient. Ball had not been affected by labor problems and was able to retain a greater percentage of its employees than its competitors. When it launched its first plastics plant, it interviewed 3,000 people for 80 open positions. Several years later, 78 of the original 80 hires were still working for Ball. Its CEO, David Hoover, joined the company in 1970 and worked his way through the ranks. Another example was Leon Madiget, chief operating officer in packaging, who had worked for the company since 1972. They typified the motivated, loyal employees that Ball had.

Give Recognition and Show Respect

Forest Labs worked hard to retain its employees, granting them recognition and respect. It had been listed on several indices as being a very good place to work, including BestJobsUSA.com's Employers of Choice 500. It ranked high on such attributes as benefits, training, diversity, growth, and technology.

Hire Skilled, Well-Trained, Energetic, and Aggressive Employees

B&B had a special culture. In 2002, it was #57 of the *Forbes* list of the 200 Best Small Companies in America. An aim of acquisitions was to increase the number of knowledgeable managerial staff and sales people. Forty percent of its managers were CPAs and were hired from major accounting firms. Newly acquired sales employees had extensive experience selling insurance, had long-time relationships with clients, and were well known in their local communities. They gained access to additional resources and a more diverse set of insurance services and products when they joined B&B. B&B's sales force was characterized as being knowledgeable, energetic, and having key analytical skills. They knew what they were selling and were vigorous in making the sales.

Between 1995 and 2001, B&B assimilated hundreds of personnel as it more than doubled the number of its employees. B&B took advantage of the sales force's innate competitiveness to assimilate them into its culture, giving them a large measure of independence, while at the same time trying to inculcate in them the level of aggressiveness that was unique to the company. The acquired companies were rolled into

Brown & Brown's aggressive "hunt if you want to eat" culture. B&B was able to retain and recruit top talent and empower employees to provide world-class service. Employees were one of its greatest strengths. Thirty-four percent of the stock was employee owned, which is just one example of how the company rewarded its employees through incentive-based compensation

Give Employees the Opportunity to Make a Difference

Dreyer's had a special culture that encouraged employee ownership and involvement. In 1988, Dreyer's instituted the "I Can Make a Difference"

---

1. People issues are the primary responsibility of managers and supervisors, not a personnel department. (Dreyer's doesn't have a typical HR department.)

2. Deciding whom to put on the Dreyer's team is very important (hiring smart).

3. People don't need to be motivated. They need to be liberated, meaning they need to be given a chance to do their job their way.

4. People involvement means just that—allowing people to get involved in Dreyer's business in a broader way than just their specific job or function.

5. Everyone is expected to own some aspect of his or her job.

6. When someone demonstrates ownership, recognize that individual with hoopla.

7. Hire highly motivated, experienced people, and train so that it imparts knowledge and skills needed for their jobs.

8. Everyone needs and deserves honest feedback from his or her manager on a regular basis.

9. We need to recognize the people who make a difference in the business.

Figure 6.3 Dreyer's "I Can Make a Difference" philosophy.

philosophy, which defined the values that Dreyer's had been exercising since 1981. This philosophy celebrated the individual, trust, and ownership of one's work. Nine "grooves" further defined the "I Can Make a Difference" philosophy. (See Figure 6.3.) The "grooves" in this philosophy, along with the dedication and integration of upper management to the philosophy, created a unique, exciting, and positive culture that cultivated innovation and dedication and reduced turnover.

Monitor and Influence Regulatory Changes, and Promptly Comply with Policies That Affect the Firm

Big winners monitored and influenced regulatory changes and promptly complied with policies that affected the firm. This lesson is illustrated by three traits that the big winners exhibited. Big winners (i) had good environmental records, (ii) promoted ethics and integrity, and (iii) willingly complied with regulations. Ball, Forest Labs, and Activition provide examples of the big winners' approach to regulation.

Establish a Good Environmental Record

One of the reasons that Ball moved toward aluminum and plastic was because containers made of these materials could be recycled. They were more environmentally friendly. Ball recycled more than 2,000 tons of material at its plants each year. It reduced material waste 80 percent from 1994 to 2002.[4] The food and beverage container industry was constantly running into environmental legislation that required that a certain percentage of its products be recycled. This situation was becoming prevalent in European countries. If a certain percentage of containers was not recycled, a deposit fee was mandated. The fee increased the expense for consumers and affected producers' bottom line. Lawsuits also were a problem because products that ended up in landfills were seen as a nuisance by environmentalists. In Europe, where Ball had many plants, packaging legislation limited the production of cans and bottles and promoted recycling.

Promote Ethics and Integrity

Pharmaceutical companies, like Forest Labs, operated in a tightly scrutinized environment. Government regulations strongly influenced the pharmaceutical industry. The 1962 Kefauver-Hams Amendments required companies to demonstrate the safety and efficacy of new drugs, show evidence of good manufacturing practices, and allow the Food and Drug Administration (FDA) to inspect manufacturing plants. The 1997 Modernization Act tried to speed up the process, but to bring a drug to market still could take 10 to 15 years, and only a small percentage of the drugs submitted actually passed FDA-mandated tests and were approved. Dependence on the FDA for the right to sell drugs presented many obstacles. Many foreign producers did not have the know-how to get products approved in the United States and were openly looking for a U.S. partner. The benefits provided to Forest's foreign partners included knowledge of the U.S. FDA approval process. One of Forest's main competencies was its ability to successfully take drugs through the U.S. regulatory process.[5] Forest acknowledged the uncertainty it faced due to legal, regulatory, and political influences. If any type of safety or quality issue related to a Forest product should surface, the media would quickly respond, and the general public would react, hurting sales. The FDA performed routine inspections of Forest's manufacturing facilities. When issues arose as a result of the inspections, the company responded by taking rapid corrective action.

But the uncertainties had to do not only with the FDA. There were Medicare and Medicaid reimbursement guidelines, set by the government, which required generic substitutes for name brand prescriptions and that often encouraged physicians to prescribe generic drugs over their name-brand counterparts. The company stayed abreast of regulatory changes and issues and tried to influence them in its favor. CEO Howard Solomon was an outspoken defender of branded prescription drugs on the basis of their health benefits. The company also aggressively promoted its organization's integrity and ethics. Due to concerns regarding drug representatives providing kickbacks and bribes to doctors, Solomon affirmed in a letter to stockholders that Forest opposed those practices and would continue to refrain from them. Forest maintained compliance programs to ensure adherence to government requirements and good professional standards. These programs addressed the interactions between the Forest sales force and physicians regarding the kickbacks and other issues.

Willingly Comply with Regulations

After the Columbine school shootings, Activision along with the rest of the video game industry came under attack for the violence, gore, and anti-social qualities of its games. In an effort to respond to these charges, Activision toned down the violence and accepted industry standards that required that it label its games by age group.

In Summary

This chapter has shown the discipline that the sweet spot companies displayed. They maintained ongoing, effective programs that reduced costs and raised quality. They took control of distribution. They smoothly managed their acquisitions. They created special cultures that got their employees involved. They monitored and influenced regulatory changes and promptly complied with government laws and requirements. They not only put themselves in sweet spots, but they also developed the capabilities to protect them. The way these companies fully exploited the sweet spots they occupied is the topic of the next chapter.

7

FOCUS

Winning companies moved into sweet spots and defended them, but they did not stop there. They deepened their position. They enlarged and extended it. They were focused. (See Table 7.1.) Their concern was with meeting the critical needs of their customers. Their global reach was consistent with these principles. They reduced their risks by limiting themselves to their core competencies and steering away from activities that might easily involve failure.

Table 7.1 Traits Showing the Focus of the Winning Companies

Company	Focus
Amphenol	Extends collaborative solution providing activities to new domains Capitalizes on overseas market growth
SPX	Derives advantage from solutions, not patented technology Makes acquisitions to extend its global presence
Ball	Streamlines by spinning off noncore businesses that detract from its mission Identifies and satisfies critical customer needs Combats domestic overcapacity with global growth
Fiserv	Uses service to be on the cutting edge of customers' needs Provides high service levels to foreign clients
Dreyer's	Has a plan to reach out through new channels
Family Dollar	Totally dedicated to the needs of its single customer
Forest Labs	Focuses away from activities that have high risk of failure Limits selling to products that have large demand
Brown & Brown	Gains flexibility by selling products while other companies take on the risks of development Carefully targets special niches
Activision	Exploits brands through sequels and related products

Figure 7.1 summarizes lessons learned with regard to focus. For each lesson in the figure, , I provide examples of the traits (Table 7.1) the big winners exhibited.

> 1. Focus on core strengths—stick to your mission.
> 2. Focus on high-growth, application-specific products for markets that have growth potential.
> 3. Extend your global reach.

Figure 7.1 Lessons learned with regard to focus.

Focus on Core Strengths—Stick to Your Mission

Big winners focused on their core strengths. They stuck to their mission. This lesson is illustrated by six traits that the big winners exhibited. Big winners (i) streamlined by spinning off noncore businesses that detracted from their mission, (ii) focused away from activities that had high risk of failure, (iii) gained flexibility by allowing other companies to assume the risks of development, (iv) exploited brands through sequels and related products, (v) reached out through new channels, and (vi) totally dedicated themselves to customer categories. Ball, Forest Labs, Brown & Brown, Activision, Dreyer's, and Family Dollar provide examples of the big winners' focus on their core strengths.

Streamline by Spinning Off Noncore Businesses That Detract from Your Mission

Ball redeployed assets and focused on a limited set of businesses associated with its core capabilities. It once had been much more vertically integrated. It had tried to gain control over the supply of its raw materials. It had absorbed zinc smelting operations, a rolling mill, and a number of manufacturers of paperboard, plastics, and rubber. It also had explored diverse businesses for expansion, including computer components, prefabricated housing, and acrylic gifts. From 1992 to 2002, it moved away from vertical integration and exited from diversified businesses, settling on packaging products for the food and beverage packaging industry as its main area of concentration. When Ball bought Heekin Can in 1992 and then spun off seven noncore businesses in 1993 in a company called Alltrista, the stage was set for it to focus on and grow this area. The noncore businesses only accounted for 12 percent of revenue, but they took a fair amount of resources in capital and management time. With the spin-off of these businesses, Ball was able to maintain a more streamlined operation, in comparison to many of its competitors, such as Alcoa and Alcan, which were vertically integrated and had stakes in extraction, smelting, and packaging.

Focus Away from Activities That Have High Risk of Failure

Forest Laboratories did not put much emphasis on the discovery or development of new drugs itself. Rather, it licensed the rights to new drugs from foreign laboratories engaged in those activities, which did not have the resources or competencies to get their products through the U.S. regulatory process or to the U.S. market without a partnership arrangement. This strategy effectively reduced the company's exposure to the high risk of failure typically associated with the discovery and development of new drugs. The company's expenditures in research and development were focused mainly in post-discovery efforts, such as clinical trials and ongoing product support for products already in the market. This strategy not only reduced the company's risk of failure, but it also limited the amount of capital tied up in a new drug before it reaches the marketplace. Forest's investment in R&D increased dramatically from 1997 levels of $40 million to 2003 levels of $205 million, but most of it was reserved for preclinical and clinical studies required for the approval of new products by the FDA.

Gain Flexibility by Selling Products While Other Companies Take on the Risks of Development

Brown & Brown positioned itself exclusively as a brokerage concentrating wholly on selling insurance to two niche markets: mid-size businesses through its retail divisions, and professionals such as doctors, lawyers, and dentists through its professional programs division. It gained tremendous flexibility by selling other companies' policies. It could enter and exit markets by offering or no longer offering a product, which helped maintain its profitability. It was not liable for any claims against the policies it sold. Its risk was mitigated, and its profits were maximized. B&B excelled at its distribution-only model, which not only provided a constant in-flow of revenue but also reduced the operational risks involved in underwriting policies. Its overhead remained small. The primary insurers sustained losses in property and casualty, but B&B assumed no responsibility, in terms of claims, for the policies it sold.

Exploit Brands Through Sequels and Related Products

Activision's strategy was to create, acquire, and maintain strong brands. It capitalized on the success of Tony Hawk's *Pro Skater* products to sign exclusive long-term agreements with Tony Hawk and many other action sports athletes. It converted popular titles into franchise-like lines, including the *Zork, Shanghai, Pitfall, Quake,* and *Hexen* series. These products served as the basis for sequels and related new products. Activision's success was attributable to a clearly defined strategy. It stayed focused on its main competencies. It eliminated noncore projects and processes and leveraged outside resources to create operating efficiencies and improve profitability. It was rewarded for its focus by overcoming threats like changing technology and industry standards, backward integration of hardware manufacturers, and consolidation of retailers.

Have a Plan to Reach Out Through New Channels

Throughout its history, Dreyer's remained focused on premium ice cream products. Its mission was to be the preeminent premium ice cream company. In 1994, it launched its Grand Plan to realize this mission. Between 1992 and 2002, Dreyer's had a clear mission based on the Grand Plan, and it was able to effectively act on that mission. It expanded its product line, and through its distribution network, extended its presence from select grocery stores in the Bay area to grocery stores, general chain stores, and convenience outlets around the world.

Totally Dedicate Yourself to a Single Customer

Family Dollar limited itself to the value sector within discount retailing. It was totally dedicated to low-income consumers. It tapped into this segment of the market that had few competitors, staying centered on this niche while it was unsaturated, and tried to dominate it. It did what it knew how to do best. It was an extreme-value discount general store with a stable product mix dominated by hard line goods. Its strategy was constant, with low prices, low overhead, and low debt being key factors.

Develop High-Growth, Application-Specific Products for Markets with Growth Potential

Big winners developed high-growth, application-specific products for markets with growth potential. This lesson is illustrated by five traits that the big winners exhibited. Big winners (i) extended collaborative solution providing activities to new domains, (ii) derived advantage from solutions and not patented technology, (iii) identified and satisfied critical customer needs, (iv) limited their selling to products with high demand, and (v) used service to be on the cutting edge of customers' needs. Amphenol, SPX, Ball, Forest Labs, Fiserv, and B&B provide examples of these qualities.

Extend Collaborative Solution Providing Activities to New Domains

Amphenol was positioned in high-growth, high margin, application-specific sectors as a solution provider. The company decreased its exposure to standard products that were under intense pricing pressure. It aligned its R&D with that of its customers, spending just 2 to 3 percent of its revenues on R&D. In a declining market, it more than held its own. Its customers preferred the company because of the broad product line. It achieved speed in product development while maintaining strong cost controls, thus earning high margins. In this way, the company was able to extend its product line to diverse markets. Among the markets it served were the converging voice, video, and data communications market, including cable television operators and telecommunication companies that entered the broadband market; factory automation and machine tools; automotive applications, including airbags, seatbelts, and other car and truck electronics; high-perform-ance commercial and military aerospace applications, consisting of avionics, flight controls, entertainment systems, missile systems, battle-field communications, and satellite and space station programs; and oil exploration, medical instrumentation, and off-road construction.

Derive Advantage from Solutions, Not Patented Technology

SPX had 68 new patent applications in 2002, up 68 percent from 2001. In total, it owned more than 600 patents and 900 registered trademarks, but it did not view patents and trademarks to be of such importance that they were critical to its business. Its focus was not mainly on patents and trademarks. Rather, it was on creating market advantage through "full customer solutions." For example, in its original specialty tool business, to reduce dependence on OEMs, it focused efforts on niche markets in the aftermarket tool and equipment market where it had the chance to offer services and not just equipment. By 2002, 40 percent of this segment's revenues came from these aftermarket niche services. An important issue was whether it was too diversified for its own good.

Identify and Satisfy Critical Customer Needs

Ball's research and development was focused on providing solutions that met the needs of the end consumer. Its R&D was aimed at giv-ing customers what they wanted. It was the first company to devel-op the 8-ounce container for the new sport drinks market. It also introduced a new plastic beer bottle, which was popular at sporting and outdoor events. Because of its leadership position in the imag-ing area, it was also benefiting the changing global geopolitical cli-mate. It was meeting high profile needs of the security and defense establishment.

Limit Selling to Products with Large Demand

Forest Labs sought solutions to high-profile U.S. health issues, such as depression, hypertension, and alcohol addiction. It limited its presence to these markets where it developed a niche—namely depression, cardiovascular conditions, respiratory illnesses, and pain and inflammation conditions. The antidepressant market, in particular, was the largest therapeutic market within the U.S. pharmaceutical industry. The company's drugs targeted the growing senior citizen population with medicines to treat hypertension, dementia, Alzheimer's, and irritable bowel syndrome. A strength was Forest's large sales force that marketed to physicians, pharmacies, and managed health care organizations (HMOs). Its sales force met directly with physician specialists. It formed strong, close, and enduring ties with them. The company targeted customers that had large growth potential, especially the HMOs that were gaining influence over which drugs were prescribed. It had a responsive sales organization and was close to its customers. To support demand for Lexapro and the other drugs, Forest Labs quickly ramped up the number of its sales representatives. It concentrated on selling, whereas other firms concentrated on developing new drugs.

Use Service to Be on the Cutting Edge of Customers' Needs

Fiserv positioned itself on the cutting edge of its customers' needs by understanding those needs and providing updates necessary to meet them. It stated that its goal was to help clients meet changing needs, expand their markets, and overcome technological challenges by "providing the highest service levels in the industry." It encouraged an exchange of ideas with customers by hosting twice-annual meetings to discuss industry, technology, and product direction. It maintained that it listened "carefully to customers' suggestions" and developed and integrated their recommendations into its products and services. Fiserv grew by extending its reach to its current customers and markets by means of value enhancements in systems it already offered. Growth in revenues came from cross-selling to its clients. It came from price increases that clients were willing to absorb because of additional services. The company found new ways to service customers. It marketed extra services to customers to address their changing needs. By extending products and services, Fiserv was able to assist its customers in many different capacities.

Carefully Target Special Niches

A key to B&B's success was its ability to identify and develop productive niche markets. It concentrated on selling retail products to small- and mid-sized companies. It gave them group policies and employee benefits. It sold property and casualty policies to these businesses. It was less involved in selling policies to individuals. It did not evolve into a "one-stop" model wherein it tried to provide for all of the financial needs of individuals. By primarily forging relationships with mid-sized companies, B&B gained large blocks of clients all at one time. Further, by staying away from extremely large corporations, it avoided having clients with too much bargaining power. No single client represented more than 1 percent of B&B's total revenues. It benefited from dealing with clients such as nursing homes and car dealers that had little in-house insurance expertise. It worked with specific groups like dentists, lawyers, doctors, professionals, and professional organizations to provide policies that met specific needs.

Extend Your Global Reach

Big winners extended their global reach. This lesson is illustrated by four traits that the big winners exhibited. Big winners (i) capitalized on overseas market growth, (ii) made acquisitions to extend their global presence, (iii) combated domestic overcapacity with global growth, and (iv) provided high service levels to foreign clients. Amphenol, SPX, Ball, and Fiserv, provide examples of the big winners' broadening their global reach.

Capitalize on Overseas Market Growth

The U.S. market for cable was saturated; by 1998, about 70 percent of U.S. households subscribed to cable programming, a number that was not growing. Because satellite technology had become a potent substitute for cable in the United States, growth would have to come from elsewhere—for instance, Europe, where the subscription rate was only 31 percent. Amphenol capitalized on the growth of overseas cable programming, the result being that its international sales of coaxial cable exceeded domestic sales in 2001. In 1997, 88 percent of its sales were in North America and Europe. Only 12 percent were from Asia. By 2002, in response to changing market needs, 24 percent of the company's sales were Asian. Its movement into Asia allowed it to tap markets that were less affected by the downturn in North America and Europe.

Make Acquisitions to Extend Global Presence

Prior to SPX's acquisition of UDI, 86 percent of its sales came from the United States, only 7 percent from Europe, and 7 percent from other countries. With this acquisition, it grew its operations overseas (it had operations in 21 countries) and increased sourcing outside the United States. From 2000 to 2002, the company's international revenues grew more than 350 percent. In 2002, the United States remained its largest market with 67 percent of sales, but Europe accounted for 20 percent, and the rest of the world was 13 percent.

Combat Domestic Overcapacity with Global Growth

In 1974, Ball entered the global arena with its first international joint venture. By means of acquisitions and joint ventures, the company continued to expand its geographic reach to China, Brazil, Hong Kong, Thailand, and the Philippines. These moves were taken to combat overcapacity in North America and to increase market share where possible elsewhere in the world. In 1997, Ball acquired 75 percent of M.C. Packaging in Hong Kong, making its subsidiary the largest beverage can manufacturer in China. When it had poor results in China, it exited the Chinese market. It closed its Chinese plants that were not profitable, although it continued to have strong ties to Thailand, Taiwan, and the Philippines. It continued to have minority or majority ownership in packaging companies in Canada, Europe, Asia, and South America. In late 2002, Ball acquired Germany-based Schmalbach-Lubeca.

Provide High Service Levels to Foreign Clients

Fiserv extended its ability to sell additional services to its customer base globally. Along with its U.S. operations, the company had sites in Argentina, Australia, Colombia, Indonesia, the Philippines, Poland, Singapore, and the United Kingdom. As of December 31, 2001, Fiserv serviced more than 13,000 clients. It operated in more than 60 countries, most with sophisticated and well-capitalized financial markets that were receptive to the advanced technological data processing solutions it offered. Significant global achievements in 2002 included the selection of Fiserv's core banking and customer servicing solutions by CITIC Industrial bank, the sixth largest bank in China, with $36 billion in assets. Fiserv had a knack for acquiring a company with a local solution and then expanding the scope of that solution at global levels. In supporting international markets, Fiserv employees were urged to speak the same language as their clients, to understand their clients' different styles in doing business, and to recognize the financial product requirements and regulations that were unique to each specific market.

In Summary

This chapter has shown the type of focus that sweet spot companies exhibited. They concentrated on their core strengths. They did not chase opportunities that were too risky. They had plans for product enhancements, extensions, and sequels. Their dedication to their customers was near total. Extensive collaboration led them to meeting the cutting-edge needs of customers for solutions. They were not in the business of providing mere isolated products, no matter how technically superior the products might be. With great care, they applied these principles to their global expansion. They identified markets with growth potential. They developed and extended the reach of their high-growth, application-specific products and deepened their penetration of global markets.

Having completed this analysis of the winning companies, I now turn to the losing firms and show how their traits differed.

LOSERS

8

COMPANIES THAT KEEP LOSING

This chapter describes nine firms that kept losing. These nine firms were selected for further analysis based on the following criteria. (See Table 2.4 in Chapter 2, "Companies That Hit and Missed the Mark.")

- *As of January 1, 2002, their ten-year, five-year, three-year, and one-year average annual market return was less than that of their industry.*

- *Their five-year average annual market return was half or less than half of their industry average.*

- *Their six-month average return, January 1 to June 1 of 2002, also was less than that of their industry.*

This chapter provides information about the industries in which the big losers competed, the products they sold, and their competitors. This analysis parallels that of Chapter 3, "Companies That Keep Winning." I look at whether the big losers are in large industries with good returns, whether their sales are concentrated or spread out, whether they have many or few direct competitors, and whether they are larger or smaller than most of the firms with which they compete.

Big losers share many characteristics with big winners, yet they are different in one crucial respect: they have more direct competitors. Because losing firms have more direct competitors than big winners, they are less able to control the classic industry forces.

In this chapter, I show that big losers did not lack opportunities for differentiation. More of the big losers than the big winners were in large industries where they could gravitate to profitable niches. Similar to the big winners (see Chapter 3), returns in the industries in which losers competed were not good. The difference is that big winners rose above these circumstances. The big losers did not. This chapter introduces the big losers that are analyzed in subsequent chapters. The sour spots they occupied and the traits of rigidity, ineptness, and diffuseness they displayed are examined in greater detail in Chapters 10 through 12.

LSI Logic

LSI Logic was in the semiconductor industry, a large industry (41 companies) that had very good average annual returns of 25.4 percent from 1997 to 2002. LSI Logic's average annual returns during this period, however, were just 3.4 percent. It was the only company in this industry that was a big loser.

The businesses in which LSI Logic competed were concentrated. (See Table 8.1) About 80 percent of its revenue in 2002 came from prewired standard integrated circuit cores. Customers were able to add unique features to these circuit cores, which were used for such purposes as video game consoles, DVD players, wireless communication infrastructure, networks, broadband, and DSL. To avoid being overly concentrated in this sector, LSI Logic also entered the storage business.

Table 8.1 LSI Logic's Primary Markets

Type of Markets	Communications (Semiconductor Business Segment)	Consumer (Semiconductor Business Segment)	Storage Systems (Storage Business Segment)
Percentage of sales in 2002	81.5% (Semiconductor segment)		18.5%
Target applications	Broadband and networking WAN aggregation platforms Customer and central office access platforms Optical, WAN switches core, edge	Dual-drive HDD DVD recorder processor Digital set-top boxes Video compact discs Video production and broadcasting	Storage components and storage adapters Servers Storage systems Data warehousing Data processing

Source: LSI Logic 2002 Annual Report

In each of these businesses, LSI Logic had numerous competitors. Two of the large firms with which it competed—Broadcom and Texas Instruments—were in semiconductors. (See Table 8.2.) Table 8.3 is a list of other competitors. The LSI Logic 2002 annual report mentioned additional firms with which LSI Logic competed. In integrated circuits, they were Strategic Markets, Adaptec, Agilent, NEC, General Systems, ST, and Toshiba; and in the storage market, the firms with which it competed included EMC, Hitachi, HP, IBM, and Sun.

LSI Logic was a relatively small company in comparison to these firms. Many of its competitors, including Broadcom, IBM, and HP, were also its customers. These companies could outsource the integrated circuits and storage that they needed from LSI Logic, or they could make these products and provide the services themselves.

Table 8.2 The Semiconductors Industry

Company Name	One-Year Return (%)	Three-Year Average Return (%)	Five-Year Average Return (%)	Ten-Year Average Return (%)
Texas Instruments	−40.8	9.6	29.0	31.8
LSI Logic	−7.7	25.1	3.4	22.8
Broadcom	−51.3	10.6	N/A	N/A
Industry Group Average	7.5	28.4	25.4	29.3

Table 8.3 Competitors of LSI Logic

	LSI Logic	Agere Systems Inc.	IBM Microelectronics (Privately Held)	Philips Semiconductors (Privately Held)
Employees	4,722	6,800	11,000[2]	31,185[2]
Revenue ($)	1.77B*	1.94B	2.00B[1]	4.29B[2]

[1] = As of 2003
[2] = As of 2002
*B = billion

Snap-On

Snap-On was in the durable household products industry, a small industry that had just five companies and low average annual 1997 to 2002 returns of just 5.9 percent. Snap-On, with an average annual return of 1.7 percent, was one of three big losers in this industry.

The products that Snap-On sold were fairly concentrated. The company developed and distributed power and hand tools and diagnostics equipment for the vehicle repair and commercial and industrial sectors. Its primary customers were technicians, mechanics, dealerships, and home tools and power equipment users. It also made tool storage products and provided software and other services for automotive diagnosis and service.

In the durable household products industry, Snap-On had two direct competitors: Stanley Works and Black & Decker. (See Table 8.4.) Danaher also competed with Snap-On. Snap-On was the same size as Stanley Works, but its performance was much poorer (see Table 8.5).

Table 8.4 Durable Household Products Industry

Company Name	One-Year Return (%)	Three-Year Average Return (%)	Five-Year Average Return (%)	Ten-Year Average Return (%)
Stanley Works	53.0	22.5	14.5	11.7
Black & Decker	−2.7	−11.3	5.8	9.8
Snap-On	24.9	2.1	1.7	7.6
Industry Group Average	27.2	2.8	5.9	8.1

Table 8.5 Competitors of Snap-On

	Snap-On	Black & Decker Corporation	Danaher Corporation	Stanley Works
Employees	12,400	22,100	30,000	13,500
Revenue ($)	2.31B*	4.64B	5.64B	2.82B
Operating Margins	5.81%	10.01%	16.02%	6.74%

*B = billion

Parametric Technology

Parametric was in the software industry. It was a large industry that had 43 firms and good average annual returns of 18.4 percent from 1997 to 2002. Parametric, with average annual returns of −21.2 percent, was one of two companies in the industry to be a big loser.

Parametric's sales were concentrated; it sold software products and tools for computer-aided mechanical design (PRO/ENGINEER) and for collaborative product development (WINDCHILL). The software was used for nearly all manufactured products, ranging from consumer goods to jet aircraft.

Some of the company's direct competitors are found in Table 8.6. Many firms competed with Parametric, including EDS, Hitachi, Zosen Delcam, Agile, i2 Technologies, and SAP.

Table 8.6 Competitors of Parametric

	Parametric	IBM/Dassault	MatrixOne	UGS PLM Solutions (Private Subsidiary)
Employees	3,500	3,966	450	5,250[1]
Revenue ($)	650.46M*	921.72M	105.33M	897.00M[1]
Operating Margins	−11.42%	28.18%	−20.29%	N/A

[1] = As of 2003
*M = million

Campbell Soup

Campbell Soup was in the food products industry. In 2002, the industry had 18 companies, and it had low returns—1997 to 2002 average annual returns were 8.8 percent. Campbell, with average annual returns of −2.8 percent, was one of four big losers in this industry.

The company developed condensed soups in the late nineteenth century. Condensed soups had a number of distinct advantages. They reduced packaging, shipping, and storage costs.

For years, Campbell had been the world's largest manufacturer and marketer of soups, but its products were fairly spread out as it acquired other brands—sauces like Pace and Prego, beverages like V8, biscuits like Pepperidge Farms, confectionaries like Godiva, and prepared food like Franco American. Campbell was the owner of more than 20 major brands.

In the food processing industry, Campbell had five direct competitors: General Mills, Heinz, Hormel, Hershey, and Sara Lee. (See Table 8.7.) Some of these firms are listed in Table 8.8. Campbell also competed with ConAgra, Cadbury Schweppes, Kraft, Mars, Nestlé, Nabisco, Pepsico, Unilever, and Hain Celestial.

Table 8.7 The Food Products Industry

Company Name	One-Year Return (%)	Three-Year Average Return (%)	Five-Year Average Return (%)	Ten-Year Average Return (%)
Dreyer's Grand Ice Cream	20.4	37.5	22.4	9.2
ConAgra	−4.8	−5.6	2.1	5.7
General Mills	19.8	13.3	13.6	8.9
Heinz (H.J.)	−9.8	−6.8	6.2	8.2
Campbell Soup	−11.3	−16.3	−2.8	6.3
Hershey	7.1	4.9	11.1	14.1
Sara Lee	−7.0	−5.2	6.0	6.8
Hormel	41.9	20.2	17.1	11.9
Industry Group Average	15.2	3.8	8.8	8.4

Table 8.8 Competitors of Campbell[1]

	Campbell	General Mills	Heinz	Kraft Foods
Employees	25,000	27,338	38,900	106,000
Revenue ($)	7.13B*	10.83B	8.41B	31.34B
Operating Margins	16.00%	18.01%	16.39%	18.02%

[1] = as of 2003
*B = billion

IMC Global

IMC (International Minerals and Chemicals) was in the specialty chemicals industry. This industry had 17 firms in 2002. Its average annual returns of 6.3 percent from 1997 to 2002 were low. IMC, with average annual returns of −18.7 percent, was the only big loser in the industry.

IMC's sales were concentrated in the area of providing vital crop nutrients to farmers. As a phosphate and potash fertilizer producer and a seller of soil and animal feed supplements, IMC was the largest supplier of phosphate and potash to domestic markets.[1] Phosphate was 61 percent of IMC's sales and 17 percent of its operating profits in 2002. IMC had 18 million tons of annual phosphate rock capacity in four mines in Florida, which accounted for 30 percent of U.S. and 9 percent of world capacity. Potash was 39 percent of its sales and 83 percent of its operating profits in 2002. Its 11.1 million tons of annual potash capacity accounted for 42 percent of U.S. and 17 percent of the world's capacity. Eighty-four percent of the potash was sold as crop nutrients, and the remainder had nonagricultural uses, mainly as animal feed.

Some of IMC's competitors are found in Table 8.9. The company also had a rivalry with Scott Company (Scott makes fertilizers almost exclusively for the home and garden market), Agrium, Terra Industries, and Mississippi Chemical. It had many competitors and compared to them, it was not that large.

Table 8.9 Competitors of IMC

	IMC	Cargill, Incorporated (Privately Held)	Norsk Hydro ASA	Potash Corporation of Saskatchewan Inc.
Employees	5,016	98,000	42,911	4,904
Revenue ($)	2.22B*	59.89B	24.82B	2.53B
Operating Margins	7.83%	N/A	16.07%	0.69%

As of 2003
*B = billion

Goodyear

Goodyear was in the automobile and parts industry. The industry had 13 firms and poor average annual returns from 1997 to 2002, amounting to just 4.7 percent. Goodyear, with average annual of –11.5 percent, was one of three big losers in this industry.

More than 85 percent of Goodyear's sales and more than 70 percent of its profits came from tires, but it also had significant holdings in other areas. It was a vertically integrated firm that was involved in everything from rubber fabrication to chemical products. The company made auto and industrial belts, hoses, and molded products of various kinds. As a tire maker, it had a leading market share in North and South America, China, and India.

The company's main competitors are found in Table 8.10. Other global players of note in the tire industry were Cooper and Chinese Enterprise Ltd. Many competitors existed even though there had been consolidation in the industry via mergers and acquisitions. Since 1999, Goodyear had been aligned with Sumitomo of Japan. The way Goodyear's partnership with Sumitomo worked was that Goodyear owned 75 percent of North American and European operations, and Sumitomo owned 25 percent. In Japan, Sumitomo owned 75 percent of the operations, and Goodyear owned 25 percent. Goodyear did the research and development (R&D) for both companies. Along with Sumitomo (in the United States, the Sumitomo brand is Dunlop), Goodyear was the world's leading tire company. (See Figure 8.1.) However, Goodyear did not match privately held Michelin in employees or revenues.

Table 8.10 Competitors of Goodyear

	Goodyear	Bridgestone	Continental	Michelin (Privately Held)
Employees	86,000	N/A	71,519	127,210
Revenue ($)	15.12B*	N/A	14.29B	19.29B
Operating Margins	−4.56%	N/A	6.73%	N/A

As of 2003
*B = billion

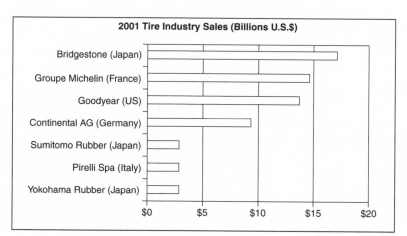

Figure 8.1 2001 tire industry sales (billions U.S.$).

Safeco

Safeco was in the property and casualty insurance industry, a large industry that had 32 firms. The industry's 1997 to 2002 average annual returns were 14.7 percent. Safeco's average annual returns were −1.0 percent and it was one of three big losers in this industry.

Safeco's sales were spread out. It derived 44 percent of its revenues from personal and auto insurance, 23 percent from commercial insurance, and 17 percent from homeowners. It was the eighteenth-largest product-casualty insurer in the United States based on 2001 written premiums. It was vertically integrated and sold insurance through independent agents; underwrote its own personal, commercial, and surety policies; underwrote its life and health insurance; and provided pension programs and annuities. In addition, the company was the leading U.S. underwriter of excess-loss insurance for employers with self-funded medical plans. It also was an asset manager and investment adviser for a family of mutual funds, variable annuity portfolios, and outside pension accounts. Safeco had 11,000 employees and 17,000 partners, who were independent agents, brokers, investment advisors, and wholesalers.

Table 8.11 breaks down Safeco's competitors in the property and casualty insurance industry. Additional competitors are found in Table 8.12. Firms not listed that competed with Safeco were Metlife Inc. and Hartford Financial Services Group.

Table 8.11 Property and Casualty Insurance Industry

Company Name	One-Year Return (%)	Three-Year Average Return (%)	Five-Year Average Return (%)	Ten-Year Average Return (%)
Brown & Brown	57.1	47.8	45.7	31.9
Gallagher (Arthur J.)	10.3	49.6	38.5	23.2
Progressive	44.4	−3.9	17.6	24.1
St. Paul	−16.9	11.2	11.5	12.6
Allstate	−21.1	−2.3	4.9	N/A
Safeco	−2.3	−6.1	−1.0	6.1
Industry Group Average	1.8	11.9	14.7	16.7

Table 8.12 Competitors of Safeco

	Safeco	Allstate	Hartford Insurance Group	State Farm (Private)
Employees	11,200	38,125	30,000	79,000
Revenue ($)	7.09B*	32.60B	20.13B	56.10B
Operating Margins	7.89%	13.27%	12.38%	N/A

As of 2003
*B = billion

The Gap

The Gap was in the retail apparel industry, an industry that was relatively large and included many firms. From 1997 to 2002, average annual returns in the industry were high, at 23.7 percent. The Gap's average annual returns during this period were 9.8 percent. A number of firms in this industry were big losers.

The Gap did not have a concentrated portfolio of products. Jeans once dominated what it sold, but the company's core products had evolved into denim, khaki, casual staples, and many types of fashion items. In 2002, the company marketed casual but stylish clothing in three distinct niches: the Gap (3,000 stores), Old Navy (850 stores), and Banana Republic (450 stores). Old Navy sold affordable fashion in an upbeat family environment. Its stores (about 40 percent of the Gap's sales) were about twice the size of those of the original Gap stores. Banana Republic (about 13 percent of the Gap's sales) provided casual luxury, sophisticated styling, and quality in an upscale service environment. With more than 3,000 locations in North America, Western Europe, and Japan, the Gap was a large and diverse operation that both sold and designed the clothes it sold.

The Gap competed with a large number of firms, some of which are found in Table 8.13 and some in Table 8.14.

Table 8.13 Retail Apparel Industry

Company Name	One-Year Return (%)	Three-Year Average Return (%)	Five-Year Average Return (%)	Ten-Year Average Return (%)
American Eagle Outfitters	−7.1	5.6	86.3	N/A
Kohl's	15.5	31.9	48.3	N/A
TJX	44.4	11.9	28.2	27.1
Abercrombie & Fitch	32.7	−9.1	26.3	N/A
Lands' End	99.7	23.0	13.6	13.1
Limited	−12.0	4.0	13.6	2.8
Gap	−45.1	−27.8	9.8	6.6
Industry Group Average	20.2	3.9	23.7	11.6

Table 8.14 Competitors of the Gap

	Gap	Abercrombie & Fitch	American Eagle	Kohl's
Employees	153,000	3,800	4,700	19,000
Revenue ($)	16.17B*	1.71B	1.58B	10.54B
Operating Margins	11.52%	19.42%	8.55%	9.72%

As of 2003
*B = billion

Hasbro

Hasbro was in the toys industry, a small industry that had four firms. Two of the four firms in this industry were big losers. Average annual returns from 1997 to 2002 in the industry—12 percent—were not high. (See Table 8.15.) Hasbro's average annual returns were −0.1 percent.

Hasbro operated in diverse markets, and its sales were spread out. It designed, manufactured, and marketed games and toys. Its core brands were Playskool, Tonka, Milton Bradley, and Parker Brothers. Games included Monopoly, Scrabble, Dungeons & Dragons, and Trivial

Pursuit. Hasbro was the second largest U.S. supplier of toys (14 percent market share) behind Mattel (23 percent market share). Some of its toys included Play-Doh and Super Soakers. It owned licensed entertainment properties such as *Batman* and *Star Wars*. It relied heavily on its key brands as core assets. In this respect, it was like Snap-On, Campbell Soup, Goodyear, and the Gap. It also depended on just a few main customers—Wal-Mart (19 percent of its sales) and Toys "R" Us (16 percent). Like Goodyear, Safeco, and the Gap, Hasbro was vertically integrated. It both made the products it sold and had retail outlets— about 85 retail stores. It also ran the Once Upon a Toy Store at Disney theme parks.

Hasbro and some of its competitors are compared in Table 8.16.

Table 8.15 The Toy Industry

Company Name	One-Year Return (%)	Three-Year Average Return (%)	Five-Year Average Return (%)	Ten-Year Average Return (%)
Electronic Arts	40.6	28.8	32.0	28.8
Activision	158.0	51.9	24.8	63.7
Hasbro	54.1	−11.2	−0.1	4.1
Mattel	19.4	−8.5	−8.0	5.4
Industry Group Average	68.0	15.2	12.2	25.5

Table 8.16 Hasbro's Competitors

	Hasbro	Jakks Pacific Inc.	Lego (Privately Held)	Mattel
Employees	6,900	316	8,297	25,000
Revenue ($)	3.15B*	322.00M**	1.61B	5.00B
Operating Margins (ttm)	10.90%	5.32%	N/A	14.93%

As of 2002
*B = billion
**M = million

In Summary

Table 8.17 summarizes what has been said about the big losers that will be analyzed in chapters nine through twelve. Many were in relatively large industries. Sweet spots might be found in these industries, but the big losers were unable to identify and move to these spots. The industries within which they operated were under intense pressure. Returns generally were low. But these circumstances were no different than those faced by big winners analyzed in chapters four through seven. Big winners overcame this disability, while the big losers did not. Big losers had more direct competitors than big winners. They were not categories of one. They were not ensconced in unassailable positions. They did not have unique products, services, and/or solutions that they offered customers. Although smaller than many of their competitors, they were still bigger than the big winners. (They had an average of $5.71 billion in revenues and 36,379 employees in 2002 compared to an average $2.66 billion revenues and 13,937 average employees for the big winners.) They were too big to be agile but not big enough to defend positions they occupied. As will be shown in the chapters that follow, these firms were stuck in cycles of rigidity, ineptness, and diffusion. They were in sour spots and had very different traits than the big winners.

Table 8.17 The Nine Losers in Relation to Their Industries and Main Competitors

	Large Industry	Good Returns in the Industry	Sales Concentrated	Many Direct Competitors	Larger Than Most Competitors
LSI Logic	*	*	*	*	
Snap-On			*		
Parametric	*	*	*	*	
Campbell				*	
IMC			*	*	
Goodyear				*	*
Safeco	*			*	
The Gap	*			*	*
Hasbro				*	

9

SOUR SPOTS

The main reason that the big losers did not do as well as the big winners is that they were in sour spots. By a sour spot, I mean that they were in competitive spaces occupied by other firms offering similar or equally good products and services. The big losers were in inhabited territory. (See Chapter 10, "Rigidity.") The products and services that they offered did not stand out as special—they did not confer distinctive benefits that customers could not obtain from other sources. (See Chapter 11, "Ineptness.") This chapter explores what it means to be in a spot that is noticeably inferior to your competitors and highly contested.

When you are in a sour spot, you are in a conspicuously poorer position than competitors. Your products and services (i) are too expensive for customers to afford; (ii) are priced too low for you to be profitable; or (iii) depend on activities that are too broad and complex for you to carry out well. These patterns involve significant misalignment with your customers (see Table 9.1), whereas the patterns of the big winners—co-designing with customers, being embedded in their infrastructure, and being a broker between customers' needs and satisfying those needs—involve significant alignment. (See Chapter 4, "Sweet Spots.")

The advice to derive from this chapter is related to the points made previously:

- *If your products and services are too expensive for your customers to afford, then:*
  - *Do not pursue technological leadership as a primary strategy, especially in an industry where commodization has taken hold.*
  - *Do not have a product-first focus—think of your customer first.*
- *If your products and services are priced too low for you to be profitable, then:*
  - *Make sure that you keep out of markets where there is overcapacity and customers have substantial power.*
  - *Do not chase market share if it means you must sell at a loss.*
- *If your activities are too broad and complex, then:*
  - *Establish a focused product portfolio that can be well-managed.*
  - *Concentrate on a particular product segment or stage in the value chain to avoid inventory and other glitches.*

This chapter provides three examples of big losers whose products and services were too expensive, three examples of big losers whose products and services were priced too low, and three examples of big losers whose activities were overly broad and complex. Along with these examples, this chapter provides recommendations that point you in the direction of greater customer alignment.

Table 9.1 Traits That Result in Distance from Customers

Sour Spot	Company	Traits That Result in Distance from Customers
Too expensive	LSI Logic	Overdesigned products Powerful customers
	Snap-On	R&D that does not meaningfully differentiate products Misalignment with customer sophistication level
	Parametric	Insufficient attention to service Competitors opening lower-priced markets
Too cheap	IMC	Competitors subsidized by foreign governments Suppliers' price increases can't be passed on
	Goodyear	No clear identity No effective process for working with customers
	Safeco	Sacrificing price for market share Poor plans for covering risk
Too broad and complex	Campbell	Inability to anticipate competitors' moves Not positioned well on price/quality continuum
	The Gap	Quality and prices not in customers' comfort zone Complex business model
	Hasbro	Few customers constitute a high percentage of sales Inaccurate prediction and timing of inventory

Too Expensive

In this section, I show how three companies—LSI Logic, Snap-On, and Parametric—became distant from their customers. In these three instances, the products and services that these companies offered were too expensive. Customers had other options. They could obtain lower-priced products and services from competitors.

Example 1: LSI Logic

LSI Logic once had very good relations with its customers. Its customers were technological leaders and it offered them highly differentiated products, but the products that LSI Logic offered became commoditized. The high-end semiconductors that LSI Logic sold became too expensive for consumer markets that were growing very rapidly. These products were not well-suited for the manufacture of DVD players, digital cameras, and wireless communication, which were gaining in popularity.

OVERDESIGNED PRODUCTS

LSI Logic made mainstream products that were overdesigned in comparison to the needs of its customers. Its products provided more features than most customers wanted. The firm's principal competitors (such as IBM, Hitachi, Texas Instruments, and Phillips) had more money to spend on research and development (R&D), and LSI Logic did not want to lag behind. To keep up, it kept its R&D expenses high as a percentage of revenues: 25 percent of total revenues in 2002, 28 percent in 2001, and 14 percent in 2000. It focused on making a very sophisticated product and not on customer service. Companies like HP and IBM were able to provide complementary services, which LSI Logic could not afford. In addition, low-entry barriers hurt the company. Small firms that entered did basic design work and outsourced the manufacturing. They entered because the industry had excess manufacturing capacity. LSI Logic shut down some of its own production facilities, and it, too, started to rely on outsourcing, but as a consequence it had less control over such critical variables as production schedules, delivery times, and product quality. Therefore, its reputation with customers went down. In the storage business, which LSI Logic entered, it occupied an entry-level space. Its products were at the low end of the market. They were seen as unsophisticated. The performance, functionality, quality, and integration of LSI Logic's low-end products were not up to par. The company was stuck; its high-end semiconductor products had too much quality embedded in them, and its storage products did not have enough.

LSI Logic's weaknesses are displayed in Figure 9.1. The company had but a few powerful customers. The firm's customers knew that LSI Logic was dependent on them. They had bargaining power over the company and exerted pricing pressure. In 2001, three customers accounted for 55 percent of LSI Logic's total revenues. In 2002, a single customer (Sony PlayStation) made up 18 percent of its revenues. These customers had a disproportionate influence on the company's lead times, its pricing, and the demand for its products. Other potential customers—firms such as Intel, Cisco, Dell, IBM, HP, and Sun Microsystems—also were competitors. They might buy semiconductors from LSI Logic, but they did not have to because they manufactured similar products. Competition from customers squeezed LSI Logic's profit margins and increased its sales volatility. If a customer could make the same products more cheaply and efficiently, it had no reason to buy from LSI Logic. LSI Logic lost sales.

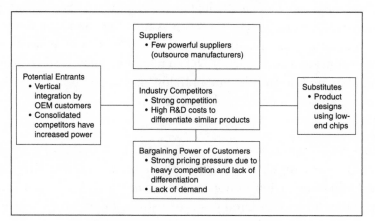

Figure 9.1 LSI Logic's weak position.

Example 2: Snap-On

Snap-On had similar issues with which to contend. It had a strong brand image, and its high-quality products had a good reputation; however, the products could not command a high enough price to justify the quality that Snap-On had placed in them.

R&D DOES NOT MEANINGFULLY DIFFERENTIATE PRODUCTS

Despite declining operating margins, Snap-On continued to pour money into R&D. Its commitment to obtaining new patents was unwavering. Nonetheless, it was unable to prevent commodization in its industry. To cost-conscious customers, the company had trouble differentiating its products. These customers wanted integrated solutions that saved them money, not individual products with advanced features that were sold one at a time. Snap-On did not respond well to the problem of being in a low-growth commodity business where there was little room for additional differentiation. It was unable to leverage its quality image into sufficiently high prices. Figure 9.2 shows that Snap-On's business units when stacked up against the competition were at best question marks (equipment and diagnostics) and at worst dogs (power tools and hand tools). The company had low market share in equipment and diagnostics and both low market share and a low business growth rate in power tools and hand tools.

PRODUCTS AND SERVICES NOT ALIGNED WITH SOPHISTICATION LEVEL OF CUSTOMERS

Snap-On was a sophisticated tools and equipment supplier for professional users who no longer were seeking so much sophistication. It continued to sell premium products with a strong brand image, when this strategy no longer made sense in its industry. In 2002, the company had 1,592 active patents, and it had many trademarks to back up its quality image. It remained a technological leader, but this path to doing well no longer was viable. (See Figure 9.2.)

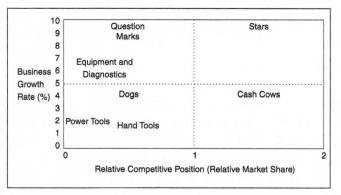

Figure 9.2 The alignment of Snap-On's businesses.

Example 3: Parametric

Like LSI Logic and Snap-On, Parametric had premium products. The ultra-sophisticated Pro/Engineer software was best in its class. Parametric proudly proclaimed its dedication to its product, but dedication to product while not paying sufficient attention to service and to competitors' low-cost alternative products placed it in a vulnerable position.

INSUFFICIENT ATTENTION TO SERVICE

In its publications, Parametric proclaimed proudly that it was a "product first" company. It identified its customers as professional engineers who continuously needed new features to meet the requirements of their jobs. Parametric saw itself as a technology leader on the cutting edge. It could tell customers what they needed, but it did not listen well to what customers wanted. It sold a suite of advanced software without providing customers the service they needed to benefit fully from this product. The company was distant from its customers, who were willing to get along with less full-featured and lower-priced solutions. It's customers did not need all the features Parametric's products provided. Competitors' products often lacked the sophisticated functions of Parametric's flagship CAD/CAM products, yet they were easier to learn how to use and perfectly adequate for most applications. Parametric's competitors sold software that was less functional but not as expensive, something that many customers appreciated.

In 1996, Parametric surpassed IBM/Dassault to become the leading supplier of CAD/CAM software, but this lead did not last. Parametric was squeezed out because of intense competition from IBM/Dassault, EDS, Hitachi, Zosen Delcam, MatrixOne, Agile, i2 Technologies, and SAP. None competed in every area. Each specialized in a part of the market and took a portion of Parametric's business. Parametric initially ignored these new entrants into the lower-priced and feature-based market. It also had problems at the high end of the market in supplying the auto and aircraft industries with what they needed. Like LSI Logic, it was in a tough position—too good for where most of the market was headed, but not good enough for the very top that had even more demanding standards than Parametric could meet.

Too Cheap

This section shows how three companies—IMC, Goodyear, and Safeco —ended up selling products and services that were too inexpensive. They lost touch with their customers' needs for specialized products and services that only they could provide, and were unable to make a decent profit from the sale of the products and services they actually sold.

Example 1: IMC

IMC was not known for providing value-added customer service. Its products were pure commodities, and it was exposed to powerful customers who had other choices for their purchases.

The company faced stiff competition from firms that were heavily subsidized by their governments. Foreign governments brought new production on line in huge blocks. The market could not absorb the new production. All the companies in the industry were looking to Asian markets for growth. The North American business was mature, but Asian producers were keeping pace with growth in demand by creating new capacity close to home. Competitors brought new production on line in Australia and India. WMC Ltd. in Australia and Oswal Chemical and Fertilizer, Ltd. in India built new capacity. They had stranded natural gas and sulfur by-products that were easily converted to fertilizer production. The Oswal Chemical plant in India was heavily subsidized, operated uneconomically, and would have been shut down were it not for government subsidy. This added capacity led to the rapid deterioration of IMC's gross margins. (See Figure 9.3.) As the world's lowest-cost producer of the nutrients phosphate and potash, IMC should have been in a good position to cope with this situation, but the company faced many obstacles simultaneously. It confronted a depressed U.S. farm economy, decreased exports because of import restrictions imposed by the Chinese government, and the supply growth of other producers.

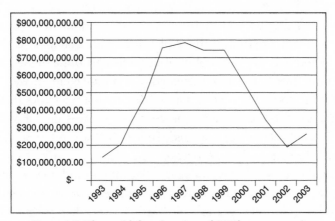

Figure 9.3 The rapid deterioration of IMC's gross margins.

IMC also confronted high raw material prices. Price volatility in natural gas markets and unfavorable supply and demand dynamics squeezed its margins. IMC operated uneconomically because of overcapacity and depressed prices, and reduced sales. Its customers could negotiate freely for discounts that IMC could scarcely afford. Because there was overcapacity in the industry, it was nearly impossible for IMC to pass price hikes on to customers.

Example 2: Goodyear

The tire industry was maturing, but Goodyear stuck to what it had always done: tires. It tried to hold a lead in market share in tires, but its profits kept falling. There was overcapacity in the industry, and customers were in a position where they could squeeze Goodyear's margins.

The tire industry was a poor one to be in. Goodyear employed nearly 100,000 workers and had regular conflicts with labor. Its large labor force had high medical expenses and huge pension liabilities that Goodyear had to finance. The rubber, yarns, wires, carbon black pigments, chemicals, and fuel that the company used to make tires were expensive. Despite owning rubber plantations in Malaysia, Goodyear was not able to put a lid on rubber prices. The corporate mission in the face of these threats remained defensive: Top management was trying to protect the company's "good name" despite many factors that were working against the company. The competition was global and very intense. Michelin (France) acquired Goodrich (the United States) and Uniroyal (the United States). Bridgestone (Japan) acquired Firestone (the United States). But Goodyear's flagship brand never had the cachet of Michelin. It did not have a clear identity. Michelin positioned itself as the high-quality and safe brand. The other global players, including Continental (Germany), Yokohama (Japan), Pirelli (Italy), Cooper (United States), and Chinese Enterprise Ltd., all had clear niches, while Goodyear did not. Pirelli focused almost exclusively on higher-margin, high-performance tires. Cooper emphasized higher-margin, replacement tires and had moved into related industries like auto parts. Chinese Enterprise Ltd. produced low-priced tires with low-cost labor.

Goodyear, in contrast, had brands that were neither upscale nor mass market. Its brands did not have clear market segments that they dominated. (See Figure 9.4.) Consumers did not really know what the company's brands stood for. Without clear identities for its brands, the company, after the Bridgestone-Firestone safety recalls, could not reposition its tires as safer and thus worthy of the higher prices it decided to

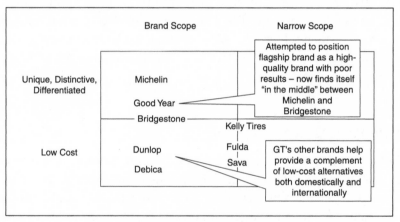

Figure 9.4 Goodyear's positioning.

charge. The market was not willing to accept that Goodyear's reputation matched its claims to a higher price.

NO PROCESS OF WORKING WITH CUSTOMERS TO BEST MEET THEIR NEEDS

Like LSI Logic, Snap-On, and Parametric, Goodyear was tied to a product, not a process of working with customers to best meet their needs. More than 85 percent of Goodyear's sales and more than 70 percent of its profits came from tires, but the tire industry was extremely competitive and labor intensive. Raw materials were expensive and exit barriers were very high. Competitors like Michelin and Bridgestone dominated in their home markets and were able to underwrite relatively low U.S. prices.

Goodyear's response was to aggressively pursue market share, but cutting prices to original equipment manufacturers (OEMs) like Ford and General Motors and selling at a loss was not a sustainable business model. The OEMs awarded contracts to lowest bidders. To obtain these contracts, Goodyear kept its prices low. The quality of its tires might not be that good—they tended to wear out quickly—but the company's low prices enticed the OEMs to select its brands. Goodyear expected to make up the difference when its customers chose them for replacement tires. However, loyalty in the market for tires was low. Individual customers, like OEMs, shopped for the lowest price. They rarely saw anything distinctive in Goodyear's design, performance, reputation, warranty, or customer service that could justify a higher price. Goodyear sunk money into R&D to make technological advances, but the advances themselves were self-defeating. They were easily copied and resulted in diminished replacement demand because the tires lasted longer.

Example 3: Safeco

Like Goodyear, Safeco's strategy was to sell standard products and services at a low price. Safeco was a high-volume producer of generic policies targeted at markets that were large and relatively homogenous. This strategy of targeting large and homogenous markets did not work.

PRICE SACRIFICED FOR MARKET SHARE

Safeco chose to sacrifice price for market share. Its discounting tactics led to its policies being underpriced, which resulted in large losses. In the insurance market where it competed (property and casualty), there was little demand for customization, and customer loyalty was low. Customers had a wide variety of choices and looked for the lowest prices. Many companies offered similar products. Safeco's original name, The General, was revealing: The general nature of its business was a reason for its being in a sour spot. As a large producer of generic policies in the auto and homeowner market, its allure was to no one in particular. It tried like Brown & Brown to enter specialty markets and offered professional liability, medical malpractice, and surplus property policies, but these policies did not fit well with the company's operations, and it did not follow through on developing these businesses. Safeco chased after market share despite the fact that large market share did not correlate with high levels of profitability. In the car and homeowner's insurance market, most people looked for the lowest prices. Internet offerings made the competition even more intense because customers were better able to compare prices and get the best deal. Fierce competition forced Safeco to keep prices low, and low prices meant poor performance.

POOR CONTINGENCY PLANS FOR COVERING RISK

In the markets in which Safeco competed, the margins were very low. Margins were low because insurance policies were not priced properly. Safeco was not only a broker of insurance policies, but it also was an underwriter. Underwriting was subject to high levels of government scrutiny, rules pertaining to solvency, limitations on investments, and required cash reserves. The risks ranged from rising medical costs affecting payouts for personal injury suits to the growing costs for asbestos removal that also came from judicial rulings to natural disasters that could not be predicted and insured against. As an underwriter, Safeco made use of a costly actuarial staff. It also had an expensive investment branch that managed the reserves from which its claims were paid. These activities were inherently risky and hard to bring under control. Safeco lowered underwriting guidelines and premiums to attract larger client bases and did not price its policies correctly. The actuarial techniques that Safeco used did not adequately cover the risks. Safeco's huge losses partially came from extreme weather events and other calamities such as terrorism that it was not able to anticipate. (See Table 9.2.) They also arose from the sudden drop in the stock market, which Safeco did not count on taking place. At the same time, with the stock market tanking, the investment side of Safeco's business was problematic. Its mutual funds did not compete well in a crowded market dominated by such giants as Putnam, which was owned and operated by its competitor, Marsh & McLennan. In addition, the market's downward turn negatively affected Safeco's reserves in the volatile equities market.

Table 9.2 Ten Largest Catastrophic Events from 1992 to 2001 ($ in Billions)

Year	Catastrophe	Total Losses
2001	World Trade Center	$20.7
1992	Hurricane Andrew	$19.9
1994	Northridge Earthquake	$15.2
1989	Hurricane Hugo	$6.1
1998	Hurricane Georges	$3.3
2001	Tropical Storm Allison	$2.9
1995	Hurricane Opal	$2.5
1993	Midwest Blizzard	$2.2
1999	Hurricane Floyd	$2.2
2001	St. Louis Hailstorm	$2.2

Source: ISO
(adjusted to 2002 dollars)

Too Broad and Complex

This section shows that three companies—Campbell, the Gap, and Hasbro—had business models that were too broad and complex to maintain a good sense for what customers wanted and needed. Because of this complexity, these companies lost touch with their markets and did not have a good command over their products. They did not have sufficient control over internal organization processes to suitably meet customer needs in a timely fashion.

Example 1: Campbell

Campbell had a very broad and complex business model. It not only competed in canned soups, where it faced serious competition from low-cost producers and highly innovative differentiated soup makers, but it had many diverse brands positioned all over the price/quality continuum. Managing this much diversity was difficult for Campbell. It was a challenge that the company had trouble meeting.

Campbell sat on its lead in condensed soups in the 1990s. It did not keep up with the movement from canned goods to microwavable and healthier ready-to-cook foods, and had underutilized condensed soup production capacity. Its performance was based on leveraging of the brand name, massive economies of scale, and little competition. The company did not anticipate the competition that emerged. In soups, the company tried to be a low-cost provider with underlying appeal because of a wholesome image and goodness quality, but it faced serious competition from two separate directions. On the one hand, the Campbell brand did not stand up to competitors that offered a better price. Store brands underpriced Campbell. Private label products and private label and generic soups were in almost all major retail outlets, and they provided serious competition at the low end of the price spectrum. On the other hand, the Campbell brand did not represent the highest quality or greatest convenience. Home Cookin' and Healthy Request introduced ready-to-serve soups to the market, which offered better taste. Condensed soups, which required the addition of water before consumption, seemed like an inconvenience. New soups had rich new flavors, more ingredients, and a premium feel. Their taste and texture were better, and they were healthier. They had less sodium and less fat. They offered convenience with larger cans, plastic containers, and other packaging innovations. Campbell was slow to counter this development. Its soups were seen as the brand for children, whereas the new entrants were the soups for adults. Campbell's traditional cash cows in the soup market—its chicken, mushroom, and tomato soups— were in trouble. General Mills acquired Pillsbury and the Progresso Soup brand, which seized 15 percent of market share with better-tasting, ready-to-eat soups. Campbell's market share dipped from more than 80 percent to less than 75 percent. It tried promotional spending, which was up 15 percent each year from 1998 to 2002, but this tactic was expensive and cut into margins. It also tried to change its advertising— to find and communicate a new brand image, but this move also was expensive and lowered margins.

Campbell also tried to grow its non-soup revenues. It had many brands on which it could concentrate other than soups. However, this approach was problematic. Its brands ranged all over the price-performance continuum. They presented formidable obstacles for consistent management. (See Figure 9.5.)

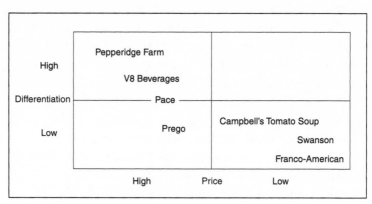

Figure 9.5 The positioning of Campbell's brands.

Example 2: The Gap

The Gap also was in a sour spot because of a complicated business model and the excessive risk and uncertainty it confronted from relying on this model. It had been at the forefront of the corporate dress-down revolution, selling classically styled, casual apparel at moderate price points, but it quickly lost its unique appeal, and its complicated business model made it hard for it to make a recovery.

The pressure on the Gap was to create products that were especially unique so that the company could obtain a high price for them. Customers had alternative sources for the high-quality casual clothing that the Gap sold. New players entered the market such as American Eagle Outfitters and J. Crew, and old competitors such as the Limited and Abercrombie & Fitch made a comeback. The Gap had three distinct niches in 2002: the Gap (3,000 stores), Old Navy (850 stores), and the Banana Republic (450 stores), which resulted in customer confusion. It became harder for customers to differentiate between these brands. The company also became overextended because it added too many stores too quickly. The specialty clothing retail market was saturated. Kohl's and Mervyn's sold similar styles at a lower price. When the economy stalled, consumers were drawn to lower priced generic items. Value shoppers were as satisfied with clothing from Target and Wal-Mart as with clothing from Old Navy. The Gap also made a fashion mishap and moved away from the basics products it had successfully sold in the late 1990s. It tried to introduce trendier and edgier clothes, but they were too hip for Gap's core customers, who did not appreciate the direction in which it headed. It saw its biggest opportunity in sales growth among teenagers, but its core customers rebelled when the Gap offered them low-cut jeans, form-fitting tops, and shear blouses linked to the popularity of teenage music and movie stars. Along with its fashion mishaps went an advertising flop—esoteric art house flick commercials with no dialogue and a subtle message that made it hard for customers to connect with the product.

COMPLEX BUSINESS MODEL

The Gap was a large enterprise with a complicated business model that was difficult to execute well. It had to be everything to everyone and had to be everywhere at once. Its customer base extended from low- to high-income families. It targeted many customer groups, from babies to teens, children, adults, men, women, U.S. customers, and a global clientele. It looked for "gaps," or what it referred to as "white spaces," in the market and added new stores for babies and maternity wear.

All this diversity brought with it complications in advertising, pricing, timing, promotion, and inventory management. Because it operated in so many different niches, the Gap had to anticipate sales revenues from different sources and create diverse growth strategies for different customer bases that put it in competition with many types of retail outlets, everywhere from the sophisticated Ann Taylor to J.C. Penney's bargains.

The company also faced the extremely complicated task of controlling the supply chain from start to finish for its different brands. It did everything from design to distribution to merchandising for each brand. Unlike its competitors, Gap designed nearly everything that it sold. Like Safeco, which must pay for high-priced actuarial and investment talent, Gap had to spend to attract talented fashion designer and marketing personnel.

The only part of the supply chain that it did not handle itself was manufacturing. The Gap had to gauge fashion trends in different market segments in a timely matter, maintain and promote favorable brand recognition, effectively market to diverse market segments, competitively price its products, overcome the risks associated with imitation, and deal with myriad global challenges.

Peak shopping was done at holidays and back-to-school times (32 percent of its sales). The company had to order the merchandise a full nine months in advance of a particular season. It had to get it right, but with this complexity, there was a loss of control. In a fashion-based business, predicting customer preferences this far in advance was hard. Poor designs and sales projections led to bloated inventories and price cuts. Gap alienated customers and had the wrong kind of products. Therefore, it faced huge markdowns.

Example 3: Hasbro

Hasbro had some of the same problems as the Gap. It designed, manufactured, and marketed games and toys and had a complicated business model that extended up and down the value chain. Like Goodyear, Safeco, and the Gap, it was vertically integrated. It both made the products it sold and had retail outlets—about 85 of them. It also ran the Once Upon a Toy Store at Disney theme parks.

FEW POWERFUL CUSTOMERS CONSTITUTE HIGH PERCENTAGE OF SALES

Like Campbell Soup, Hasbro depended on a few key customers for a high percentage of its sales. In 2002, it was extremely dependent on its top 5 customers, who accounted for more than 50 percent of its revenues. Wal-Mart made up 19 percent of its sales in 2002, and Toys "R" Us made up 16 percent of its sales in that year. These customers demanded low prices and imposed rigorous demands. Demography, moreover, did not work in the company's favor. There was a decreasing number of U.S. families with children—60 million and going down. Although Hasbro tried, it was not successful in global markets, where spending per child was a paltry $34 compared to $400 in the United States. Globally, it faced great challenges because of piracy and an inability to protect its registered trademarks and copyrights.

BUSINESS MODEL REQUIRES ACCURATE PREDICTION AND TIMING
Hasbro had a complicated business model that depended on accurate prediction and timing. It had to provide products exactly when its retail customers needed them; otherwise, they were stuck with unsold inventory that had to be sold at discount. Its products had a limited selling season. Like the Gap, it had to anticipate and understand what consumers would want months in advance for adequate stock to be available. It had to correctly forecast demand during peak seasons to control inventory.

Hasbro's large customers required that it respond quickly and adjust to the smallest movement in customer demand so that inventory was neither over nor under supply. Mistakes were costly, and when made, they hurt the relationship and made it difficult to work with a customer. Preferences for toys and games changed wildly from year to year. It was challenging to predict what would be popular even with highly exact forecasting models. The company recycled its old brands and redesigned existing toys and games, but it was unable to consistently come up with new hits.

A big disappointment for Hasbro came when a movie licensing deal with LucasArts Entertainment for the *Star Wars'* property flopped. Hasbro paid way too much ($600 million) and lost $150 million on the deal. In contrast, Mattel paid just $20 million for a 15-percent royalty stake in *Harry Potter* books and films and reaped huge returns.

New competition came from the home entertainment and gaming industry. Sony and Microsoft competed in the hardware area, and Electronic Arts and Activision competed in software. Hasbro failed to successfully enter the rapidly growing electronic game market. In 1995,

Hasbro attempted to take existing games like Monopoly and put them on CD-ROMs for gameplay on PCs. In 1998, it acquired Tiger, Microprose, and a library of Atari games. It tried to develop its own virtual reality games and planned for an online site (Games.com) where people could play games. However, by 2000, Hasbro realized that none of these efforts would bear fruit, so it decided to sell these holdings.

In Summary

Companies find themselves in sour spots when they lose control over the classic five industry forces, the most important of which is customers. You can avoid losing control by doing the following: (i) make sure that you are able to sell your products and services at prices that your customers can afford; (ii) price these products and services at levels that enable you to make a profit; and (iii) have business models that are simple enough that you can carry out the tasks and activities well.

Being in a sour spot means distance and misalignment with customers. It means that you are unable to sell them sufficient quantities of goods and services to be consistently profitable. Your customers' switching costs are low, and it's easy for them to abandon you.

This chapter has provided examples of sour spots you should avoid. Here are the lessons to learn:

- Do not over- or underdesign your products.
- Have more than a few powerful customers.
- Don't keep pouring money into R&D if the R&D does not meaningfully differentiate your products.
- Align your products and services with the level of sophistication of your customers.
- Don't be a product-first company that does not pay sufficient attention to service.
- Don't ignore competitors in the lower-priced-based market.

- Be wary of competing with foreign government subsidized products.

- Be in a position where you can pass suppliers' price increases on to customers.

- Have a clear identity.

- Be tied to a process of working with customers to best meet their needs.

- Don't sacrifice price for market share.

- Have good contingency plans to adequately cover risk.

- Anticipate your competitors' moves.

- Know where to position yourself on the price/quality continuum.

- Justify your product's price with especially unique products within your customers' comfort zone.

- Keep to a simple business model.

- Don't depend on a few powerful customers for a very high percentage of your sales.

- Don't rely on a complicated business model that requires very accurate prediction and timing.

Losing companies got into these sour spots by rigidity, ineptness, and diffuseness. The next chapter's focus is on the first of these attributes.

10

RIGIDITY

Big losers were not passive. They, too, moved (see Table 10.1), but often it was in the wrong direction, or their timing was off. Big losers moved because they had to in response to a threat. Their moves were defensive, not offensive. They moved without good knowledge of their customers. Big losers did not move toward positions where they could be more fully aligned with their customers' needs. It was a movement driven by products and technologies, not by markets. Figure 10.1 summarizes the lessons learned from big losers. For each lesson in Figure 10.1, I provide examples of the traits (Table 10.1) the big losers exhibited.

Table 10.1 Rigidity: The Movement of Losing Companies

Company	Rigidity
LSI Logic	Moves toward standard, low-end products Fails to keep up the pace in new product offerings
Snap-On	Sticks to an original business that loses promise Buys weak-performing firms in the same industry
Parametric	Stays in a niche that is out of favor Does not maintain skills in new product development Lags in recognizing the need for enhanced customer service
IMC	Moves further toward commodities Allows substantial debt to build because of acquisitions Responds slowly to core market decline
Goodyear	Expands into nonprofitable business Moves further toward products sold to original equipment manufacturers Buys commodity businesses Does not take advantage of blunders by competitors
Safeco	Sticks with a weak business line Moves further toward risky products with declining prices Overpays for acquisitions Does not move to profitable niches
Campbell	Ignores noncore brands Misses changes in demand
The Gap	Does not keep expansion in line with growth in sales Loses touch with core customers Does not anticipate demand
Hasbro	Ventures too far from core strengths Engages in risky royalty partnerships Fails to enter new markets rapidly Does not prepare for change in consumer tastes Gets bogged down in bureaucracy

- Do not rely exclusively on expansion of your core products for growth.
- Avoid over-reliance on hard-to-differentiate commodity products sold on the basis of price.
- Do not accumulate additional capacity at high prices when there is insufficient demand.
- Respond vigorously when you're experiencing a decline in your core business area.
- Don't lag in recognition and reaction to changes in your customers' tastes.
- Bigger is not necessarily better.

Figure 10.1 Lessons learned from losing companies about rigidity.

Do Not Rely Exclusively on Expansion of Your Core Products for Growth

Big losers tended to rely on the expansion of their core products for growth. This fault is illustrated by five rigid traits that they exhibited. They (i) stuck to original businesses that were losing promise, (ii) remained in niches that were out of favor, (iii) expanded unprofitable businesses, (iv) failed to abandon weak business lines, and (v) overemphasized their core brands. Snap-On, Parametric, Goodyear, Safeco, and Campbell provide examples of the big losers' over-reliance on their core products for growth.

Do Not Stick to an Original Business That Loses Promise

Although Snap-On had many competitors (see Figure 10.2), it stayed true to what it always had done. In response to changing industry conditions, it did not move quickly or far. It did not waver from its mission despite the fact that it had little control over its customers and suppliers. The barriers to entering the industry in which it competed were low and the market offered numerous substitutes. The company continued

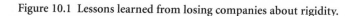

to create sophisticated tools. It had strong brands and premium-quality products: hand tools, power tools, diagnostic tools (from hand-held scanners to high-end diagnostic systems), and storage units. It further refined and developed these products even though its market share was small compared to its competitors. Snap-On had trouble moving toward selling applications that solved problems rather than selling tools for professional users. It continued in the same direction it had been going despite the fact that the automotive industry was a poor candidate for growth, profit margins had shrunk, and there was a decline in capital investment among its customers. This decline that started in 1998 continued through the recession of 2001 and only added to Snap-On's woes.

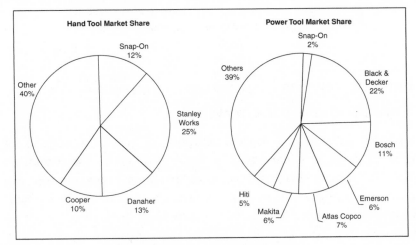

Figure 10.2 Snap-On's 2002 market share.

Do Not Stay in a Niche That Is Out of Favor

In a market that was maturing, Parametric was a one-product company that did not offer a low-priced, user-friendly version of its software. Until 1998, it ignored price wars raging in the industry. In the early 1990s, it had landed major corporate accounts with firms such as Ford Motor Company and Caterpillar, Inc. By 1991, it commanded a 10-percent market share in CAD/CAM (computer aided design/computer aided manufacturing) software with its PRO/Engineer product. Throughout the 1990s, Parametric charged a premium for this software.

Typical packages were priced between $1,500 and $9,500, with standard bundles of six to eight units being sold for around $18,000. However, the software had many functions that customers did not need.

In 1998, the company introduced an entry-level version of Pro/ENGINEER, but the version was no better than those of its competitors', and Parametric's version was higher priced. As sales flattened in the mid-1990s, Parametric saw an opportunity in Product Lifecycle Management (PLM) software. PLM software was used in product development. It tracked and controlled data. In 1998, Parametric released Windchill, a Web-based program that provided infrastructure for collaborative product development on the Internet. Windchill was meant to be easy to use and install, but it did not live up to its promise. It required more than 18 months of installation time.

In 2001, Parametric introduced a more easily deployable application of Pro/ENGINEER. This application had links for management records. It was meant to assist engineers, customers, and sales forces in working together to customize product designs and manage projects on the Web. The company upgraded the quality of its products, integrated acquired technologies into Pro/ENGINEER and Windchill, and increased their functionality, but even with these improvements, Parametric's progress in this fast-moving industry was slow. It had not advanced quickly enough from being a single product company in a mature market with limited growth potential.

Do Not Expand into a Nonprofitable Business

Goodyear was in a mature industry that had low profit margins. The market for tires had too much capacity. Labor and raw material costs were high and hard to control. In response to Bridgestone's merger with Firestone and Michelin's mergers with Goodrich and Uniroyal, Goodyear finalized a global alliance with Sumitomo Rubber Industries. This alliance added another $2.5 billion to its 1999 tire sales and reestablished Goodyear as the world's largest tire producer. Sam Gibara, who was CEO at the time, wanted this status. His aim was to grow the company's tire revenues from $12 billion to $23 billion. With the Sumitomo alliance, Goodyear acquired the Dunlop brand of tires and achieved access to Sumitomo's European manufacturing and distributing operations. Even with this alliance, Goodyear did not reach the revenue goals it was seeking. The price of the alliance was too high, and declining cash flows combined with growing debt in an industry like tires where rivalry was intense hurt Goodyear.

Do Not Stick Within a Weak Business Line

Safeco derived about three-quarters of its sales from the property and casualty (P&C) insurance market. The market was populated by a large number of firms that offered similar products. Safeco's President and CEO Mike McGavick said about his company's customers: "People buy our products, especially auto and business insurance, because they are compelled to do so by banks, by states, or by logic—it is not a 'happy' purchase." Traditional property and casualty products, such as car and homeowner's insurance, were obligatory purchases for most people. State law mandated the purchase of auto insurance, and lending institutions required the purchase of homeowner's insurance. The consumer was price sensitive, which caused companies to compete on the basis of price to maintain market share. Safeco lowered premiums to compete. Company executives reasoned that if their premiums were lower than those of the competition, the company would gain market share. Safeco tried this tactic from 1993 to 1994 and again from 1998 1999, but its discounting did not work. Lower rates helped it retain customers, but not win new ones. Because it undercut its prices to maintain market share, it incurred large losses of more than $1 billion from 1999 to 2001.

Do Not Ignore Noncore Brands

Campbell was one of the first U.S. firms to achieve national distribution. By eliminating most of the water, condensed soups made packaging, shipping, storage, and overall distribution simpler and cheaper. Starting in 1915, with the purchase of Franco-American, the company shifted to other product lines. In 1948, it continued to diversify with the acquisition of V8 juice. In 1955, it bought Swanson, in 1961 Pepperidge Farm, in 1966 Godiva Chocolatier, in 1978 Vlasic Pickles, and in 1982 Mrs. Paul's Seafood. Between 1981 and 1992, it added Prego spaghetti sauces to its product lines. Campbell expanded its product offerings to many food types, including canned pasta (Spaghettios), snack crackers (Pepperidge Farms Goldfish crackers), and sauces (Prego and Pace).

However, the company failed to take good advantage of the product lines it added. Such brands as Pace, Picante, Pepperidge Farm, Godiva, and V8 had unrealized potential. Within Campbell, their status was second to soups. For instance, customers enthusiastically endorsed V8's Splash line of juices when they were introduced in 1999, but sales slumped when the company failed to follow through with a strong marketing campaign.

Uninspired management coupled with stiff bureaucracy meant that Campbell was slow to take advantage of opportunities outside of soups. In 2002, 66 percent of earnings continued to be from soups. Condensed soups generated 35 percent of the firm's profits, but the sales of condensed soups had been flat or waning in the United States since 1970. Worldwide, soup sales were down by 21 percent since 1998. Only by moving to frozen, dry, premium (Campbell's Select and Home Cookin') and healthy (Healthy Request) varieties did Campbell remain the leading U.S. soup maker, with roughly 70 percent of the market. In 2002, soup shipments continued to decline. The only Campbell brands that showed signs of life were the new ones that the company introduced—Home Cookin' and Healthy Request. Behind the decline were customers clamoring for product improvements and healthier alternatives that Campbell was not providing.

Avoid Over-Reliance on Hard-to-Differentiate Commodity Products Sold on the Basis of Price

Big losers tended to rely on hard-to-differentiate commodity products sold on the basis of price. This fault is illustrated by five traits. Big losers moved toward (i) standard, low-end products, (ii) commodities, (iii) products sold to original equipment manufacturers, (iv) risky products, and (v) products that did not match up well with their core strengths. LSI Logic, IMC, Goodyear, Safeco, and Hasbro provide examples of the big losers' over-reliance on commodity products.

Do Not Move Toward Standard, Low-End Products

LSI Logic moved from ASICs (application-specific integrated circuits) to standard integrated circuits (CoreWare mix-and-match technology). Instead of continuing to work with its customers to manufacture custom-made computer chips, it sold standard computer chips to which its customers added their proprietary logic and systems.

In response to Wintel's success, LSI Logic made the move to CoreWare. CoreWare could integrate with almost any application or system in the industry. LSI Logic acted to fill voids in its CoreWare portfolio with the acquisitions of SEEQ Technology and ZSP Corporation in 1999, but the standard product it offered was not a differentiating point between itself and the competition, and the company did not receive the orders it needed to justify the movement it made to this product.

Best known for leading-edge technologies, LSI Logic was adversely affected by competitive pricing and lower margins in standard chips. It had to compete on price with other manufacturers, something it was not good at.

In response to losses LSI Logic suffered in 1998, 2001, and 2002, it moved into the storage area network (SAN) business through its 1988 acquisition of Symbiosis, a data storage company, the 2000 acquisition of Syntax, a software company for the storage management market, and the 2002 acquisition of Mylex from IBM. In the storage area business, LSI Logic competed with its customers (NCR, IBM, Sun Microsystems, and Raytheon). It had a low-cost strategy in a highly competitive commodity business dominated by large, resource-rich competitors. Its gross profit margins therefore declined from 43 percent to 23 percent in 2001. LSI Logic abandoned custom-made products for standard products sold on the basis of price, and it did not pay off.

Do Not Move Further Toward Commodities

IMC operated almost exclusively in the bulk fertilizer market. Its primary products were commodities that experienced cycles of oversupply and decreased demand, depressed prices, and low margins. In the fertilizer business, there was intense global competition for a shrinking market.

Thomas C. Meadows formed the predecessor to IMC, United States Agricultural Corporation, to provide basic fertilizer nutrients to U.S. growers in the early 1900s.The original company was primarily a phosphate mining operation. In 1909, Meadows teamed with Waldemar A. Schmidtmann, whose holdings included a thriving potash mine in Germany and fertilizers.

IMC's attempts to diversify out of the fertilizer business in the 1990s failed. It found itself overleveraged. By 2002, it sold off almost all its noncore operations. The huge debt load hurt profit margins and forced it to sell an Ogden, Utah solar evaporation facility and Australian soda ash business.

The fertilizer business did not allow for much product differentiation. Being the lowest-cost provider was the main option. As a low-cost producer, IMC was able to capitalize on a healthy market and exploit economies of scale. However, in North America, the market was mature, and it offered limited possibilities for growth. The company shipped between 25 and 30 percent of its fertilizers to China, Australia, India, Japan, and Brazil. Export demand also started to turn down, and with the decline, the company's credit worthiness slipped. It had negative free cash flow, and its lenders demanded higher payments, which impaired its ability to diversify.

Do Not Move Further Toward Products Sold to Original Equipment Manufacturers

Companies like Goodyear competed on the basis of price in the tire industry selling commodities to hard-pressed original equipment manufacturers (OEMS). The automobile companies who made up 25 percent of Goodyear's sales were not in a position to cut the company any slack. They drove down prices to the point where Goodyear was selling its tires below cost. The company sold cheap, nondurable tires to automakers in the hope that the vehicle owners would be loyal to the brand, and when their tires wore out, the vehicle owners would ask for Goodyear tire replacements. Unfortunately, the vehicle owners shopped for tires with the lowest cost regardless of brand. Tires were a commodity, so customers were not loyal to a brand. Goodyear could not get out of this predicament. It was in a fiercely competitive, mature industry with low profit margins, and it had trouble differentiating its product in a meaningful way.

Do Not Move Further Toward Risky Products with Declining Prices

Brutal competition in the property and casualty insurance business continued to force Safeco to slash prices. Safeco purchased other companies such as American States Financial Corporation (AS), WM Life Insurance Company, and R.F. Bailey to broaden its geographic base. With its business spread out more broadly, Safeco executives believed that the company would be in a better position to recover from natural disasters that struck in one part of the world. The company no longer would be devastated by calamities that hit a single region of the U.S. After the acquisitions, Safeco lowered its auto insurance and homeowner policy rates. It used discounted underwriting and pricing to retain customers, but these efforts cut the company's slim operating margins. Insurance payouts were growing, but premiums for most lines were stagnant or declining. The Internet made it increasingly easy for consumers to compare prices and switch providers. With short (usually six-month) policies, customers were not locked in for long. Selling hard-to-differentiate commodity products was a difficult business for Safeco to be in.

Do Not Venture Too Far from Core Strengths

In the face of mounting competition from fast-growing computer gaming companies, Hasbro understood that it could not rely solely on its core toy and game products. It tried to enter the computer gaming industry. A subsidiary, Hasbro Interactive, developed computer games based on the company's popular board games, such as Monopoly, Risk, and Battleship. The digitization strategy went further when Hasbro acquired Tiger, Microprose, and a library of Atari games in 1998. Tiger was an established company in the hand-held computer game market. Microprose and the Atari assets were meant to assist Hasbro in starting an online interactive gaming venture that it intended to call Games.com.

These ideas never got off the ground. In 2000, Hasbro gave up on Hasbro Interactive and Games.com after each venture had losses in excess of $100 million. They were sold to Infogames Entertainment, for stock, cash, and net assets. The sale was written off as a $104 million operating loss. When Infogames' share prices slid, another $32 million had to be written down on this investment. Hasbro experienced steadily declining revenues after the sale and ended the year 2000 with a net loss of $170.7 million.

Do Not Accumulate Additional Capacity at High Prices When Demand Is Insufficient

Big losers tended to accumulate additional capacity at high prices when there was insufficient demand. This fault is illustrated by six traits the big losers exhibited. They (i) bought weak-performing firms, (ii) allowed their debt to build because of their acquisitions, (iii) acquired commodity businesses, (iv) overpaid for the companies they acquired, (v) expanded too rapidly, and (vi) had risky royalty and licensing arrangements. Snap-On, IMC, Goodyear, Safeco, the Gap, and Hasbro provide examples of this fault.

Do Not Buy Weak-Performing Firms in the Same Industry

From 1992 to 1999, Snap-On made 25 acquisitions, almost all of them in the domestic auto repair industry. (See Figure 10.3) Its acquisitions had a high failure rate. The companies it bought were not positioned for strong growth. Many did not do well. They did not drive large enough incremental sales to offset their high costs.[1] Because of these acquisitions, Snap-On wrote off $36.5 million in goodwill in 1998. It wrote off another $16.9 million in goodwill in 1999. The company's profit margins declined, and it had to reduce costs and close factories. Moody's Investors Service lowered its senior unsecured debt rating in 2003.

Figure 10.3 Selected Snap-On acquisitions: 1992 to 1999.

Do Not Allow Substantial Debt to Build Because of Your Acquisitions

Following a series of mergers and acquisitions in the 1990s, IMC was in strategic and operational control of the world's largest phosphate operations, made more potash than any company (see Figure 10.4), and was the world's third largest fertilizer company. IMC Global's two core businesses—phosphates and potash—had come together in 1909. In 1988, the firm combined its fertilizer assets and went public. In 1993, it entered into a joint venture with Freeport McMoran Resources

1989 Purchased a 50-percent partnership interest in a subsidiary of W.R. Grace & Co, the Four Corners phosphate rock mine, and related properties in west central Florida.

Purchased phosphate reserves and rock processing facilities from Hopewell Land Corporation.

1993 Joint venture with Freeport-McMoRan Resource Partners.

1995 Acquired substantially all of Central Canada Potash division of Noranda, Inc. (CCP).

Acquired the animal feed ingredients business of Mallinckrodt Group Inc.

1996 Merged with The Vigoro Corp.

Acquired retail distribution operations, Madison Seed and Agri-Supply, and precision farming operation, Top-Soil.

1997 Acquired Western Ag-Minerals Company, a subsidiary of Rayrock Yellowknife Resources.

Sold its rail care repair operations to Fitzgerald Railcar Services Inc.

Acquired Freeport-McMoRan Inc.

Merged with FTX.

Completed smaller acquisitions, including buying several retail distribution operations and a storage terminal company.

1998 Acquired Harris Chemical Group Inc. and its Australian affiliate, Penrice Soda Products Pty. Ltd.

Sold Vigoro to Pursell Industries Inc.

1999 Sold its Agribusiness retail and wholesale distribution unit, including its nitrogen production facilities in East Dubuque, Illinois and Cincinnati, Ohio to Royster Clark.

Sold its oil and gas business.

2001 Sold Penrice Soda Products Pty. Ltd. to Castle Harlan Australian Mezzanine Partners Pty Ltd.

Sold IMC Salt to Compass Minerals Group.

2002 Discontinued the remaining portion of its chemicals business.

Completed the acquisition of the sulfur transportation and terminal assets of Freeport-McMoRan Sulphur LLC.

2003 Sold White River sodium bicarbonate mine and plant to Natural Soda AALA, Inc.

Figure 10.4 IMC's acquisitions, joint ventures, and divestitures.

Partners to create IMC Phosphates Company M.P., a phosphate mining and fertilizer company in Florida and Louisiana. This joint venture made it the world's largest phosphate producer.

Throughout the 1990s, IMC did not stop expanding its phosphate and potash businesses. However, many of the deals it struck did not work out.[2] Management failed to recognize that in spite of attempts to grow, the company was vulnerable. In 1998, it overpaid for Harris Chemicals N.A. It funded this entire $1.4 billion acquisition with borrowed money.[3]

The company was the most financially leveraged of North American fertilizer producers. (See Figure 10.5.) During the period from 1995 to 1999, IMC's acquisitions left the company with huge debt just as the market for fertilizers started to decline. Its phosphate sales dropped from 7.3 million tons in 1998 to 6.0 million tons in 2001, reflecting less demand. (See Figure 10.6.) The company lost its investment grade credit ratings, and its interest expenses grew. It had to address the debt situation or risk bankruptcy. Because of these financial woes, IMC was forced to sell assets at only a fraction of the price it had paid for them.

Do Not Buy Commodity Businesses

In the late 1980s and early 1990s, Goodyear made a series of divestitures, beginning with its aerospace division in 1987; its South African tire division in 1989; its Scottsboro, Alabama tire plant in 1991; its food, industrial, and polyester businesses in 1992; and its roofing and wheel and brake businesses in 1993. But Goodyear reversed course thereafter. In reaction to ongoing consolidation in the tire industry, it began to acquire other tire companies. In 1993, it bought Kelly Tires. In 1994, it purchased Tecbelt Pacific, a 75-percent share of Dalian Tire Company in China, and a 60-percent share in a rubber company in China. In 1995, Goodyear tried to strengthen its European tire business by buying a 50-percent stake in Dacki Swedish, a tire retailer, besides one-third ownership of TC Debica, Central Europe's leading tire producer. In 1996, Goodyear acquired Belt Concepts of America. In 1997, it bought a stake in the Sava Group, and in 1999, it completed its joint venture with Sumitomo.

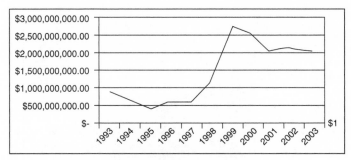

Figure 10.5 IMC debt levels.

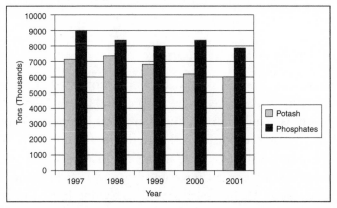

Figure 10.6 IMC's phosphate and potash sales volumes: 1997-2001.

However, demand never picked up to the levels that Goodyear expected, and it suffered from overcapacity in many plants. Moreover, the
acquisitions were financed by significant amounts of debt. As the debt
level rose, the firm's bond ratings fell, the cost of interest to maintain its
debt increased, and the company developed a serious liquidity problem. In 2002, it owed more than three times what it was valued. (See
Figure 10.7.)

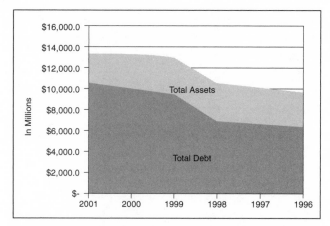

Figure 10.7 Goodyear's total assets to total debt: 1996 to 2002.

Do Not Overpay for Acquisitions

Historically, Safeco had concentrated its operations west of the Rockies. However, it took a major step in geographic and product diversification in 1997 with its acquisition of American States Financial Corporation (AS). This acquisition transformed Safeco into a national player in the property and casualty (P&C) insurance marketplace. It doubled its independent agency distribution force and became a leading underwriter. The acquisition of AS, however, proved costly due in part to the high price. Safeco had revenues of $4.8 billion when it paid $2.8 billion for AS in 1997. In that year, it also acquired WM Life Insurance Company, a unit of the Washington Mutual Bank of Seattle, and formed a strategic alliance with Washington Mutual to distribute annuities via the bank's multistate network. Around that same time, Safeco purchased the naming rights to the Seattle Mariner's ballpark and acquired London-based R.F. Bailey to establish a firm international presence.

Safeco was attempting to increase its market share in the P&C insurance market, from which it derived about three-quarters of its sales. However, the premiums for most property and casualty lines during the 1990s were stagnant or declining, even while insurance payouts were increasing. The discounting policies that Safeco adopted failed because of the company's failure to correctly anticipate losses that came from exposure to weather-related catastrophic events in the Midwest and to other nonweather-related claims.

Safeco had been forced to issue a substantial amount of debt to finance the acquisitions. Its balance sheet deteriorated and its credit rating was downgraded. In 2001, the company wrote off $1.2 billion in goodwill pertaining to the AS acquisition and $13 million in goodwill pertaining to the R.F. Bailey acquisition.

Keep Expansion in Line with Growth in Sales

In the 1990s, the Gap's CEO, Millard "Mickey" Drexler, was lauded as the "king of retailing." With Drexler at the helm, the company was a pioneer in the corporate dress-down revolution. It expanded rapidly to meet consumer demand. The Gap's 1997 annual report to shareholders said, "If there is a gap, we'll fill it." The company was true to its motto not only expanding its core brand, but also moving into many specialty segments.

The number of Gap stores doubled from 1995 to 2002. The company entered Japan and Germany during this period. It also launched Gapkids, babyGap, GapBody, GapMaternity, and online shopping at Gap.com, and it increased the worldwide recognition of its brands.

Between 1998 and 2001, square footage at Gap Inc.'s three chains—Gap, Banana Republic, and Old Navy—almost doubled. The company continued to add 20 to 25 percent more retail space each year from 1999 to 2001. (See Table 10.2.) The three-year compound annual growth rate in its retail space was 25 percent per year. The new locations that the Gap opened to boost sales, however, were costly to bring on line. Gap had to pay about $1 billion in rent for its 3,000 plus stores in 2002. The impressive growth in space was not matched by growth in sales, which declined from $548 per square foot in 1999 to $394 per square foot in 2001.

In 2001, growth in earnings growth came to an abrupt halt, when the Gap lost $7.8 million. Its overly rapid expansion saturated the market, bringing on the challenge of operating in different segments in a mature market. The company had too many stores in too many different market niches. Rapid store growth and weak financial performance left the Gap saddled with debt. (See Figure 10.8.) The downgrading of its debt rating meant high interest costs and insufficient access to capital.

Table 10.2 The Growth in the Number of Gap Stores

Year	Total Number of Stores
2001	3,740
2000	3,018
1999	2,428
1998	2,130
1997	1,854
1996	1,680
1995	1,508
1994	1,370

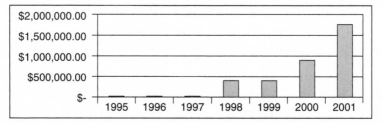

Figure 10.8 The Gap's long-term debt.

Avoid Risky Royalty Payments

Because Hasbro licensed other firms' hit properties, its royalty expenses were huge—$427 million, $296 million, and $210 million, or 7.3 percent, 10.2 percent, and 10.5 percent of net revenues in 2000, 2001, and 2002. Hasbro suffered a setback in the late 1990s when a key alliance did not work as expected. Its partnership to promote *Star Wars* figurines was an almost total bust. Due to the sequel's lack of popularity, it did not yield the expected profits. The 1999 episode of *Star Wars* that George Lucas fans anticipated so highly did not generate demand for related products that Hasbro expected. *Star Wars* action figures had been huge sellers in the past, and Hasbro risked a huge amount of money signing up the rights to the three sequels. The generous contract that Hasbro gave Lucas called for an initial minimum payoff of $581 million. In contrast, Mattel, Hasbro's main competitor, paid a paltry $20 million for the rights to the more popular *Harry Potter* books and films. Hasbro made a huge bet on *Star Wars'* popularity that failed.

Respond Vigorously When Experiencing a Decline in Your Core Business Area

Big losers did not respond vigorously when experiencing a decline in their core business. This fault is illustrated by five traits. Big losers did not (i) keep pace with new product offerings, (ii) maintain skills in new product development, (iii) respond rapidly to core market decline, (iv) keep up with changes in demand, and (v) rapidly enter new markets. LSI Logic, Parametric, IMC, Campbell, and Hasbro provide examples of the big losers' inability to respond vigorously to a decline in their core business.

Keep Up the Pace in New Product Offerings

In the capital-intensive semiconductor industry in which LSI Logic competed, the company had to make high-level investments to upgrade facilities and purchase new equipment. LSI Logic was not able to make rapid adjustments. It was slow to move unless faced with threats. In 1985, most of its customers were large military and aerospace contractors. It abandoned this market because military spending started to decline.

The years 1996 through 1998 were difficult ones for LSI Logic. In 1998, the company reported losses of $126 million. With virtually nothing remaining of its military business, the company started to provide standard chips for PCs and the consumer electronic market (such as Sony PlayStation, DVDs, digital cameras, and wireless communications), but this market did not pan out as well as expected. LSI Logic's specialized chips were too expensive for the market, and its application-specific integrated circuits (ASICS) no longer were paying off, because both large (Motorola, Texas Instruments, Toshiba) and small (Agere Systems, Adaptec, Qlogic) companies entered this market and squeezed the company's profits.

From 2001 to 2002, total demand in the market for ASIC chips decreased by 45 percent. The number of manufacturers went from more than 100 in the mid-1990s to 12 by 2002. Competitors rapidly consolidated to reduce costs. Their products were higher quality, faster, and less expensive than LSI Logic's. LSI Logic switched to less expensive chips.

Maintain Skills in New Product Development

Parametric acquired companies with related capabilities, but it was not successful at leveraging the acquisitions. Unsuccessful attempts to expand through mergers and acquisitions in addition to lack of attention to competitors' advances put Parametric in a poor position.

In 1995, Parametric acquired Evans & Sutherland Computer's design software division and Rasna. The acquisitions gave it capabilities for product operations simulations. In 1996, it acquired Greenshire License Company, Computervision, and ICEM Technologies. Greenshire License Company gave it project modeling and management capabilities. Computervision, a direct competitor, was a leading provider of product design and development software. Its acquisition expanded Parametric's customer base and increased the company's presence in industries such as automotive, aerospace, and shipbuilding. ICEM Technologies provided advanced surfacing and reverse engineering software tools widely used by the automotive and aerospace industries.

In 1998, Parametric acquired InPart Design, a firm known for its comprehensive Internet-based library of mechanical parts. In 1999, it acquired Division Group, a data visualization specialist strong in Web-based development. Parametric's strategy was to create software that permitted individuals, regardless of their roles in the commercialization process, to participate in product development, but it was late in using the knowledge and skills it acquired to create new products.

To compete more effectively against the niche providers, Parametric developed a suite of preconfigured modules for Windchill that offered specific functionalities. Customers could pick and choose a functionality that satisfied their needs at a cost significantly lower than

Parametric's packaged solution, but Parametric was slow to find a solution when the needs of its customers changed. While it introduced an upgraded version of PRO/Engineer, its competitors made a series of unanswered product launches. Consumers lost confidence in Parametric CAD/CAM software and began switching to competitors who had what they perceived to be more reliable, user-friendly, and in some cases, lower-cost solutions.

Respond Rapidly to Core Market Decline

A primary reason for the lowered application rates of fertilizers was an unhealthy U.S. farm economy. IMC was highly dependent on export markets, with sales to these markets being between 55 percent and 60 percent of its total sales from 1997 to 2002. In 2000 to 2001, however, the Chinese government imposed tight fertilizer import restrictions.

To further compound these problems, as demand slipped, supply grew. Several competitors in Asia brought new production facilities online. New capacity came online in large blocks that could not be absorbed immediately. The new capacity that competitors brought online was closer to end markets.

Therefore, the transportation costs to service it were lower. The new capacity did not have sunk costs, which allowed the developers to pick good locations. IMC thus found itself competing against rivals that had lower costs. IMC's average selling price for phosphate fertilizer fell from approximately $178 per short ton in 1998 to approximately $128 per short ton in 2001. Each $10 decline in the price per ton reduced its pre-tax profits by $65 million.

IMC made organizational changes, sold units, exited businesses, right-sized assets, and tried to adjust operations to match demand and improve cash flow. It tried to differentiate itself via better customer service and e-commerce. It introduced a culture of continuous improvement. But the oversupplied fertilizer industry was in a down-cycle. It was a difficult environment in which to introduce these changes. The changes came too late and were too little.

Do Not Miss Changes in Demand

Campbell Soup's competitors made significant gains. Taking market share were rivals such as General Mills' Progresso. Progresso positioned its scope as a "grown-up" alternative that was upscale and commanded a premium price. Consumer preference was moving toward high-quality, easy-to-prepare foods, not condensed brands, which required the addition of water.

Campbell was slow to capitalize on growing demand for healthier, more convenient foods. It lost ground because it did not acknowledge soon enough that consumers wanted convenience, quality ingredients, full-bodied taste, and creative packaging. It spent its time fighting off store-brand and generic imitations that sold at a discount and making acquisitions (Pace Foods, Fresh Start Bakeries, and Homepride) that gave the appearance of growth. Much of the growth in the biscuits and confectionary segment, for instance, came from the acquisition of Arnott's in Australia. (See Table 10.3.)

To secure its position as the leader in soups in Western Europe, Campbell acquired Erasco Group of Germany in 1997 and Liebig of France in 1998. Its 7-percent increase in international soup sales in 1999 was driven mainly by the Liebig acquisition. In 1999, Campbell acquired the Stockpot premium refrigerated soup business. In 2001, it bought Unilever's European soup and sauces holdings, and in 2002, it purchased Erin Foods, Ireland's second largest dry soup business.

However, these moves did not enable Campbell to keep up with nimble, innovative competitors. In 2001, it finally decided to get into the "convenience meal" product arena with its Campbell's Supper Bake, but the meal took 35 minutes to prepare and cook, which was at least 10 minutes longer than most of the competing products. There was also some question as to whether this product was even an innovation, because it was basically a soup recipe with the ingredients in a box.

Campbell started a three-year "Transformation Plan" in 2001. It increased spending on advertising, made product quality initiatives, and tried to improve sales execution. The company invested in new technology ("cold blending"). It updated advertising themes, brought back the "M'm M'm Good" tagline, and enlisted 2002 Winter Olympic star Sarah Hughes to appear on the label of Chicken Noodle, the most popular condensed soup flavor. To pitch Chunky Soup, the company relied on an "It fills you up right" campaign and used the NFL for its ads. The company introduced specialized varieties of Select Soups, including Roasted Chicken with Rotini and Penne Pasta, Honey Roasted Chicken with Golden Potato, and Italian Style Wedding Soup. More of its products had easy-to-open packages. Net sales in 2002 increased by 6 percent, but earnings were off by 19 percent.

Table 10.3 Campbell's Acquisitions and Divestitures: 1992 to 2002

Year	Move	Company	Products and Location	Notes
1992	Acquisition	Sanwa Foods	Ramen soups (United States)	Helped drive 5.5-percent increase in soup volume
1993	Acquisition (increase ownership to 58 percent)	Arnott's	Biscuits (Australia)	$170 million increase in sales, noted as primary reason for earnings increase
1993	Acquisition (increase ownership to 100 percent)	Spring Valley Juice	Juices (Australia)	
1994	Acquisition	Dandy Mushrooms	Fresh mushrooms (Australia)	
1994	Divestiture(s)	Campbell Foods, PLC; Casera Foods; La Forest Perigord SA; Quadelco Limited; Torreo y Ribelles SA	Various (most foreign)	
1994	Acquisition	Fray Bentos	Canned meat (UK)	Helped increase sales over 1993 for International division
1995	Acquisition	Pace Foods	Salsa, other sauces (United States)	Sales increase of $127 million
1995	Acquisition	Fresh Start Bakeries	Bakery products	

Table 10.3 Campbell's Acquisitions and Divestitures: 1992 to 2002

Year	Move	Company	Products and Location	Notes
1995	Acquisition	Stratford-upon-Avon Foods	Canned vegetables and fruits (UK)	
1995	Acquisition (increase ownership to 65 percent)	Arnott's	Biscuits (Australia)	
1996	Acquisition (increase ownership to 70 percent)	Arnott's	Biscuits (Australia)	
1996	Acquisition (50 percent ownership)	PT Helios (Arnott's Indonesia)	Biscuits and snack foods (Indonesia)	
1996	Acquisition	Greenfield Healthy Foods	Fat-free cookies (Ireland)	
1996	Acquisition	Homepride Cooking Sauces	Cooking sauces (UK)	Significant contribution to 1-percent earnings increase of $136 million
1996	Acquisition ("controlling interest")	Cheong Chan	Asian cooking sauces (China)	Significant contribution to 1-percent earnings increase of $136 million
1996	Divestiture	Mrs. Paul's	Frozen seafood (United States)	
1996	Divestiture	Campbell's Groko	Frozen vegetable processor (Denmark)	
1996	Divestiture(s)	Ripe and Spanish olive processor	Olives	
1997	Acquisition	Erasco Group	Soups (Germany)	
1997	Acquisition (by Arnott's)	Kettle Chip Company	Salty snacks (Australia)	
1998	Divestiture	Continental Sweets	Confections and (related) distribution business	Led to sales declines
1998	Divestiture	Melbourne Mushrooms	Mushrooms (Australia)	Led to sales declines
1998	Divestiture	Spring Valley Juice	Juices (Australia)	
1998	Divestiture	Delacre	Biscuits/confections	Excluding this transaction, sales increased 7 percent in biscuits/confections

Table 10.3 Campbell's Acquisitions and Divestitures: 1992 to 2002

Year	Move	Company	Products and Location	Notes
1998	Acquisition	Liebig	Dry soups (France)	Sales increase $7.5Mq
1998	Acquisition (increase ownership to 100 percent)	Arnott's	Biscuits (Australia)	
1998	Divestiture	Boas B.V.	Fresh mushrooms (Australia)	
1998	Divestiture(s)	Poultry and can-making operations	(United States)	
1998	Divestiture	Fresh Start Bakeries	Bakery products	
1999	Acquisition	Stockpot	Premium refrigerated soup (United States)	Helped drive 12-percent earnings increase
2000	Divestiture	MacFarms of Hawaii	Macadamia nuts (United States)	
2002	Acquisition (by Arnott's)	Snack Foods Limited	Salty snacks (Australia)	
2002	Acquisition	Erin Foods	Dry soup (Ireland)	
2002	Acquisition	Velish	Soup (Australia)	

Enter New Markets Rapidly

Hasbro's moves were poorly timed. In 1992, it began to entertain ideas for the electronic marketplace, but it established Hasbro Interactive only in 1995, when it took existing Hasbro games and put them on a CD-ROM so people could play them on personal computers. The company expected that the demand for these products would boost sales for its board games. People who played the computer versions would want the board game versions and vice versa. Stimulating this demand was important because typically a family who purchased a board game like Monopoly would not need to buy another Monopoly set for many years. With the Internet's increase in popularity, the company wanted to take advantage of its reputation for great games by creating a site where people could play these games. It did more than rely on existing games, venturing into virtual reality by working on a new product it planned to call Sliced Bread. It spent $40 million trying to develop Sliced Bread. The company's entry into technology and interactive gaming came late, however, and its decision to pull out did not work well.

Don't Lag in Recognition and Reaction to Changes in Your Customers' Tastes

Big losers lagged in recognizing and responding to changes in customer tastes. This fault is illustrated by four traits that big losers exhibited. They lagged in (i) recognizing the need for enhanced customer service, (ii) responding to competitors' innovations, (iii) staying in touch with core customers, and (iv) preparing for changes in their customers' tastes. Parametric, Campbell, the Gap, and Hasbro provide examples of the big losers' lagging in their recognition and reaction to changes in their customers' tastes.

Don't Lag in Recognizing the Need for Enhanced Customer Service

Parametric's strategy was to develop a technologically superior product. It was hobbled by a deeply held notion that it was a product development company, not a customer service organization. The company faced stiff competition from niche and full-scale enterprise solution providers that were offering much higher levels of service than it was willing to provide. Product development, the company stated, was its "only business," and product sales the sole determinant of success.

Starting in the early 1990s, management decided to opt for aggressive sales quotas, which forced the sales force to adopt "hit and run" tactics. This method usually left customers with expensive software they had to handle on their own. Customers received almost no product integration support. With aggressive quotas, sales representatives were only allowed short periods to assist customers after the initial sale. Commission and compensation plans were designed to encourage them to spend as little time as possible with customers. Sales force training revolved around the concept of getting customers to sign on the dotted line.

The company always had distributed products through a mix of direct sales and third-party resellers based on the belief that the mix of distribution channels addressed the differing sales and support needs of a broad customer base. However, it shifted the mix more toward third-party resellers, presenting it with the problem of training and managing this distribution channel. The shift meant a loss of direct contact with its customers. Although Parametric had pride in its product development abilities, it bungled the 2000 rollout of the new version of PRO/Engineer called Wildfire. Wildfire had programming errors that caused it to crash frequently. The rollout was fraught with errors, bringing on a backlash from customers who refused to upgrade to the new version. As the company lost touch with customers, its sales and net income slipped. (See Figure 10.9.)

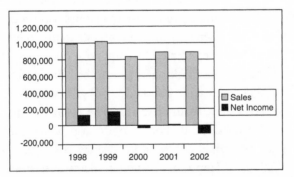

Figure 10.9 Parametric's sales and net income: 1998 to 2002.

Don't Lag in Responding to Competitors' Innovations

Campbell lost track of what its customers wanted. Progresso delivered a product that consumers perceived to be differentiated in a category that had become homogeneous. It spent money in improving its soups' taste and texture with new technology, but Campbell backed off because of retooling costs estimated at $100 million. Campbell blamed its inactivity on capital infrastructure that would be expensive to replace or modify.

Campbell's ready-to-serve brands did not differ much from its condensed soups. They had nondescript vegetables and tasted bland. To ensure the death of lethal microorganisms, they endured high heat treatments, which made the vegetables soft and caused deterioration in the flavor. In condensed soups, Campbell's main change was the addition of more meat to chicken noodle soup. Ready-to-serve soups were offered in low-sodium and low-fat varieties, but similar changes were not made in condensed soups.

The company never strayed from its "M'm, M'm, Good" wholesome image advertising campaign. By the year 2001, the highest priority was getting the core condensed soup business back on solid footing. Under the "Transformation Plan," there was a heavy emphasis on updated marketing efforts and increased spending on infrastructure to improve product quality. There was a concerted attempt to reduce inefficiencies and costs in production. The cooking time of the soup was cut back to improve taste. Vegetables were handled more gently and cooked less to preserve their flavor and retain crispness. The company spent more on advertising. It also introduced "Pop 'n' pour" tops and resealable plastic bottles. The company had a new store display concept. It launched a product called Soup at Hand that could be microwaved in the container, required no spoon, and could be consumed on the go.

These initiatives were late in coming. Sales of condensed soups continued to stagnate, falling from $1.55 billion in 1998 to $1.33 billion in 2002—a drop of 14 percent. Progresso continued to increase its U.S. market share, which grew from 9.2 percent to 13.5 percent.

Don't Lose Touch with Core Customers

The Gap began to lose touch with what mainstream shoppers wanted. Its "cooler than cool" commercials deviated from the company's prior image—casual comfort and confidence. The company used educated guesses to discern what customers were seeking. Its consumer research was weak. Its guesses had been right enough of the time in the past. But now it cranked out trendy merchandise aimed at a younger audience—low-cut jeans, form-fitting tops, and shear blouses linked to the popularity of teenage music. Its 30-something customers were repelled by the purple men's shirts and the fashion aimed exclusively at slender figures. They fled the Gap for more solid retailers. The company's attempt to reposition itself as an edgier and more youthful apparel retailer failed. It alienated the group that had been its main customers—young career workers. The decision to seek growth among teenagers and people in their early 20s was a mistake. These customers had other options. The Gap did not pick up sufficient numbers of this group to make up for other groups it lost.

Prepare for Change in Consumer Tastes

Facing the challenges of a mature industry with tremendous competition, Hasbro misinterpreted market movements. When the U.S. economy started to decline in the late 1990s and fell into a recession in the early part of the twenty-first century, the toys and games industry was threatened because it was delivering want versus need items. For most consumers, toy and games were discretionary purchases. They took on secondary importance when times were hard. However, in the immediate post-9/11 period, people also were spending more time at home. There was an opportunity to sell families more board games to occupy their time. From its years of experience in the industry, Hasbro's management should have understood these trends, but the company did not have a workable or robust plan to deal with them. There were not enough new products in its pipeline to take up the slack.

Bigger Is Not Necessarily Better

Big losers' bigness led to rigidity. This fault is illustrated by four traits that big losers exhibited. They were unable to (i) take advantage of blunders by competitors, (ii) move to profitable niches, (iii) anticipate demand, and (iv) escape bureaucracy. Goodyear, Safeco, the Gap, and Hasbro provide examples of big losers' being handicapped by bigness.

Take Advantage of Blunders by Competitors

Goodyear's expansion efforts made the company larger but also less profitable. Its sales grew by an average of 4 percent per year between 1999 and 2002, but it posted only one-quarter of its net profit during this time. Goodyear's size was a disadvantage. It was not able to capitalize when one of its main competitors, Firestone, took a blow to its reputation. In 2000, Firestone's tires were linked to several fatal rollover accidents, and the company had to undertake a massive recall of 6.5 million tires. Demand for tires other than Firestone soared, but because of inventory issues, Goodyear was unable to meet the demand. Goodyear decided to raise prices (by 7 percent in January 2001) to match Michelin instead of making increased supply available to its distributors. But it could not support these prices with a perception of quality or safety. Customers, looking for the best deal, were not willing to pay the markup. When the increase in demand subsided, Goodyear's market share dropped from 31 percent to 28 percent. By the summer of 2002, it had to reduce prices.

Move to Profitable Niches

As of 2001, Safeco had about 12,000 employees. Safeco also had more than 17,000 partners, including independent insurance agents, brokers, investment advisors, and wholesalers. Its revenue was around $7 billion, while Brown & Brown was a billion. Nonetheless, Safeco sales of property and casualty insurance gave it no significant advantage over its smaller competitor. It battled over price to no avail, while competitors thrived in niche markets.

Anticipate Demand

The Gap was too large for its own good. As it opened new stores each year, it started to see declining sales. The anticipated demand did not materialize to support the increased retail space. The stores were too close to each other. Because of poor placement, cannibalization occurred between Old Navy and Gap. The company's expansion efforts led to slower inventory turns. When inventory started to pile up, the Gap had to heavily discount merchandise. When it then tried to raise prices, customers did not stay loyal. Customers expected discounts, and because they had other low-cost alternatives, they abandoned the Gap.

Avoid Bureaucracy

Hasbro's size was an obstacle to finding the next big hit. The company was bureaucratic and inflexible. Its feuding internal divisions made it hard for the company to act promptly and decisively. It was not succeeding in the creative part of the business. It failed in its efforts to develop new products internally. It concentrated instead on redesigning and recycling old hits, thus exploiting its existing brands for additional gain rather than using them as a stepping stone for new departures. Bureaucracy stifled Hasbro's creativity.

In Summary

This chapter has shown the failed moves of the big losers. They tended to rely exclusively on the expansion of their core products for growth. These products were hard-to-differentiate commodity products sold on the basis of price. Big losers accumulated additional product capacity at high prices even though there was insufficient demand for their product. They did not respond vigorously when they experienced a decline in their core business. Their size took away from their flexibility. Because they were rigid, they inhabited sour spots. The next chapter shows how ineptness ensconced them in these sour spots.

11

INEPTNESS

Ineptness kept the big losers even more deeply ensconced in their sour spots. (See Table 11.1.) They did not have the skills to create best-value positions for their customers. They did not have the skills to defend the positions they occupied. Without these skills, they were not able to protect the positions they occupied. They were vunerable to displacement by more capable competitors.

Because of their ineptness, the big losers did not escape sour spots they occupied. They lacked the underlying discipline to provide best-in-class service and customizable offerings at low cost. They did not gain mastery over the supply chain. They were not able to effectively manage acquisitions nor did they keep their employees well motivated. They also did not avoid accounting and other scandals.

Table 11.1 Ineptness

Company	Ineptness
LSI Logic	Does not develop long-term customer ties
	Has snags in managing mergers and acquisitions
Snap-On	Fails to deal effectively with productivity challenges
	Experiences disarray in implementing new systems
Parametric	Provides less service and support when losses mount
	Has an accounting scandal
IMC	Allows cost savings to erode levels of service
	Withholds product from the market
	Does not effectively deal with environmental challenges
Goodyear	Turnaround efforts do not improve service, lower costs, and define unique niches
	Alienates distributors and dealers
	Does not achieve synergies
	Has troubled relations with unions
	Fails to comply with government regulations
Safeco	Underprices products
	Overpays for acquisitions
	Fails to sufficiently motivate the sales force and hold it accountable
	Does not effectively manage government oversight
Campbell	Cost-cutting leads to a neglect of R&D and innovation
	Fails to cope with powerful retailers
	Lags in responding to competitors' innovations
The Gap	Loses touch with changes in fashion
	Loses touch with core customers
Hasbro	Repeated restructuring does not work
	Fails to accommodate major retailers
	Resorts to price fixing

Figure 11.1 summarizes the lessons learned from the big losers' ineptness. For each lesson in the figure, I provide examples of the traits (Table 11.1) they showed.

> 1. Develop capabilities to provide best-in-class service and customizable offerings at low cost.
> 2. Gain mastery over the supply chain.
> 3. Be effective in managing your acquisitions.
> 4. Make sure your employees are motivated so that your moves will be well-executed.
> 5. Maintain high ethical standards and develop capabilities to manage regulation.

Figure 11.1 Lessons about ineptness.

Develop Capabilities to Provide Best-in-Class Service and Customizable Offerings at Low Cost

Big losers did not develop capabilities to provide best-in-class service and customizable offerings at low cost. This fault is illustrated by seven traits. Big losers (i) did not deal effectively with productivity challenges, (ii) cut back on services and support when their losses mounted, (iii) allowed cost savings to erode service levels, (iv) failed in their turnaround efforts, (v) underpriced products, (vii) neglected R&D and innovation, and (viii) repeatedly failed in restructuring efforts. Snap-On, Parametric, IMC, Goodyear, Safeco, Campbell, and Hasbro provide examples of the big losers' failure to develop these capabilities.

Deal Effectively with Productivity Challenges

Snap-On did not effectively deal with productivity challenges it confronted. Its management recognized inefficiencies in processes and infrastructure. The company's cost structure was excessive. As demand declined, the company had to make changes. In 1998, Snap-On announced a restructuring program dubbed Project Simplify. The goal was to make its business operations simpler and more effective through internal rationalization and consolidation, flattening of the organizational structure, and the sharing of services among departments. Snap-On discontinued product lines, closed 13 facilities (both manufacturing plants and warehouses), and eliminated nearly 1,100 positions. Its efforts to improve productivity absorbed more than $300 million in restructuring charges after 1998 but made no serious dent in the productivity problems that the company faced. In 2001, Snap-On introduced another program of internal rationalization and consolidation to replace Project Simplify. The new program was called Driven to Deliver. (See Figure 11.2.) The goals were to achieve $40 million in yearly pretax savings and to institutionalize continuous improvement into the fabric of the corporate culture. Driven to Deliver had the goal of saving tens of millions of dollars by cutting plants, distribution centers, nonprofitable businesses, and labor. The restructuring initiatives that Snap-On undertook were expensive and they removed capital from new product initiatives, but they did not yield the outcomes that Snap-On wanted.

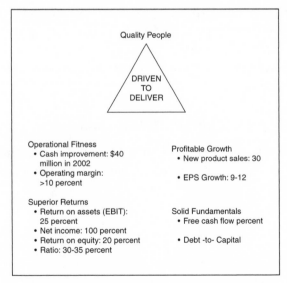

Figure 11.2 Snap-On's Driven to Deliver model.

Do Not Provide Less Service and Support When Losses Mount

Parametric had net losses of $10.1 million and $93.6 million in 2001 and 2002, respectively. Threatened by competitors who offered lower-cost products, it was not in a position to take well-thought-out, calculated risks. Restructuring charges and write-downs of investments were $52.9 million and $32.2 million. To address declining revenues, the company took several measures to slash costs in a short period of time. It reduced the sales staff while keeping its core engineers and software developers. It cut sales and marketing expenditures by 17 percent and R&D expenditures by 9 percent from 2001 to 2002. Employees in sales and marketing were reduced by 13 percent. The company relied more on indirect marketing channels, which had lower overhead expenses than the direct sales force. Relying more on this channel meant distancing itself from customers. Parametric was less able to provide critical program integration support and services that customers wanted.

Do Not Allow Cost Savings to Erode Levels of Service

As a way of reducing organizational debt, IMC was forced to push costs as low as possible while still maintaining high quality. Trying to push costs down was a logical response given the challenges the company faced. In a marketplace where price was the major factor in a purchaser's buying decision, being a low-cost producer was necessary for survival.

Given the prolonged depressed state of the markets IMC served, the company's efforts to keep costs down were far reaching. It took many steps to slash costs, including reducing overhead, rightsizing, reorganizing, process redesign, and leveraging its distribution and transportation network. To keep costs low, the company started a program called Project Profit in 1998, Rightsizing in 1999, and Six Sigma in 2001.

Project Profit consisted mainly of restructuring in the phosphate business. Within a year, the savings were $65 million through the consolidation of various mines and plants. Rightsizing was done to simplify core businesses by reducing the asset base, consolidating, lowering fixed and overhead costs, and cutting corporate expenses. Six Sigma was initiated to achieve quality and process improvements. The program included more than 40 projects and generated annualized savings of about $8 million. Altogether, the company programs reduced expenses by more than $160 million.

Though IMC emphasized reduced expenses, it also had to consider service quality. One way it improved on this dimension was by upgrading its Web site. Customers could track orders, obtain sales and marketing contact information, and learn more about the company's products and services online. A second improvement was operating personnel visits to major customers. The visits were supposed to yield additional sales. IMC also held periodic educational seminars where customers could learn how to realize the "full potential" of using its products. The firm also was active as a strategic investor in Rooster.com, agriculture's leading e-business network.

But the company's highest priority was to reduce costs, not improve service. According to management, fertilizer companies had to compete on price first. Branding, patents, and other intangibles played a far smaller role. Yet some of IMC's competitors had innovated in these areas. They successfully marketed value-added services. Some offered custom-made products that had additional, slow-releasing micronutrients that were better suited to particular soils. Others provided consulting services to farmers who needed assistance in fertilizer application. IMC's stress on cost meant that its products were not as differentiated as those of its competitors.

Turnarounds Need to Improve Service, Lower Costs, and Define Unique Niches

Goodyear's repeated turnaround attempts got nowhere. Its attempt to turn the company around in 2002 was simply a replay of what it had tried and failed to accomplish in the past: simplifying sales and the supply chain, achieving cost-cutting, clarifying the brand's image, strengthening distribution channels, growing the business through product introductions and sales, and stabilizing margins and market share. The company had a revolving door of business line presidents and a new CEO in 2002, Robert Keegan, who came from Kodak. Goodyear continuously failed to define the niches in which it operated. To what extent was it upscale and to what extent mass market? Did it make tires mainly for original equipment manufacturers or for individual consumers?

Do Not Underprice Products

By choosing to position its products as generic and low-priced, Safeco opened itself up to competition from numerous other low-cost providers. This approach prevented it from generating a perception of value with its customers, thereby weakening its bargaining power with them. Safeco was a large, high-volume producer and broker of generic policies targeted at automobile owners, homeowners, and small business owners. In an attempt to compensate for relatively modest growth, property and casualty firms like Safeco aggressively competed on cost to capture additional market share. As Safeco sought to lower its prices to compete in the low-cost, generic insurance policy business, its operating margins fell, and it was unable to cover the payouts from claims on the policies it was underwriting. The company attempted but failed to enter the specialty services market with its Select Markets division. It was unable to effectively provide professional liability, medical malpractice, and surplus property products. These businesses did not fit well with Safeco's other products and core competencies.

Do Not Allow Cost-Cutting to Result in a Neglect of R&D and Innovation

Campbell was constantly under the gun to become more efficient. In the 1980s, under CEO Gordon McGovern, it had been organized into 50 autonomous business units to foster creativity. David Johnson, who became CEO in 1990, reversed this policy. To improve productivity, he restructured the company into three separate units, cut down on nonstrategic businesses, and consolidated plants to reduce costs. His aim was to increase earnings by 20 percent through cost cutting and lower prices.

The first target was to consolidate high-cost and underutilized plants and to place them in more cost-effective locations. The company shut down six manufacturing plants and started construction on a new $150 million world-class manufacturing facility. It also began to prune low-return, nonstrategic business units that detracted from its earnings. Throughout the 1990s, under Johnson and Dale Morrison, who became CEO in 1997, Campbell emphasized efficiency and productivity over R&D and innovation. It went through regular episodes of restructuring and reconfiguring. It increased operating margins by 11 percent as a result of cost cutting and selected price increases. The board approved programs to re-make the company six times from 1992 through 2002, including every year from 1996 to 1999. Campbell continued to reconfigure and close production plants. It had facilities in 18 U.S. states and 15 foreign countries. Campbell reduced administrative and other staff and divested underperforming and nonstrategic business.

The costs for these programs averaged $215 million per year. The number of Campbell employees went from 46,920 in 1993 to 24,250 in 1998 following the spin-off of Vlasic and Swanson and overseas units and leveled off at about 25,000 in 2002.

The culture was risk-averse and dominated by financial controls. R&D as a percentage of operating expenses was cut to about 3 percent per year, as below competitors Kraft and General Mills, which typically spent more than 5 percent on R&D over operating expenses per year. The low R&D spending meant fewer new product introductions. The company also did not quickly adopt scanners and other computer technologies in distribution and inventory. Other than minor product improvements, packaging changes, and slight adjustments in distribution and inventory, the company did not innovate much during the 1990s.

Make Sure That Repeated Restructuring Works

In 1997, Hasbro started a Global Integration and Profit Enhancement Program to reduce costs. It closed five manufacturing facilities in order to consolidate operations and it laid off 2,500 people. The company wrote off the costs of the program at $140 million, estimating that it would save $50 million per year. In 1999, it once again restructured in the hope of reducing costs. It closed two more manufacturing plants and laid off an additional 850 people to further consolidate its U.S. manufacturing. In Europe, it streamlined marketing and sales. The company traditionally had created separate marketing campaigns for different regions in Europe. It determined that it would be more cost efficient to consolidate such efforts. The restructuring again cost Hasbro $14 million, and it hoped for savings of $50 million per year. It repeatedly restructured in an attempt to turn itself around. However, these efforts did not prevent a 12-percent drop in revenues in 2000 and a $144.6 million net loss.

Gain Mastery Over the Supply Chain

Big losers did not gain mastery over the supply chain. This fault is illustrated by six traits. Big losers (i) did not develop long-term customer ties and increased power over suppliers, (ii) maintained prices by keeping product from the market, (iii) alienated distributors and dealers, (iv) did not cope well with powerful retailers, (v) lost touch with changes in fashion, and (vii) could not accommodate retailers' demands. LSI Logic, IMC, Goodyear, Campbell, the Gap, and Hasbro illustrate these problems.

Develop Long-Term Customer Ties and Increase Your Power Over Your Suppliers

LSI Logic did not have monitoring devices in place to correctly appraise fluctuations in supply and demand and the possibility of price erosion. Its relationships with its customers were such that they provided little help in achieving forecasting accuracy, resulting in idle, excess assets and capacity in addition to customer service issues.

The company also had few guarantees about its future markets because it did not have long-term contracts with customers. As a result, demand for its products was irregular. LSI Logic filled customer's overflow-manufacturing orders and had to carry large inventories. It produced on demand and was in no position to effectively monitor, anticipate, plan for, and accommodate marketplace changes.

LSI Logic also did not have much power over suppliers. The company purchased raw materials, such as advanced plastic or ceramic packaging for integrated circuits, from a limited number of suppliers. The constant challenge was to secure low-cost raw materials in a timely fashion from the same group of suppliers used by the entire industry.[1]

In the semiconductor market, to get products to the market quickly before they became obsolete was essential. The industry required high levels of R&D expenditures. R&D represented 30 percent of LSI Logic's sales in 2001, but the R&D was not paying off. LSI Logic was falling behind in design capabilities, performance, time-to-market, price, and product features. It was not doing a good job of improving current products and finding new ones to meet its customers emerging needs.

In the late 1980s, the company expected a boom in defense expenditures that never materialized. Therefore, it made heavy investments in factories that it was not able to use. It repeated the same mistake in the late 1990s. It expected the boom in consumer electronics to continue and again overinvested in production.

To meet what it thought would be endless demand, LSI Logic vertically integrated production that previously had been outsourced. It centralized production capabilities in the United States, making significant investments in its own wholly owned advanced manufacturing facility in Oregon even though it operated internationally.[2] When worldwide demand for new, faster microprocessors declined after 2000, the high fixed costs associated with the U.S. plants and equipment resulted in overcapacity and substantial net losses.

The company's revenues declined by almost $1 billion between 2000 and 2001 while expenses increased by almost $350 million, for a net loss of almost $1 billion in 2001. The Oregon facility never operated above 60 percent capacity. When the tech bubble burst, LSI Logic's revenues dropped, and it had to cut product lines and eliminate more than 1,400 positions.

Do Not Withhold Product

IMC tried to increase prices by tightening supply. As North America's largest supplier of phosphate, it attempted to use its market power to affect prices. It tried to limit phosphate supplies through both permanent and temporary shutdowns at facilities. In 1999, it permanently closed two phosphate mines. In February 2003, it temporarily idled one of its Louisiana and one of its Florida mines. Its supply restriction policies, however, did not met with much success. They did not give the company greater control of the supply chain.

Do Not Alienate Distributors and Dealers

Goodyear started a program in inventory control in 1998. It initiated the program because of the extremely competitive nature of its industry. It had to keep costs in line. Labor and raw materials were largely out of the company's control, so managing inventory was one of few means available for cost reduction. Goodyear segmented its businesses. Each was responsible for profits and losses, inventory control, and cost reduction. The business units restricted dealers from gaining access to special deals when inventory was not at peak levels. Goodyear's large network of 1,000 owned stores and 2,500 independent dealers had less flexibility with respect to order terms and timing.

Goodyear's decision to sell its tires through Montgomery Ward, Just Tires, and Penske stores and discount chains like Sam's Club and Wal-Mart alienated the dealers. Dealers could not compete with these large chains and responded by severing their exclusive ties with Goodyear. During the Firestone recall, the dealers could not obtain product they needed from Goodyear, so they stepped up the selling of other brands.

Another opportunity that Goodyear failed to exploit was customer response to a positive review of the Dunlop brand in *Consumer Reports*. Demand for Dunlop tires grew, but Goodyear failed to supply the dealers with tires quickly enough to meet the demand, further straining its dealer relationships.

Cope with Powerful Retailers

Because of its immense buying power, Wal-Mart had a major influence on Campbell's success. Wal-Mart's share of retail food was 15 percent and growing. It accounted for more than 12 percent of Campbell's sales. It was the company's largest customer, and it had specific expectations about what its suppliers would do to lower costs and share in the distribution burden. Along with other warehouse superstores such as Costco, Wal-Mart was changing the way food companies like Campbell did business. Other retail food outlets through whom Campbell sold, such as Kroger and Safeway, reacted to the challenge posed by Wal-Mart by going through many consolidations, which also changed the way they dealt with suppliers. By 2002, the top-five U.S. retailers accounted for 40 percent of grocery sales.

Consolidation was global. Belgian-based Delhaize Group became the fifth-largest supermarket company in the United States, and Dutch-based Royal Ahold the sixth-largest supermarket company. In their constantly shifting relationship with suppliers, the retailers were gaining the upper hand, and Campbell had trouble coping with the situation.

Do Not Lose Touch with Fashion

The Gap's dependence on changing fashion was risky, because each season's product line again had to prove its sales-worthiness. Gap's performance depended on successfully gauging fashion and seasonal trends. Thirty-two percent of sales took place in the back-to-school season. If the company misjudged where trends were headed, it meant lost revenues, markdowns, and reduced profits. Predicting customers' preferences was difficult. The company had to figure out what would sell nearly nine months before that merchandise was available for sale. It had to purchase the inventory in advance of the peak selling seasons, order the merchandise, and have it delivered just at the start of the season. If the style the designers chose was not a hit, the company had to sell inventory at reduced pries.

In 2001, the Gap had a significant problem when its styles did not match what consumers wanted to buy. When the company changed its merchandising strategy from casual fashion basics to trendy apparel targeted to young customers, the merchandise did not fit the needs of customers, who were interested in classic Gap clothing like khakis, jeans, and plain shirts. Customers wanted fewer and simpler styles; they wanted the Gap to return to its roots—style, taste, and quality at a moderate price. But Gap's stores were filled with product offerings that were too fashion-forward for its customers. In 2002, the company missed consumer trends in men's apparel during the third and fourth quarters, resulting in a 7.1-percent decline in sales and a 146.5 percent decline in earnings compared to the previous year.

Understand How to Accommodate Major Retailers

As the retail industry consolidated, Hasbro became dependent on fewer distribution channels. The company's top five retail channels accounted for 41, 48, and 52 percent of its net revenues in 2000, 2001, and 2002 respectively. Its main customers, Wal-Mart and Toys "R" Us, represented 30 to 35 percent of its net sales in this time period. The rapid consolidation meant that the retailers had more clout over prices. They made additional demands. The improved quick-response inventory management system that Toys "R" Us installed in 1998 resulted in lost revenue for Hasbro.

Other retailers put similar pressures on the company. They expected their suppliers to be precise in the timing of deliveries. They wanted more products from suppliers during the holiday season and less during the rest of the year. Companies like Hasbro either had to manufacture at a rapid pace immediately prior to the holiday season or suffer stiff inventory holding costs the rest the year. It was difficult for Hasbro to accommodate these demands. It did not want to risk holding excess inventory, but it also did not want to ramp up production in uneven spurts without knowing what the outcome would be.

Hasbro ran the risk of rapid changes in consumer tastes, which were costly if it was left with excess inventory that buyers no longer wanted. To rectify this problem, Hasbro took steps to redesign its distribution systems, and it started to cut back on the number of its manufacturing plants, but these efforts did not fully work.

Be Proactive in Managing Your Acquisitions

Big losers were not proactive in managing their acquisitions. This fault is illustrated by three traits they exhibited. Big losers had (i) snags in purchasing new companies, (ii) problems in achieving synergies, and (iii) paid too much for firms they acquired. LSI Logic, Goodyear, and Safeco provide examples of the big losers' problems in managing their acquisitions.

Avoid Snags in Managing Mergers and Acquisitions

LSI Logic's purchase of Para Voice, Data Path, Intraserve, and divisions of NeoMagic and Cacheware resulted in devaluing intangibles associated with R&D soon after the acquisitions were completed. The 2001 acquisitions of C-Cube and RAID, a division of AMI, enhanced its presence in the cable modem, cable set-top box, and DVD and expanded its reach in China, but these acquisitions again led to the devaluation of R&D-related intangibles. The time needed to integrate the businesses coupled with other merger snags and problems diluted the advantages that the acquisitions were supposed to achieve.

Achieve Synergies

Goodyear bought companies throughout the world in the hope of creating global manufacturing and distribution synergies, but the company did not effectively integrate the new companies. The synergies it hoped for failed to materialize, and there were significant costs associated with managing the new companies. Goodyear accumulated debt and was slow to divest underperforming units. It tried to divest noncore operations and rationalize operations, but its efforts often did not succeed. In 1998, for instance, it closed an older Alabama plant and tried to consolidate its operations in the company's more efficient facilities. However, Goodyear subsequently had to reopen this plant to attempt to meet demand associated with the Firestone recall. Both the closing and reopening of the plant came with significant costs.

Do Not Overpay

Safeco's acquisition of AS proved costly due in part to the high price. The firm had revenues of $4.8 billion when it paid $2.8 billion for AS in 1997. In that year, it also acquired WM Life Insurance Company, a unit of the Washington Mutual Bank of Seattle, and formed a strategic alliance with this bank to distribute annuities via its multistate network. Around that same time, Safeco purchased the naming rights to the Seattle Mariner's ballpark. It also acquired London-based R.F. Bailey to establish a firm international presence.

Safeco overpaid for AS, and the two corporate cultures did not blend well. Merging the two companies was costly, and the integration proved difficult. Safeco did not want to risk losing any AS clients. Therefore, the company made the decision to lower underwriting guidelines and reduce the premiums charged. Safeco took on additional risk when it lowered underwriting guidelines. It began to sustain large underwriting losses, and the company operated at a loss. (See Table 11.2.) The three largest components of property and casualty, which represented the largest division of the company, were personal auto, homeowners, and business insurance. All three units suffered large underwriting losses that outweighed what their premiums generated.

Table 11.2 Safeco Operating Results (Dollar Amounts in Millions, Except Per-Share Numbers)

	2001	2000	1999	1998	1997
Gross premiums	$4,472.80	$4,709.10	$4,645.00	$4,441.80	$2,9837.40
Underwriting loss	($837.50)	($521.90)	($366.70)	($109.40)	$36.20
Per-share income	($7.75)	$0.90	$1.90	$2.51	$3.31

Make Sure Your Employees Are Motivated

Big losers were not good at motivating their employees. This fault is illustrated by three traits they exhibited. Big losers (i) experienced disarray when they implemented new systems, (ii) did not have good relations with unions, and (iii) were unable to motivate sales and make it accountable. Snap-On, Goodyear, and Safeco provide examples of this problem.

Shun Disarray in Implementing New Systems

In the same year that Project Simplify began, Snap-On decided that it needed a new enterprise-level computer system to efficiently coordinate activities. It started to install the new computer system, but the company lost $50 million in sales in the first half of 1998, primarily due to snafus related to the installation. The failure had negative effects on employee productivity and service levels. Computer World rated it the second worst IT fiasco of the 1990s.

The effort to integrate various business units via the new computer system and implement shared services went poorly, causing lower sales and productivity, higher labor and freight costs, and business process problems. The new system did not work properly, which slowed deliveries and disrupted the supply chain, causing disarray in purchasing and inventory and resulting in a decline in operating income.

The installation of the new computer system was not an isolated event. Another example of the problems that Snap-On had in executing was its efforts in e-commerce. Snap-On's strategy was to bring the store to its customers. Its independent dealers sold products via vans that they drove to work sites (such as automotive body shops, marinas, and airports, where professional service technicians worked). Because almost all career mechanics owned their own tools, this model put the company's tools within arms' reach of primary customers. Unfortunately, many of the mechanics who bought the tools were unable to keep up with the payments. As an answer to this dilemma, Snap-on started an e-commerce initiative. The mechanics would buy their tools over the Internet. They would not have to sacrifice convenience, and Snap-On would be more certain of payment. In January 2000, it announced an e-commerce alliance with Genuine Parts (GP), which allowed it to connect its online repair products with GP's online part ordering infrastructure. This alliance was supposed to eventually result in a full-blown "store without walls," but Snap-On delayed opening its online store due to concerns about channel conflict. Dealer resistance meant it was unable to make the full transition to e-commerce. The dealers were not motivated to work with the new system.

Foster Good Relationships with Unions

Goodyear had a history of adversarial relations with its unions. It had a difficult time scaling back wages to get them in line with declining production. In 2002, Goodyear accepted a labor pact that called for reducing labor costs by $1.15 billion over three years and eliminating 3,000 jobs, but in exchange, Goodyear had to retain and invest in all but two of its U.S. factories and limit imports from abroad. Its union thus gained power to keep the company from outsourcing. Adding to the labor problems was an aging workforce that imposed a huge pension fund liability on the company. As Goodyear stock plummeted, the pension fund became severely underfunded, and at the end of 2002, Goodyear owed the pension fund more than $2 billion.

Motivate the Sales Force and Hold It Accountable

Safeco had internal weaknesses related to difficulties in retaining and attracting good employees while weeding out poor performers. It was still perceived as a company that took care of its employees until retirement instead of an incentive-based company that was capable of recruiting top performers. Without incentive-based compensation at Safeco, the sales force was unmotivated and had been slow to move product and provide good customer service. The company had been complacent about its sales staff, thinking they could sell its products even without the incentives because the products were priced so low. In 2001, Safeco let go of 1,000 underperforming agents, and it was looking to cut up to 1,200 more positions. Safeco was trying to reenergize its the sales force to reignite sales, launch a "zero-defect" service mentality whenever sales touched customers, and lock in progress with better measures to hold people accountable.

Maintain High Ethical Standards and Develop Capabilities to Manage Regulation

Big losers were not good at maintaining high ethical standards and developing capabilities to manage government regulation. This fault is illustrated by five traits the big losers exhibited. They (i) were unable to avoid accounting scandals, (ii) did not effectively deal with environmental challenges, (iii) failed in the area of regulatory compliance, (iv) did not effectively manage regulations, and (v) had occasion to resort to price fixing. Parametric, IMC, Goodyear, Safeco, and Hasbro provide examples of these lapses.

Avoid Accounting Scandals

Parametric's financial statements for 2001, 2000, and 1999 were restated because it miscalculated deferred maintenance revenues from 1999 through 2002 due to implementation of a new accounting system. The restatement resulted in service revenue reductions of $12.0 million, $2.8 million, $14.5 million, and $4.1 million for fiscal years 2002, 2001, 2000, and 1999, respectively.

Multiple class action suits were filed against the company. They charged that Parametric issued a series of materially false and misleading statements to the public between October 19, 1999 and December 31, 2002. The lawsuits claimed that Parametric violated generally accepted accounting principles and misinformed investors about its true financial situation. Parametric countered with a request to dismiss the lawsuits on the basis that they were without merit. The U.S. District Court for the District of Massachusetts subsequently denied the request. Parametric claimed that it would continue to vigorously contest the lawsuits. In addition, a delay in filing the 2003 annual report on Form 10-K prompted the NASDAQ to issue a letter to Parametric notifying it that it was not in compliance with filing requirements for continued listing with NASDAQ. Parametric responded to the potential delisting by complying with NASDAQ's requirements and releasing a revised 2002 annual statement, a move that avoided the delisting.

Deal Effectively with Environmental Challenges

IMC had a severe accident at the start of the 1990s and thus was subject to close regulatory surveillance. Its mining operations were subject to many federal, state, provincial, and local environmental, health, and safety laws. The laws related to air and water quality, management of hazardous and solid wastes, management and handling of raw materials, and land reclamation. Specific agencies that had oversight over IMC's operations included the U.S. Environmental Protection Agency and the Saskatchewan Department of Environmental and Resource Management. Laws to which it was subject were the 1990 Amendments to the Clean Air Act, Process Safety Management (PSM) standards under the Occupational Safety and Health Act (OSHA), and the Comprehensive Environmental Response Compensation Liability Act (CERCLA), which was otherwise known as Superfund.

Comply with Regulations

Several discrepancies came to light in Goodyear's accounting practices. The company was involved in a potential scandal that threatened to damage its image. Goodyear also was subject to heavy safety and environmental regulation. The National Highway Traffic Safety Administration (NHTSA) had standards for tires sold in the United States for highway use. It had the authority to order the recall of products. Its regulatory authority was expanded in 2000 as a result of the enactment of the TREAD (Transportation Recall Enhancement, Accountability, and Documentation) Act. This act imposed numerous new requirements with respect to tire recalls, including the requirement that tire manufacturers remedy tire safety defects without charge for five years. Compliance with its regulations increased the cost of producing and distributing tires. The tire industry also had to focus on tire reuse, recycling, and safe disposal. Tires that were not disposed of properly could pose an environmental hazard (fire, stagnant water, and so on). The United States and Europe had fairly strict controls regarding tire disposal.

Manage Government Oversight

As an underwriter, Safeco was subject to substantial governmental oversight. The company operated in a highly controlled regulatory environment that included rules pertaining to solvency, licensing of agents, limitations on investments, barriers to entering new markets, and requirements on cash reserves. Like other companies in the insurance industry, Safeco was highly dependent on the government's actions.

Don't Resort to Price Fixing

The British government fined Hasbro millions of dollars for price fixing, which resulted in a lot of bad press. In the political/legal arena, Hasbro had bad publicity.

In Summary

This chapter has shown the ineptness of the big losers. They did not develop capabilities to defend the positions they occupied. They lacked skills to provide customers best-in-class service and customizable offerings at low cost. Also, these losing companies did not gain mastery over the supply chain and were ineffective in managing their acquisitions. They neither motivated their employees to ensure that their moves were well-executed, nor did they adhere to high ethical standards and have the capabilities to manage regulation. They were in sour spots not only because of rigidity and ineptness, but also because of a lack of focus, as the next chapter will show.

12

DIFFUSENESS

Big losers were too diffuse to deepen, enlarge, or extend the positions they occupied. (See Table 12.1.) They did not establish clear connections among disparate business units, stick to long-term merger or acquisition plans, and create common goals among diverse divisions. They emphasized research and development (R&D), which was of little use to their customers or to the promising growth markets to which their customers were devoted. Their globalization was meant to overcome domestic inadequacies, but it only bred additional problems with which they did not cope well. Figure 12.1 summarizes lessons learned from big losers with regard to their diffuseness. For each lesson in Figure 12.1, I provide examples of the traits (Table 12.1) the big losers exhibited.

Table 12.1 Diffuseness

Company	Diffuseness
LSI Logic	Is unable to maintain connections among its businesses
	Emphasizes product R&D and is distant from markets
Snap-On	Does not effectively integrate global acquisitions
Parametric	Relies on intermediaries for direct customer contact
	Is unable to maintain service levels when selling globally
IMC	Is unable to create synergy among its businesses
	Does not stay on top of policy changes in key export markets
Goodyear	Has too many unrelated holdings
	Is unable to sufficiently expand international presence
Safeco	Is involved in too many ends of the value chain
	Is unable to identify and pursue promising markets
Campbell	Does not have a long-term plan for acquisitions and divestitures
	Is unable to support rapidly growing product lines
	Global expansion does not compensate for its domestic weakness
The Gap	Expands the scope of its operations rather than simplifies
	Deals with the complications of managing many different brands
Hasbro	Does not make sure its divisions have common goals
	Is insufficiently aggressive in pursuit of global opportunities

1. Maintain a clear strategic direction—do not spread yourself too thin.
2. Focus on markets that have future promise.
3. Do not rely on a global focus to fix domestic problems.

Figure 12.1 Lessons about diffuseness.

Maintain a Clear Strategic Direction—Do Not Spread Yourself Too Thin

Big losers did not maintain a clear direction—they spread themselves too thin. This fault is illustrated by seven traits big losers exhibited. They did not (i) maintain linkages among their main businesses, (ii) create synergy, (iii) establish relationships among their holdings, (iv) have long-term merger and acquisition plans, (v) stay concentrated on specific parts of the value chain, (vi) simplify their operations, and (vii) impose common goals on their divisions. LSI Logic, IMC, Goodyear, Campbell, Safeco, the Gap, and Hasbro provide examples of these faults.

Maintain Connections Among Your Main Businesses

Over the years, LSI Logic's core businesses became increasingly broad-based and stretched thin. The company was less focused on its strengths. In 2002, LSI Logic had two separate businesses that were not well related to each other—high-end chips (80 percent of sales in 2002) and low-end storage (20 percent of sales in 2002). It was difficult for the company to manage advanced and complex products in the former business while it was involved in the commodity-like storage business.

Create Synergy

IMC's management lost focus as it began to drill for oil and gas and operated salt and soda ash businesses that provided minimal synergies with its core crop nutrients business. The company was involved in an assortment of nonprofitable efforts outside of its core businesses, contributing to a lack of focus. IMC in the early- to mid-1990s tried to enter related markets. During this time, it was attempting to become a "full-line provider" to global agricultural markets. It moved into salt, soda ash, other farming-related chemicals, and oil and gas markets to achieve this end. The cost to move into these markets, however, was not cheap. For example, to finance the acquisition of Harris Chemical Group, Inc. and its affiliate Penrice Soda Products Pty. Ltd. in 1997,

IMC spent $450 million in cash and assumed approximately $950 million of debt. Unfortunately, as the company assumed this debt, fertilizer prices fell sharply, which put IMC in a difficult position.

The company rewrote its strategic plans three times thereafter. In an effort to rebound, it sold assets to reduce debt. It cut capacity and restructured. By 2003, it had sold essentially all noncore assets, but it was not much better off. The depressed state of agricultural markets offset any positive results it had hoped to achieve. Having inconsistent executive management led to varying strategies that resulted in unfocused decisions. The company's strengths were in mining. It made poor growth decisions by acquiring companies outside its core. It did not have transferable capabilities that it could move easily to the new industries it entered.

Have Related Holdings

Goodyear had little continuity in its strategy. Divestitures in the 1980s were followed by acquisitions in the 1990s, which spread the company thin by putting it in many market positions simultaneously. With the purchase of Kelly and Dunlop, Goodyear shifted from the lower to the higher end of the market, but its products were neither the lowest in price nor the highest in quality. They did not stand out.

Bridgestone and Michelin chose particular market segments and stuck to them. Smaller, niche rivals like Cooper concentrated only on the replacement market. Cooper diversified into the related auto parts' business. Pirelli made high-performance tires. Goodyear did not have such a focus. Alternating attempts to position itself as an upscale, higher-priced brand and as a low-cost, mass-market brand confused consumers and dealers. Goodyear was not focused in how it competed with other brands on design, performance, price, reputation, warranty, customer service, and customer convenience.

In addition to tires, Goodyear manufactured and marketed rubber and other products for industrial and consumer markets. It had a line of chemical products that it made and sold. It owned rubber plantations in Malaysia. The company also had retail outlets that provided automotive repair and other services.

Goodyear was in all ends of the business from raw materials (the rubber plantations), to manufacturing, to related product lines, to retail distribution. It produced oil for fuel (divested in 1998). It made chemicals that went into the tires. It produced the isoprene, nylon and polyester, yarn and wire for synthetic rubber. It provided warehousing and distribution. It marketed and sold to OEMs and retail stores and repaired and retreaded the tires, as well as developing and designing them. It had independent retailers and placed product in discount retailers. Its dealers competed with its business partners. The company's noncore businesses, such as chemical products, were in commodity industries, giving it little chance for differentiation. The disarray of these diverse holdings was hard to manage.

Establish a Long-Term Plan for Acquisitions and Divestitures and Stick to It

Campbell struggled with where to focus. It had a long-standing commitment to quality products and "good, wholesome, high-quality food." The company started as a soup firm, but it did not maintain the focus on soups for long.

In 1915, Campbell began to acquire other firms with the purchase of the Franco-American Food Company. Additional acquisitions included V8 Vegetable Juice (1948); C.A. Swanson & Sons (1955), the originator of the TV dinner; Pepperidge Farm (1960); Biscuits Delacre (1960); Goldiva Chocolatier, Inc. (1966); Vlasic Foods, Inc. (1978); and Swift-Armour S.A. Argentina (1980). In 1992, Campbell bought Arnotts, Ltd., the seventh-largest biscuit manufacturer in the world. In 1993, it purchased Fray Bentos, the United Kingdom's leading brand in premier canned meat. In 1995, it bought Pace Foods, the world's leading producer and marketer of Mexican sauces. It also purchased Green Healthy Foods and Fresh Start Bakeries Inc. in that year. In 1996, Campbell's acquisitions included Erasco, a canned fruit and vegetable company in England. In 1998, they included a canned soup firm in Germany, Forton Foods. The company's acquisitions in 2001 included Oxo, Batchelors, Heisse Tasse, Bla Band, and Royco, which were leading instant dry soup and bouillon brands in Europe. In 2002, the company bought Snack Foods Limited, a leader in the Australian salty snack category, and Erin Foods, Ireland's second largest dry soup business.

Campbell had a full array of domestic and international brands. The problem was the haphazard pattern of how it acquired and divested these firms. Its strategy changed about every three years. It did not have the patience to follow through with long-term plans. In 1993, the company recorded restructuring charges of $353 million in closing two frozen food plants and selling of nonstrategic businesses, many of which served niche markets. In 1997, it sold Fresh Start Bakeries, a business it had acquired only two years earlier. In 1998, it carried out another major series of divestitures in a continued portfolio reconfiguration, selling off Continental Sweets, Melbourne Mushrooms, Spring Valley Juice, Specialty Foods (Vlasic), and Swanson.

Avoid Involvement at Too Many Different Ends of the Value Chain

Safeco showed a lack of focus in determining which market and product segments to operate in. It had 18 different business lines, many of which were counterproductive to its core business—property and casualty insurance. It needed to focus its business around what it was really good at. Since its founding, Safeco had been a vertically integrated firm. It physically underwrote its own policies and assumed the risk that went hand in hand with underwriting. Underwriting insurance policies was a risky business, because a large number of different events could trigger claims against the policies.[1] Firms as vertically integrated as Safeco had to have in place an infrastructure to assess, manage, and hedge against potential losses and risk. Premiums had to provide sufficient capital to maintain operations and generate dividends to stockholders, even in difficult capital market conditions. The company had to employ a costly actuarial staff, investment department, and accounting department, all of which was difficult to do simultaneously.

Simplify Instead of Expanding What You Do

Many of the Gap's problems were due to the company's lack of focus. It was involved in all aspects of brand development—from product design and distribution to marketing, merchandising, and creating the right shopping environments. It controlled these activities internally. It designed almost all of its merchandise in-house, but it outsourced the manufacturing through a network of more than 1,000 vendors.

Attracting and retaining key personnel in fashion design and marketing was a challenge. Overcoming international obstacles was a challenge. About 90 percent of its production units were made outside of the United States, with approximately 13 percent coming from China and Hong Kong. Getting the advertising right was another challenge. Merchandise was advertised heavily through a variety of media, including major metropolitan newspapers, major newsweeklies, lifestyle and fashion magazines, mass transit posters, exterior bus panels, bus shelters and billboards, and TV and radio ads.

The company had too much to do in controlling the shopping environment and all aspects of brand management, including product design, distribution, marketing, and merchandising. It's strategy was complex. Its customer base was everyone from low- to high-income families, babies, teens, adults, men, and women, both in the United States and globally. This diverse focus brought complications in advertising, pricing, timing, and inventory management. It exposed the company to risks from other brands, rapid expansion, and design, production, marketing, and selling issues.

Ensure That Your Divisions Have Common Goals

Hasbro's problems also were related to an undefined and unfocused strategy. The company was in many businesses simultaneously—toys, games, and retail in the United States and abroad. Its toys (35 percent of its revenues) ran the gamut from action figures, vehicle playsets, and creative play products to toys for young boys, young girls, preschoolers, and infants. Its brands included both Playskool and Tonka. It made *Star Wars* action figures in addition to Disney. It owned the rights to Mr. Potato Head, GI Joe, My Little Pony, Transformers, Pokémon, Furby,

Hungry Hippo, Twister, Barney, Sit n' Spin, Teletubbies, Cabbage Patch Kids, Play-Doh, Nerf balls, and *Harry Potter*.

Internally, it was never quite clear how Hasbro should manage all these properties. The company's games (34 percent of its revenues) were equally diverse. They included board games, card games, puzzles, hand-held electronic games, children's electronic games, electronic learning aids, trading cards, and role-playing games. It's brands included both Parker Brothers and Milton Bradley. It owned the rights to Monopoly, Scrabble, Dungeons & Dragons, and Trivial Pursuit.

Hasbro also operated approximately 85 retail stores under the Wizards of the Coast and Game Keeper names, which not only sold games directly to the consumer, but also provided locations for tournaments and other organized play activities.

Overall, its different divisions struggled to work together for common goals. A weakness of Hasbro's was the constant internal struggles that came about because of the diversity. In 1996, after a failed takeover attempt by Mattel, an outside consultant was brought in to reorganize. The reorganization did not help; the divisions continued to fight with each other.

Focus on Markets That Have Future Promise

Big losers did not focus on markets that had future promise. This fault is illustrated by six traits big losers exhibited. They (i) focused on product R&D and not markets, (ii) concentrated their R&D on limited user groups, (iii) failed to maintain direct contact with customers, (iv) did not identify and pursue promising markets, (v) did not sufficiently support rapidly growing product lines, and (vii) did not avoid the complications of marketing diverse brands. LSI Logic, Snap-On, Parametric, Campbell, Safeco, and the Gap provide examples of these problems.

Emphasize Markets, Not Product R&D

LSI Logic saw itself as a technological leader. It spent 9.8 percent of revenue on R&D in 1995 (see Figure 12.2), 19 percent in 1998, and 28 percent in 2001. In 2002, it estimated that more than 60 percent of its employees were engineers pursuing technological advances. But its focus of this R&D was on products, not markets. The company was committed to updating the products even without long-term customer support for the innovations it was making. It operated with the assumption that an unusual or outstanding technology would drastically improve the health of its business. This assumption did not always prove to be true.

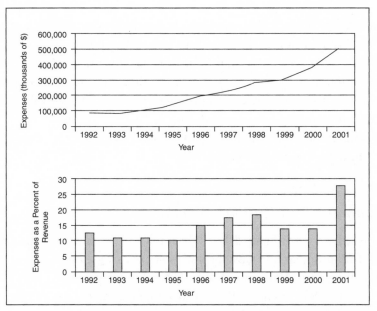

Figure 12.2 R&D expenses at LSI Logic.

Avoid Concentrating R&D on Limited User Groups

Snap-On's focus was mostly on product development and brand. It wanted to extend its reputation for innovative, high-quality tools for the professional user, such as the automobile mechanic. For its brand to continue to command a premium price, it was very conscious of R&D, and it had to be protective of its patents. Snap-On's R&D facility in Bensenville, Illinois opened in 1978. The company continued to increase R&D spending throughout the late 1990s despite the company's financial woes. In 1996, Snap-On spent $42.4 million on R&D. That number grew to $50.2 million in 2001. As a consequence, the company boasted one of the broadest and deepest lines of products in the industry and held 1,592 patents in 2002, with another 637 applications filed or pending.

Snap-On maintained that it wanted to break out of its vehicle service niche and reinvent itself. It was trying to extend its market niche beyond vehicle service to other industrial and commercial applications. It was attempting to provide software solutions and training programs focused on its technologies and products. However, it was still a product-based company for a limited group of users, who were becoming increasingly cost conscious. Snap-On was not effectively modifying itself to meet these customers' needs.

Maintain Direct Customer Contact

In 1998, Parametric named Rand Technologies as "master distributor" of its core products and gave them almost exclusive selling rights in various countries. Likewise, Rand covered most of the training and support services for PRO/Engineer. Rand distributed Parametric's core products to small businesses, which offloaded small account sales activity and enabled Parametric to focus its internal sales staff on larger accounts.

However, Rand, which was free to sell products for other software providers, also developed a relationship with IBM/Dassault Systems. Parametric did not have a way to effectively remedy this problem. Instead, it rolled out an indirect sales model called the Challenge Advantage Reseller program. This program focused on increasing alliances with other resellers and systems integrators and training them as full-service, single-point-of-contact providers. Parametric also developed relationships with the largest consulting firms (including Accenture and Deloitte) to sell and integrate its products.

By relying on these various indirect distribution channels consisting of third-party systems integrators, resellers, and other strategic partners, Parametric lost contact with its customers. Innovative methods in software design that were being developed by competitors, which were based on customer requests and research, were not given the attention they deserved.

Indeed, the marriage between Parametric and Rand ultimately turned sour. In early 2003, Rand filed a $100+ million lawsuit against Parametric, claiming that Parametric had breached the contract in several ways.

Identify and Pursue Promising Markets

Safeco had the goal of being the financial services company that individuals and corporations looked to for all of their needs. It did not focus on a particular market or product, struggled with its identity, and lacked strategic direction.

From 1992 to 2002, the company regularly changed emphasis. Along with offering standard automobile, homeowner's, and life insurance, it also sold hospital insurance policies and had a presence in Canada. Safeco's operations included commercial lending and leasing, investment management, general insurance, and financial services distribution operations. The company underwrote personal, commercial, and surety lines of insurance including automobile, homeowner's, fire, commercial multi-peril, worker's compensation, miscellaneous casualty, and fidelity policies. Its life insurance products included individual products, retirement services (pension), and annuity products. It provided property and casualty insurance, bonds, life insurance, annuities, retirement services, commercial credit, and asset management. It had its own asset management company to manage its mutual funds, a trust company, and outside accounts. Because the mutual funds it administered were not sold through banks, Safeco was moving in the direction of partnering with banks. It was a small mutual fund player, so this was a huge challenge. Safeco credit provided loans and equipment financing to businesses, insurance agents, and affiliated companies. Although the credit operations were profitable, they also tied up nearly $1.5 billion in assets. Safeco found it increasingly difficult to justify this business while other segments of the company were struggling to survive. The diversity of company holdings was difficult to manage effectively. The company had failed to identify promising markets and was not committed itself to pursuing them.

Support Rapidly Growing Product Lines

Campbell had four different segments in 2002: (1) North America Soup and Away from Home: $2.524 billion in revenues; (2) Biscuits and Confectionery: $1.507 billion in revenues; (3) North America Sauces and Beverages: $1.182 billion in revenues; and (4) International Soup and Sauces: $920 billion in revenues. Condensed-soup shipments continued to slide, but sales from new products in the Pepperidge Farm division, such as Goldfish Colors crackers, rose. Yet management continued to declare that Campbell's highest priority was to restore the soup business. Indeed, Campbell tended to view soups as a snacking alternative: "The more we study today's consumers, the clearer it becomes that few foods are better suited to their needs than soup—as a meal, a snack, a beverage, (or) an after-school pick-me-up." The competitors in the snack arena were strong. They included everything from SnackWell's cookies to reduced-fat, no-fat, and baked potato chips.

Sales from Biscuits and Confectionery were increasing primarily due to the performance of Pepperidge Farm, Arnotts, and Godiva. Thus, the indulgent snack category seemed to have particular promise. So did the North America Sauces and Beverages Division, but Campbell did not give either group sufficient support to grow. The company didn't favor products that had promise, such as V8 vegetable juice, Pace Mexican sauces, and Prego sauces, in terms of resource allocation. Campbell didn't put forth sufficient marketing or R&D support toward product lines like Pace and Godiva, which were growing at double-digit rates between 1992 and 2002.

Avoid the Complications of Different Brands

The Gap was serving different market segments utilizing three separate brands and trying to control almost the entire supply chain for all these brands from initial design to retail sale. The Gap's brands covered all segments of the population from value-conscious to high-end. The strategy of different sales channels required different growth strategies for each channel, putting the Gap in equal competition with the sophisticated style of Ann Taylor and the bargain clothing at J.C. Penney. The tasks that Gap had to accomplish were complicated.

After building the Gap brand on high-quality, moderately priced, casual styles for men, women, and children, the company expanded its portfolio to include fashion-forward, high-end Banana Republic and family-oriented budgeter, Old Navy. The company was unable to create a robust enough market distinction between the brands. The differentiation between Gap and Old Navy, for instance, was not great. Both sold casual clothes of similar type, variety, and quality.

Do Not Rely on a Global Focus to Fix Domestic Problems

Big losers relied on global fixes for domestic problems. This fault is illustrated by six traits big losers exhibited. They were unable to (i) avoid failure in global acquisitions, (ii) maintain service levels to increase global sales, (iii) rely on global expansion to overcome domestic weakness, (iv) stay on top of policy changes in key global markets, (v) expand their international presence to meet market needs, and (vi) stay aggressive in pursuing global opportunities. Snap-On, Parametric, Campbell, IMC, Goodyear, and Hasbro illustrate these problems.

Avoid Failure in Global Acquisitions

Snap-On acquired companies to expand product lines and compete internationally, but the acquisitions did not succeed. With global expansion, it offered products in more than 150 countries, but growth for these products was slim. The market for most of the products shifted downward soon after Snap-On bought the companies. Globally, Snap-On was spread very thin. In 2001, it generated $2 billion in sales in 150 different countries, but sales outside the United States and Europe were only 5 percent of its total, and Snap-On's global businesses were not positioned for strong future growth.

Maintain Service Levels to Increase Global Sales

Approximately half of Parametric's employees were located in the United States, with the other half operating in foreign countries such as Canada, France, Germany, and Japan. Despite its global presence, Parametric was unable to make the best of its reach because of decisions it made about what it should concentrate on.

Customers who bought the software felt that they had to invest significant amounts of their own time and money to train their personnel and to integrate the software. Customers found Parametric to be ill equipped and unresponsive about working with them on integration. Although the company had a technologically sophisticated product, Parametric did little to effectively service its client base. The result of these practices was that Parametric was unable to generate subsequent sales from its existing customer base. When Parametric attempted to reacquire a customer to generate follow-up sales or sell product upgrades, it was confronted with frustrated and hostile customers.

Don't Expect Global Expansion to Overcome Domestic Weakness

By means of its acquisitions, Campbell had developed a global focus, selling products in 120 countries. Its products were often tailored for specific foreign markets, such as dry soups in Europe. Overseas markets presented Campbell with good opportunities to expand its customer base and product markets. The company moved aggressively to take advantage of these opportunities, building an extensive dry soup concern in France, which it used to leverage its growth in the dry soup line in the rest of Europe. Campbell also made several acquisitions of other overseas leading producers of soups, including Erin Foods and McDonnell's in Ireland and Velish in Australia.

Campbell had success with its Arnotts brand (a leading snack foods company) in Australia. It strengthened its presence in the snack market with the acquisition of Snack Foods Limited, the number-two salty snack company in Australia.

But Campbell's global expansion did not make up for its domestic weakness. For the period 2000 to 2002, overall sales were down, and Campbell's results were mixed. (See Table 12.2.)

Table 12.2 Campbell's Global Net Sales (In Millions): 1996, 1999, and 2002

Region	2002	1999	1996
United States	$4,339	$4,804	$5,332
Europe	$843	$630	$1,122
Australia/Asia Pacific	$554	$616	$614
Other countries	$502	$438	$733
Adjustments and eliminations	($105)	($64)	($123)
Consolidated	$6,133	$6,424	$7,678

Stay on Top of Policy Changes in Key Export Markets

IMC focused on strengthening exports to several key countries, including China. Rather than providing protection against market swings, however, these ties made them worse. China was a major customer, but its demand for IMC's products basically went away when the country imposed import restrictions, causing a large reduction in sales. The reduction in sales caused available capacity to go idle, which hurt IMC's profitability.

Expand International Presence to Meet Market Needs

In comparison to such competitors as Bridgestone, Michelin, and Continental, Goodyear was not sufficiently global. The company's highest growth in 2002 came from Eastern Europe, Africa, and the Middle East. The Asian and European Union markets also were strong, but the U.S. market was slumping. Without growth in global markets, Goodyear was likely to continue to lag behind its competitors. It had the leading market share in tires in North America, Latin America, China, and India, but not Japan, where Bridgestone continued to be number one, or Europe, where Michelin dominated.

Be Aggressive in Pursuing Global Opportunities

About a quarter of Hasbro's revenues were from its international operations. The U.S. market was saturated. To sustain growth, it was necessary to attract the attention of children around the world. With India and China accounting for more than 700 million potential toy consumers, it was in Hasbro's best interests to pursue the opportunity. Hasbro's most successful international brands in 2002 were ActionMan, Play-Doh, Monopoly, and FurReal Friends, in addition to licensed toys from Disney, Star Wars, and Pokémon. However, Hasbro was not being aggressive enough in pursuing these global opportunities.

In Summary

This chapter has shown the lack of focus that the big losers showed. They spread themselves thin and failed to maintain clear strategic direction. They were unable to identify and emphasize markets with future promise. They tended to rely on global business to try to fix domestic problems. None of what they did worked quite as intended.

Having completed the analysis of the traits of the big winners and losers, I turn to the following—what were the overall traits that distinguished one group of companies from the other? What constitutes best practices for achieving sustained competitive advantage and avoiding sustained competitive disadvantage? What are the secrets of long-term success and how do you avoid being a long-term loser?

CONCLUSION

13

WINNING AND LOSING PRACTICES

The big winners did so much better than the big losers for four reasons:

- *They occupied sweet spots.*

- *They had the agility to move into these spots.*

- *They had the discipline to protect these spots.*

- *They had the focus to exploit and extend these spots.*

The big losers had the opposite characteristics:

- *They were in sour spots.*

- *They were too rigid to move out of these spots.*

- *They were inept at defending the positions in which they found themselves.*

- *They were not able to hone in on these spots and extend and exploit them.*

This chapter summarizes the traits that distinguish the big winners from the big losers. It recapitulates the main argument of the book about what it takes to succeed in the long run. It revisits the idea of a sweet spot, agility, discipline, and focus and provides additional examples.

A Sweet Spot

A sweet spot is being in a noticeably better position than your competitors, a position that is virtually uncontested. You are in a niche where you are nearly a category of one. One of the main reasons that the big winners did so much better than the big losers is that they occupied sweet spots, whereas big losers occupied sour spots.

Being in a sweet spot means:

- Staying close to your customers.

- Being intimate in your understanding of their needs.

- Catering to groups of customers whose desires you know well and with whom you have developed trusting relationships.

- Building your business around a clear value proposition for the customer groups you know well.

The key to being in a sweet spot is to regularly deliver more value to your customers than your competitors.

Positioning is the place that these products and services occupy in consumers' minds relative to the products and services of competitors. It is the "complex set of perceptions, impressions, and feelings" that customers have about these products and services.[1]

You need to have a well-executed niche strategy in which your products and services are well-positioned.

- In what ways are your products and services distinctive?

- How do they bring superior value to selected customers?

Great business models start by bringing superior value to customers. You can only bring superior value to customers if you are close to them.

You have to be totally dedicated to serving your customers and bringing them something of special value.

You must provide customers the best value for their money.[2] To do so, you have to understand your customers well. You have to know who they are and understand their needs.

- What exactly do your customers want?
- In what way are you best positioned to satisfy their needs?

Are you best positioned to satisfy customers' needs by selling undifferentiated products and services (mass marketing), or should you relate to a distinct group of buyers? The examples of winning companies in this book suggest that you are better off relating to a distinct group. Niche marketing rather than mass marketing is more often associated with long-term success.

Big winners know how to satisfy the specialized needs of a distinct group of customers. If you are able to understand and meet the needs of a distinct group, you will face less competition in the long run. Your products and services will be more valued and your margins will be higher. In addition, you will be less subject to imitation.

Generic items quickly become commodities. Specialized items, based on precise customer understanding, still must be continuously updated to retain their appeal. The more specialized and the more based on intimate customer knowledge your products are, the more likely you can stay a big winner for a long time. You will maintain your lead and not lose it.

You must regularly ask yourself who your target customers are and why you chose them. You cannot back off from these questions.

- Who precisely are you serving and why?
- What type of value do you bring to this segment?
- Why will this segment not switch to your competitors—why will it remain loyal to you?

Remember that segmenting a business market is different from segmenting a consumer market. Likewise, segmenting a global market is different from segmenting the domestic market. Consider usage opportunity, rate, and readiness on the part of your customers to buy.

Each segment you serve is distinct. It might merit a different product and service mix. You must individualize your products and services to the concrete needs of target customers. The more individualized they are, the more likely they will have an enduring appeal. The more individualized, the greater attachment and bond you will create with your customers. Ongoing success depends heavily on the degree to which you can establish this attachment and the degree to which you can deepen it over time.

You have to treat each customer group you serve differently. Divide your customers by the type of benefits they seek. Take into account many variables: age, income, gender, lifestyle, social class, personality, and geography. Big winners show this sensitivity to markets and customers. Big losers tend to treat all customers alike. To the losers, customers are just a big, homogenous blob. Is it any wonder that customers are so willing and ready to abandon them?

After you have decided which customer groups to serve, you can bring them superior value in various ways. You can combine and bundle features, or you can keep features separate. You can promote one or two product and service lines as best in a class, or you can develop a whole set of different product and service lines that extend broadly across different categories.

The message from the big winners is to meaningfully differentiate your products and services based on the benefits they offer. The distinguishing features are many—style, design, durability, reliability, image, training, and expertise. Customers can derive many benefits from what you sell. Big losers tended to miss the importance of selling something other than just standard products and services, on the one hand, or ultra-sophisticated products and services, on the other Meaningful differentiation lies between these extremes. The unimaginative product offerings of the losers are not in touch with customer needs. Thus, customers have no reason to stick with the losers. They have better alternatives than staying with them. Without delivering value to customers, you will be a loser and you will be in a vulnerable position.

You must try to make your products and services vastly superior to your competitors. You need a unique selling proposition that you present to your customers. Regularly reexamine and renew your selling proposition because it is why you remain in business and are able to prosper. In the end, to achieve long-term business success, you have to provide something of exceptional value. Expect long-term failure if you cannot do so.

An Example of the Search for a Sweet Spot: The Market for Painkillers

A good example of the search for a sweet spot is the hunt for a highly effective, extremely gentle pain reliever. (See Figure 13.1.)[3] Consumers' perceptual map of pain relievers consists of two dimensions—effectiveness and gentleness—against which products can be arrayed. At one time, Excedrin, Anacin, and Bufferin were in the high-effectiveness, low-gentleness category. Excedrin had the highest effectiveness and lowest gentleness. Bufferin had the highest gentleness and lowest effectiveness. Anacin was somewhere in middle. All three products were better than aspirin, while Tylenol had the gentleness space to itself. This was the source of Tylenol's strength. Its weakness was that it was not as effective as the other analgesics.

Not all the positions in the gentleness/effectiveness space, however, were taken. Other options made their presence felt; the existing array left open spaces for additional painkillers and painkilling methods. Some of the pain relievers filling the spaces, such as Ibuprofen and Aleve, claimed to be even more effective. Some, such as Celebrex and Vioxx, were more specialized. Others, such as Darvon and Percodan, were more powerful and required prescriptions; they were narcotics for

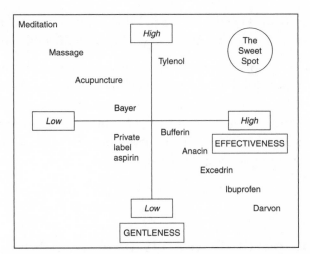

Figure 13.1 Finding a sweet spot in the market for painkillers.

patients in extreme pain. But some painkillers were totally different. Meditation, acupuncture, electrostimulation, massage, acupressure, and relaxation were high on gentleness, but did they really eliminate pain? If someone were to find the truly highly effective, extremely gentle pain reliever, this person would be in a sweet spot, a truly unassailable position until it could be matched by a competitor.

Positioning for Advantage

Big winners thus position themselves for advantage. Big losers do not; their relationship to their customers is not in sync. Positioning for advantage involves several aspects.

First, it means having a customer orientation. You must incorporate something of great distinctiveness into your products and services that you offer. Big losers are product, not customer, oriented. Their understanding of their customers is not sufficiently focused. (See Table 13.1.) They do not understand the specific needs and concerns of their customers.

Table 13.1 Oriented Toward Customers and Not Products

	Customer	Product
Distinct	Sweet spot	
Diffuse		Sour spot

Second, you need to offer integrated solutions. Customers want more than just products and services.

You must understand the world from your customers' perspective. How can what you offer solve the specific problems your customers have? Think through the issue from the perspective of your customers. Be aware that customers struggle with how to use products. (See Figure 13.2.)

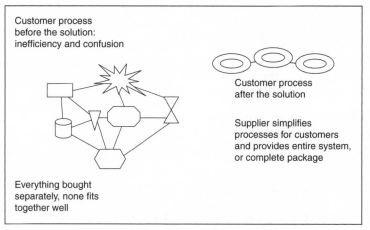

Figure 13.2 Providing customers with solutions.

The third consideration to keep in mind is that your involvement with customers must be firsthand. You cannot become detached or distant. (See Table 13.2.) Your understanding of customer needs should be based on dialogue with your customers. You have to know how to elicit information from them. Closeness allows you to better forecast your customers' future needs. You will know what to do next. You can only solve your customers' problems if you know what they are. Thus, you have to maintain ongoing and intimate customer contact.

The final element is to bring your knowledge to bear. Be sure that you use it to create a distinctive niche. Have an area of distinctiveness. (See Table 13.3.) All the big winners had an area of distinctiveness.

Table 13.2 Achieving Knowledge of Customers

Winning Companies' Approach to Customers	Losing Companies' Approach to Customers
Close and involved	Distant, detached
First-hand experience, reciprocal relations, intimate exchanges	Faith in formal methods of gaining customer knowledge and objectivity
Looking for exceptions; interested in singular and atypical	Hoping to flatten experience; interested in typical and ordinary
Calculations about customer needs based on ongoing dialogue with customers	Calculations about customer needs based on predictions about general behavior
Tailors offerings to meet specific customer needs; willing to cater to the unusual	Often provides generic offerings to average customers; outfitter of the masses
Grows markets through customer feedback and interaction	Grows markets through high volumes and increasing scale of activities
Goal to innovate new classes of customers	Goal to achieve high market share

A sweet spot means being oriented toward customers and not toward products. (See Table 13.2.) It means focusing on solutions and not products. (See Figure 13.2.) It means having regular, sound knowledge of your customers' needs (see Table 13.2), and it means developing distinct ways of relating to customers. (See Table 13.3.)

You remain a big winner because you have elicited long-term customer loyalty. Long-term customer loyalty is the best way to gain power over Porter's classic five forces, starting with customers and extending to suppliers, existing competitors, new entrants, and substitutes.

Table 13.3 Having Distinct Ways of Relating to Customers

Big Winners	Area of Distinctiveness
Amphenol	Co-creates unique, high-value products with its customers
SPX	Offers its customers high-level system-wide manufacturing solutions that cross engineering disciplines
Fiserv	Provides essential backoffice services to its customers who are unable to provide these services on their own
Dreyer's	Efficiently distributes its competitors' products and its own to many kinds of customers
Forest Labs	Successfully commercializes foreign products that U.S. customers otherwise would not have the ability to access
Ball	Innovates new concepts in partnerships with its key customers
Brown & Brown	Fashions custom-designed programs and plans that meet the needs of underserved customer niches
Family Dollar	Conveniently provides basic necessities at low cost to low-income customers
Activision	Creates hits mostly for its young male customers by being at the center of a producer-distributor network

Co-Designing, Embedding, and Brokering

The big winners had three main means of creating customer loyalty. (See Chapter 4, "Sweet Spots.") They were:

- Co-designing products and services with their customers
- Embedding themselves in the infrastructure and processes of their customers
- Brokering relationships between their customers and their customers' suppliers

The concrete advice that derives from what the big winners did in this regard is that:

- You should endeavor to co-design with your customers.
- You should customize your products and services to meet your customer's distinct needs.
- You should make your closeness to your customer physical and tangible.
- You should establish a presence on-site with your customers.

- You should understand where your products fit into your customers' value chain.

- You should act as intermediaries between your customers' desires and those that can meet these needs.

Avoiding Misalignment

In contrast, the big losers had patterns that yielded substantial misalignment with their customers needs. Big losers:

- Had products and services that were too expensive for their customers

- Had products and services whose price was too low to earn a profit

- Relied on activities that were too broad and complex to be performed competently

The advice that derives from what the big losers did is that:

- You should have a customer-first, not product-first focus.

- You should not pursue technological leadership as a primary strategy, especially in industries where commoditization is taking hold.

- You should abandon markets where there is overcapacity and customers have substantial power.

- You should recognize that it is futile to chase market share under conditions in which you have no choice but to sell at a loss for a long period.

- You cannot maintain an unfocused product portfolio.

- You should concentrate on a particular product segment or stage in the value chain to avoid inventory and other glitches.

A Diagnostic for Knowing if You Are in a Sweet Spot

How do you know if you are or are not in a sweet spot? Here is a series of questions you can ask to make this determination.

Are we co-designing products and services with customers?

- Are we engaged in niche marketing?
- Do we have sufficient leverage with suppliers and customers?
- Are we moving toward being a fully integrated supplier?
- Are we aiming to move to niches that have especially high growth potential and good margins?
- Do we have multiple growth platforms?
- Are we designing unique products that help customers with brand differentiation?
- Are we altering basic product characteristics in a timely fashion to meet customers' changing needs?
- Are we gaining increasing recognition for our prices, service, quality, and performance?

Are we embedded in our customers' infrastructure?

- Are we seamlessly integrated with our customers' systems?
- Are we giving our customers a broad array of solutions?
- Are we taking advantage of our customers' need for outsourcing?
- Are we taking advantage of our customers' need for independent, unbiased vendors?
- Have we chosen a sufficiently challenging niche, such as distribution?
- Have we taken enough steps to build our brand?
- Have we chosen markets that others are not serving well?
- Have we secured openings where other companies cannot operate?
- Are we thriving because of the simplicity and predictability of our operations?

Are we being a broker between our customers' needs and the fulfillment of their needs?

- Are we introducing a new model into an industry whose attractiveness is waning?
- Are we reducing risk by bringing to market products successfully sold abroad?
- Are we building capabilities to market foreign products?
- Are we an outlet for products that other companies develop?
- Do we understand customers' needs for products and services in niches where the competition is less intense?
- Can we get our customers the best deal?
- Do we have control over a well-defined niche?
- Have we become the hub in the spoke of a wheel—do we bring many parties together?

A Diagnostic for Avoiding a Sour Spot

There is a similar group of questions for avoiding a sour spot.

Are our goods and services too expensive?

- Do we overdesign our products?
- Are we too reliant on a few powerful customers?
- Are we pouring money into research and development (R&D), even though the R&D does not meaningfully differentiate our products?
- Are we aligning products and services with our customers' level of sophistication?
- Are we "product-first," and therefore not paying enough attention to service?
- Are we ignoring lower-priced competitors?

Are our goods and services too cheap?

- Are we competing with products subsidized by foreign governments?
- Can we pass on suppliers' price increases to customers?
- Do we have a clear identity? Do we know what we stand for?
- Do we have a process of working with customers to best meet their needs?
- Are we sacrificing price for market share?
- Do we have good contingency plans to adequately cover risk?

Is our business model too broad and complex?

- Are we well-positioned on the price/quality continuum?
- Are we able to anticipate competitors' moves?
- Do we have unique products that are within our customers' comfort zone?
- Are we staying with a relatively simple business model that we can reproduce again and again?
- Are we too dependent on a complex business model that is hard to reproduce because it requires extremely accurate prediction and timing?

Agility, Focus, and Discipline: Finding a Balance

Finding a sweet spot is important, but it is just one of the secrets of long-term success. The others emphasized in this book are agility, discipline, and focus.

You need to identify a sweet spot, but just identifying it is not enough. You must have the agility to move to it, the discipline to protect it, and the focus to fully exploit it. To better understand these attributes and how they relate to each other, let us look at a few examples.

Agility

Best Buy epitomizes the trait of agility. The company began as a high-quality stereo retailer for audiophiles, with just a few stores in the Twin Cities. Then it moved to its current niche as a mass-market low-cost electronics outlet and evolved into a hybrid. (See Figure 13.3.)[4] It now sells both high-margin myth products and low-margin commodity ones. The high-margin products are mainly for profits, and the commodities are mainly for growth. The company also tries hard to make its stores exciting and fun. The value for the money package it creates gives customers a choice by taking away pressure that would be applied by a commissioned sales force. These moves have been taken to position Best Buy against Circuit City and they were very successful. In 1991, Best Buy's sales were $.66 billion, substantially behind Circuit City's sales of $2.36 billion, but by 1996, Best Buy beat Circuit City, with sales of $7.21 billion compared to Circuit City's $7.02 billion.

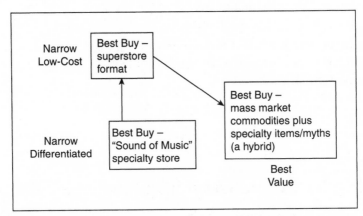

Figure 13.3 Best Buy: The move to best value.

Best Buy surpassed Circuit City by rapidly making moves that Circuit City did not match. Each phase in its development was built around a previous one. As the company repositioned itself again and again, it held onto elements of its old identity even as it branched out and created a new one.

In this regard, Best Buy might be compared to Ivory Snow. (See Figure 13.4.)[5] Ivory Snow started as a differentiated product, a pure and mild soap as opposed to the crude, inexpensive ones with which it competed in late nineteenth-century America. Ivory did not have harsh ingredients. It floated and was heavily advertised as being "99.44 percent" pure. Until it was challenged by Dial, the first deodorant soap, and by Dove, the first beauty bar, Ivory sold at a premium price. In response to these competitors, Procter & Gamble, the maker of Ivory Snow, had to be agile. It repositioned Ivory as a basic, no-frills, but good-value soap. While Procter & Gamble didn't give up on the product's original features, it sold the product in simple bundled packages as a great value for the money. The advertising slogan, "We probably should charge more for a great soap like Ivory," represents the new position that Ivory occupied.

Best Buy and Ivory share something in common: They moved on. They grew and changed, but they also retained aspects of their prior identities. They built on what they once were.

Agility is not just about change, but about change within the context of continuity, as the Best Buy and the Ivory examples illustrate.[6]

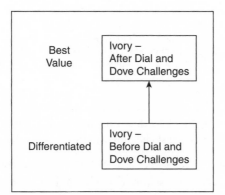

Figure 13.4 Ivory: The move to best value.

Discipline

In industry after industry, this type of movement takes place. But movement by itself is not enough. It must be combined with discipline. An example of agility not being combined with discipline comes from the securities industry. (See Figure 13.5.) Morgan Stanley, a full-service broker, purchased Dean Witter in 1997 and obtained more than 10,000 brokers whose clients were not the high-net-worth individuals to whom it had traditionally catered. Its culture of exclusivity had to be combined with a more common touch as the firm merged these two powerful but different organizations. Morgan Stanley did not abandon the culture of exclusivity. It did not let go of its old identity but built upon it.

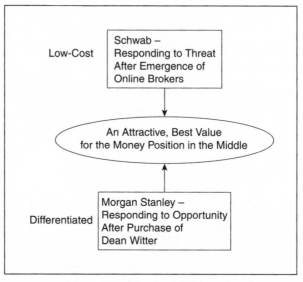

Figure 13.5 Schwab and Morgan Stanley:
From low cost and differentiated to best value.

A short time later, Schwab, starting in a different position than Morgan Stanley, also repositioned itself, taking aspects that once had been foreign to it and forging a new image. Unlike Morgan Stanley, which was nothing but highbrow, Schwab had pioneered the discount broker niche. It eliminated advice, reduced commissions, and offered transactions from a salaried sales force. With overhead far lower than a full-service broker like Morgan Stanley, it could afford to be a low-cost operator.

But the story of Schwab, like that of many other companies, is one of constant upheaval and change. The company could not stay where it was indefinitely. Outflanked by the extreme low-cost positions that were staked out by a group of aggressive new entrants, the online brokers, whose margins were even more razor thin than its own, Schwab had to move.

Many firms occupied or tried to occupy the extreme low-cost niche. They included TD Waterhouse, E-Trade, Siebert and Company, Ameritrade, and Datek. The extreme discounters were a thorn in Schwab's side. Their entry into the industry forced Schwab to take more of a "best-value" approach. Schwab moved upscale. It set up services for the super wealthy by relying on a group of affiliated professional account managers and purchasing US Trust, a traditional investment bank. With the latter move, Schwab began to compete for some of the same customers as Morgan Stanley.

From being poles apart, the two firms of Morgan Stanley and Schwab began to converge. They were occupying a similar space, offering comparable but distinct, attractive, value-for-the-money packages to the same group of customers. However, the territory to which these firms moved was a crowded one. In the high-end space, companies like Salomon Smith Barney, Goldman Sachs, and Merrill Lynch competed with Schwab and Morgan Stanley. In the middle, companies like Edward Jones, AG Edwards, Prudential, RBC Dain Rauscher, Piper Jaffrey, and UBS Paine Webber competed with these companies.

The success of Schwab and Morgan Stanley was in question not because they were not agile but because they did not have a means of protecting the spots they occupied. Neither firm had a unique set of capabilities and competencies that protected them from copying by competitors. They moved, but the territory that they entered was highly contested, and neither Schwab nor Morgan Stanley had the discipline to stand out. Neither company could defend the new niches they occupied.

Focus

So, movement for the sake of movement does not distinguish big winners from big losers. The movement must be accompanied by discipline. You must have discipline to protect the space you occupy and the focus to fully exploit it. Focus is the ability to reap as much of the benefits of the sweet spot you have occupied as possible. It is obvious but important to note that it takes discipline to be focused.

Dell is an excellent example of the combination of discipline and focus. (For more about Dell's discipline, see the insert at the end of this chapter.)[7] Dell grew its worldwide market share in PCs from about 5 percent to nearly 15 percent from 1998 to 2003, while other companies faded. Its growth was almost entirely organic. It was not propped up by mergers and acquisitions. Rather, Dell's aggressiveness forced its major competitors, HP and Compaq, to merge.

Dell sought to grow and to keep growing; it wanted to double its revenues every five years. But it recognized that exclusively selling more PCs, with prices rapidly declining at the end of the 1990s, was not the answer. The company, therefore, decided to transfer the capabilities and competencies that constituted the discipline it had with PCs and laptops to other products such as servers, storage, printers, handheld devices, and switches.

Dell took the same basic model it used in PCs and laptops and extended it to other products. It quickly gained a foothold in the handheld PDA market. In entry-level servers, it went from a 10-percent U.S. market share in 1997 to more than 29 percent by 2003. In workstations, it took the market lead with a 44-percent share. In storage, it had the sixth-largest market share, and its sales were growing at a rate of more than 25 percent per year. Another market that Dell entered was switches. The company extended its model and reproduced it in many product categories. The ability to extend a business model and reproduce it is the essence of focus.

Lessons

Achieving long-term advantage is hard because it means managing the tension of being able to change direction quickly (agility) with digging in, refusing to budge, and reinforcing a space (discipline). You are extending this space so that you have reaped all the benefits (focus). It's important to manage this tension creatively. If you manage it well, you will have realized one of the rarest, most valuable, and hardest-to-reproduce capabilities that your firm can possess. If you manage it poorly, you are destined to endure hard times.

Big winners managed this tension well. Big losers did not. It is that simple.

What are the lessons for you? How do you manage this tension well? I have summarized these lessons in Figure 13.6. They have agility, discipline, and focus on one side, and rigidity, ineptness, and diffuseness on the other. What you have to do to achieve agility, discipline, and focus is often the other side of the coin of what you have to do to avoid rigidity, ineptness, and diffuseness.

The difficulty is in emphasis—when is agility called for, and when is focus and discipline? In dynamic industries under conditions of disequilibrium and disruptive technology, agility is called for. The future is unpredictable, and you need revolutionaries in your firm who will break the rules. In static industries under conditions of equilibrium and sustaining technologies, discipline and focus are called for. The future is most likely going to be like today, and you need controllers and improvers in your company who will enforce and fix the rules.

But how do you know if you should make the transition from agility to discipline and focus? Today in business, it is never completely clear, so you must maintain elements of all these traits simultaneously. You must have the requisite variety of these qualities to meet every contingency.

Balance makes for a resilient company that is able to thrive in the long run under all circumstances. Many managers make the mistake of thinking they know which way things are headed, so they throw all their eggs in one basket. They purposefully become unbalanced only to regret it later when conditions change. In the heyday of the tech boom, Intel was way out in front in agility only to regret it later when company executives realized they had sacrificed discipline for agility and allowed arch-rival AMD to creep precariously close in the firm's core microprocessor markets.

The way to prepare for future scenarios of different kinds is to maintain a balanced portfolio of qualities. The unbalanced firm might achieve short-term successes, but it will not sustain long-term success.

Agility	Rigidity
1. Move toward new and promising markets where customers have specialized needs that only you can meet. 2. Be an aggressive acquirer, taking advantage of the opportunities to broaden and enhance your product offerings. 3. Be sufficiently diversified so that you can compensate for a decline in one segment with strengths in another segment. 4. Respond swiftly to threats and opportunities. 5. With smaller size comes greater flexibility. 6. Grow your business in accord with your customers' changing needs.	1. Do not rely exclusively on expansion of your core products for growth. 2. If there is insufficient demand, do not accumulate additional capacity at high prices. 3. Avoid overreliance on hard-to-differentiate commodity products sold on the basis of price. 4. Respond vigorously when experiencing a decline in your core business area. 5. Bigger is not necessarily better. 6. Don't lag in recognizing and reacting to changes in your customers' tastes.
Discipline 7. Maintain ongoing, effective programs that reduce costs and raise quality. 8. Control distribution. 9. Make for smooth transitions in managing your acquisitions. 10. Create a special culture to get your employees involved. 11. Monitor and influence regulatory changes and promptly comply with policies that affect the firm.	**Ineptness** 7. Develop capabilities to provide best-in-class service and customizable offerings at a low cost. 8. Gain mastery over the supply chain. 9. Be effective in managing your acquisitions. 10. Make sure your employees are motivated and your moves are well executed. 11. Maintain high ethical standards and develop capabilities to effectively manage government regulation.
Focus 12. Focus on core strengths—stick to your mission. 13. Focus on high-growth, application-specific products for markets that have growth potential. 14. Extend your global reach.	**Diffuseness** 12. Maintain a clear strategic direction—do not spread yourself too thin. 13. Focus on markets that have future promise. 14. Do not rely on a global focus to fix domestic problems.

Figure 13.6 Lessons from the big winners and losers: managing the tension.

Distinct Patterns

Big winners combine agility, discipline, and focus into distinct patterns. Table 13.4 shows how each big winner did so. The first column refers to the lessons in Figure 13.6. The table illustrates how each big winner combined a subset of positive traits under each of these lessons. For instance, Amphenol had four agile, three disciplined, and two focused traits. Together, these nine traits formed a unique and hard-to-copy pattern that contributed to the company's success. This blend of qualities supported the sweet spot it occupied. Without it, Amphenol would be hard-pressed to sustain a winning position. Similarly, Ball had a pattern of six agile, four disciplined, and three focused traits for a total of 13 attributes that constituted a winning pattern that was hard for competitors to reproduce or copy.

In this way, the big winners combined agility, discipline, and focus. They brought together these hard-to-unite, contrasting traits. These traits formed difficult-to-copy patterns. The performance of the big winners was not a result of a single positive trait but of multiple positive traits that reinforced one another.

The big winners avoided rigidity, ineptness, and diffuseness. Big losers combined these traits into overall patterns that made for their prolonged failure. The first column in Table 13.5 again refers to the lessons found in Figure 13.6. Based on these lessons, the table illustrates how the big losers combined a subset of negative traits. LSI Logic, for instance, had two rigid, two inept, and two diffuse traits for a total of six qualities that contributed to its persistent losing. Similarly, Goodyear had a pattern of four rigid, five inept, and two diffuse traits for a total of 11 attributes that contributed to its persistent losing.

In each instance, the losing firms brought together elements of rigidity, ineptness, and diffuseness; their poor performance was not a result of a single bad quality but of multiple weaknesses that reinforced each other. The losing firms were condemned to fail because of a pattern of bad traits, not because of any single weakness.

Each winning and losing firm had a distinct pattern. These patterns are further illustrated in Appendix D, "Patterns of Winning and Losing Companies," where you can see how each of the winning firms

Table 13.4 Traits of Winning Firms: Patterns of Agility, Discipline, and Focus

Lesson	Amphenol	SPX	Fiserv	Dreyer's	Forest	Ball	B&B	Family Dollar	Activision	Total
Agility										
1			X	X		X	X		X	5
2				X	X	X		X	X	5
3	X	X	X	X	X	X	X		X	8
4	X	X	X		X	X	X	X	X	8
5	X	X	X			X	X		X	6
6	X	X	X		X	X	X		X	7
Subtotal	4	4	5	3	4	6	5	2	6	
Discipline										
7	X	X	X	X		X	X	X	X	8
8	X			X			X	X	X	4
9	X	X	X			X	X			4
10				X	X	X	X		X	5
11					X	X				2
Subtotal	3	2	2	3	2	4	4	2	3	
Focus										
12				X	X	X	X	X	X	6
13	X	X	X		X	X	X			6
14	X	X	X			X				5
Subtotal	2	2	2	1	2	3	2	1	1	
Grand Total	9	8	9	7	8	13	11	5	10	

Table 13.5 Traits of Losing Firms: Patterns of Rigidity, Ineptness, and Diffuseness

Lesson	LSI	Snap-On	Parametric	Campbell	IMC	Goodyear	Safeco	Gap	Hasbro	Total
Rigidity										
1		X	X	X		X	X			5
2		X			X	X	X	X	X	7
3	X				X	X	X		X	5
4	X		X	X	X				X	5
5						X	X	X	X	4
6			X	X				X	X	4
Subtotal	2	2	3	3	3	4	4	3	5	
Ineptness										
7		X	X	X	X	X	X		X	7
8	X			X	X	X		X	X	6
9	X					X	X			3
10		X				X	X			3
11			X		X	X	X		X	5
Subtotal	2	2	2	2	3	5	4	1	3	
Diffuseness										
12	X			X	X	X	X	X	X	7
13	X	X	X	X			X	X		6
14		X	X	X	X	X		X		6
Subtotal	2	2	2	3	2	2	2	3	1	
Grand Total	6	6	7	8	8	11	10	7	9	

combined agility, discipline, and focus and how each of the losing firms united rigidity, ineptness, and diffuseness.

The patterns of winning and losing firms reinforced and supported each other. The former guaranteed the winners' continued success. The latter ensured the losers' ongoing failure. Prolonged competitive advantage and disadvantage are not the result of a few good or bad traits in isolation, but of a package of traits combined in these distinct patterns.

Managing the Tension

The key to being a winner, then, is to do a good job in managing the tension that exists among agility, discipline, and focus.[8] Your aim should be some kind of balance, or proportionality. You should set up harmonious relations among these traits based on a creative tension. If you can establish such a balance, your company will be much better off, not only now but in the future. If it thrives in more than one of these domains simultaneously, its horizon will stretch; it will expand from the present where discipline is needed to be profitable today, to the near future where focus is essential for growth, to a more distant time when your company can feed off its ability to identify new niches and occupy them quickly.

You do not achieve long-term success by building these traits separately. You must combine them into larger wholes so that your success is ensured both now and afterward.

The trade-offs you will have to make cannot be trivialized, however; they are hard ones. On the one hand, you have to move swiftly to the sweet spots. On the other hand, you have to be steadfast in protecting the positions you currently occupy.

Consider the following:

- Moving to a sweet spot depends on new product concepts and imaginative marketing methods. Autonomy and risk taking are the driving forces. Bureaucratic obstacles have to be cleared away so that the new concepts can be brought to the market rapidly. An innovative niche must be grasped and occupied before a competitor discovers and inhabits it. Getting to this type of niche, however, might necessitate rule infringement, which cannot be tolerated easily in a disciplined and focused organization.

- Employees in agile companies are likely to rebel against the time, budget, and other constraints found in disciplined and focused organizations. Making products again and again in a flawless way for established markets rests on different temperaments and skill sets than people in an agile organization generally have. Standardization, reliability, and rigid adherence to procedure are what people in disciplined organizations generally do best. In a disciplined and focused firm, the goals are likely to be zero defects and minimum variation. These goals conflict with the agile firm's forbearance for error. In the disciplined firm, the acceptance of mistakes must be suppressed. Disciplined and focused companies primarily recruit and retain reliable, stable, and methodical people who are capable of adhering to this regime, while they are likely to view the employees hired by agile firms as unsteady and impractical.

To be a big winner, you must cultivate attributes that will allow you to operate at both ends of this spectrum, however contradictory they might be. Being a big winner means finding the right balance between agility on the one hand and discipline and focus on the other. You have to be innovative but also execute without a glitch.

Persistent winning rests on mastering traits that represent opposing qualities. Momentum will be on your side if you are able to do so. You will not have just a few strokes of good luck but many years of sustained accomplishment.

Big losers manage the tension poorly. Something gets out of whack. Negative trait is layered upon negative trait. Big winners manage the tension well. Positive traits build on each other. They cohere into something greater than the sum of their parts.

Exploration for new niches is not necessarily incompatible with the exploitation of existing niches. You have to aggressively expand yet aggressively protect what you already enjoy. Being in a sweet spot and having the agility to get there requires creativity, the generation of new ideas, and innovation, while discipline and focus rest on conformity to current rules and standards, efficiency, and scrupulous attention to detail. You must cultivate and master all these traits at the same time to assure your long-term success.

A Diagnostic: Knowing Your Level

Your aim should be to achieve a balance between agility, discipline, and focus. (See Figure 13.7.) However, most firms are somewhere in the middle. They are not big winners or big losers. They have some things going for them and some things going against them. They must figure out what their pluses and minuses are and how to get better. Usually, they do not have much time to do so. They have to act quickly against the state of partial unbalance in which they find themselves. For instance, they might be inept even though they are currently in a sweet spot and have mastered focus and agility. In this instance, they are unlikely to hold on to the sweet spot they occupy for long. Their ineptness will be their undoing.

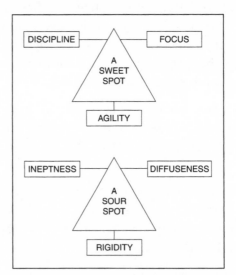

Figure 13.7 Balance and imbalance.

Other firms might be diffuse even though they are in a sweet spot and have discipline and agility. In this instance, it is unlikely they will be able to take full advantage of the good position they occupy.

Still other firms might be rigid even though they are in a sweet spot and have discipline and focus. In this instance, they are sacrificing the future for the present. They are not destined to go beyond what they currently do well. Their superior performance will soon come to an end.

There are many partial and in-between states. (See Figure 13.8.) A company can be considered relatively lucky if it only has a single weakness, or one negative trait it must fix. Many firms have multiple flaws—more than a single weak trait that they manifest at the same time. For instance, a company is rigid at the same time it is in a sour spot; although it is disciplined and focused, these qualities do it no good. Its rigidity prevents it from engaging in the movement that it must have to escape from a sour position.

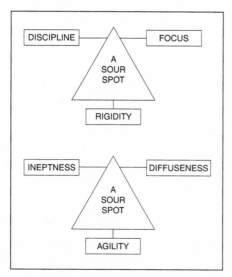

Figure 13.8 Partial and in-between states.

A company can be inept and diffuse and in a sour spot. Even if it were agile, it would get nowhere, for it would be unable to consolidate the position to which it arrived. Desperately searching for a future because it has no present, this company never comes to rest.

Most companies have combinations of positive and negative traits. They are neither performing at their absolute best nor their absolute worst. They need a diagnostic to help them evaluate what to do.

What should firms in the middle do? How should they assess their position? How can they identify their strengths and weaknesses? How can they act to make improvements?

Each firm has its tendencies. Understanding them requires rigorous soul-searching. I would suggest that you start by asking yourself some of the questions listed next. This line of questioning should suggest where your strengths and weaknesses are. Then it's up to you to address the weaknesses and compensate for them.

Doing so will put you on the path toward becoming a big winner.

A Diagnostic for Knowing if Your Company is Focused, Disciplined, and Agile

Is our company diffuse?

- Are we maintaining a clear strategic direction—are we spread too thin?
- Are we focusing on markets that do not have future promise?
- Are we avoiding domestic problems by relying on global expansion?

Is our company focused?

- Are we focused on our core strengths—are we sticking to our mission?
- Are we focused on high-growth, application-specific products for markets with growth potential?

- Are we extending our global reach in a way that supports our overall mission?

Is our company inept?

- Does our company lack the capabilities to provide best-in-class service and customizable offerings at a low cost?
- Are we not paying sufficient attention to the supply chain? Have we gained mastery over it?
- How good are our acquisitions? Have we managed these acquisitions well?
- Does our company motivate employees so that they execute well?
- Are we maintaining high ethical standards?
- Do we have the capabilities to deal effectively with government regulations?

Is our company disciplined?

- Does our company maintain ongoing, effective programs to reduce costs and raise quality?
- Does our company have good control over distribution?
- Does our company smoothly manage acquisitions?
- Does our company have a special culture that gets employees involved?
- Does our company promptly comply with the public policies that affect it?
- Does our company do a good job of monitoring and influencing government regulatory changes?

Is our company rigid?

- Is our company relying exclusively on the expansion of its core products for growth?
- Are we accumulating additional capacity at high prices even when there is insufficient demand for these products?
- Are we overreliant on hard-to-differentiate commodity products sold on the basis of price?

- Are we responding vigorously enough when we experience a decline in our business?
- Do we grow and get bigger simply for the sake of getting bigger?
- Are we slow in recognizing and reacting to changes in customers' tastes?

Is our company agile?
- Is our company moving toward new and promising markets where customers have specialized needs that only we can meet?
- Is our company an aggressive acquirer, taking advantage of opportunities to broaden and enhance our product offerings?
- Is our company sufficiently diversified so that it can compensate for a decline in one segment of the market with strengths in another segment?
- Is our company able to respond swiftly to the threats and opportunities it faces?
- Is our company small and flexible enough to respond quickly?
- Does our company grow in accord with our customers' changing needs?

Being a big winner should be the aim of every firm. You do not want to have to depend on some lucky streak to do well. You want your winning to last. You should not be satisfied with one-time successes. The aim should be to be a dynasty. Achieving ongoing success means doing it all well. You have to find a sweet spot and be agile, disciplined, and focused *at the same time.*

In Summary

This chapter has explained what it takes to be a consistent long-term winner. It takes finding a niche that no one else occupies, but that is not enough. You need the agility to move to that space, the discipline to protect it, and the focus to fully exploit. You must do it all. Anything less, and being a big winner will be beyond your reach.

Dell's Focus and Discipline[9]

Dell's unique configuration of resources, capabilities, and competencies had been perfected over a period of almost 20 years. When Michael Dell began to sell computers out of his University of Texas dorm room in 1984, he realized that he could eliminate a high proportion of the selling costs by circumventing the dealer and selling directly to customers. Michael Dell believed that he could sell customers low-priced, built-to-order machines, taking orders and delivering products one at a time. This system did away with the reseller and retail markup; it eliminated inventory risks and provided a cost advantage.

Born of necessity, these principles became the central tenets in Dell's business model. Eliminating alternative channels to customers, Dell concentrated on its relationships with suppliers and customers. Direct relationships with customers and suppliers created valuable information, which formed the basis for mass customization and just-in-time manufacturing. Virtual integration allowed a small company to beat IBM, a much larger company that was its main competitor at its origin. Dell won with its superior capabilities for coordinating resources and putting them to productive use. Because it was virtually integrated, Dell was able to more fully take advantage of the resources it possessed.

You cannot understand the success of a company like Dell without understanding how Dell shaped the value chain. The aim was to maximize value to the parties with whom the company interacted. Key capabilities that were at the center of how the company succeeded are listed next.

Relationship suppliers—At the inception of the PC industry, companies basically had to create all the components themselves—disk drives, memory chips, and application software. As the industry matured, specialized companies produced them. This specialization allowed Dell to leverage the investments that other companies had made and focus on delivering solutions to its customers. With its suppliers, Dell had two tasks: to set quality objectives and build data linkages. It stitched together its business by treating its suppliers as if they were nearly inside the company.

Fast inventory movement—The company worked with the suppliers to reduce inventory and increase speed. Holding assets as inventory and having accounts receivable were unnecessary risks of doing business. Dell increased the velocity of its business through rapid inventory turns and tight management.

Performance metrics—Inventory velocity was one of a handful of key performance measures that Dell watched closely. Other critical real-time performance measures were margins, average selling price, the overhead associated with selling, and fundamentals such as profit and loss statements on a monthly basis. Dell used these metrics to help manage operations. It divided them by product, customer segment, and geography, and it used them to ensure quality and prevent quality breakdowns, which might slow the flow of goods and materials.

Keeping track of customers—None of Dell's customers represented more than 1 to 2 percent of its revenues; therefore, one week one customer was buying and the next week it was another customer. Ninety percent of Dell's sales was to institutions, businesses, or government, and 70 percent was to large customers who bought more than $1 million in PCs per year. For years, Dell did not actively pursue the consumer market because it could not reach its profit objectives. So it let its competitors introduce machines with rock-bottom prices and zero margins. Dell built only in response to a customer's order, thus avoiding the typical stop and start cycles in the industry where companies stuffed channels to get rid of old inventory and meet short-term financial objectives.

Forecasting—Forecasting was a critical skill for Dell. Account managers led customers through a discussion of their future PC needs. They communicated with staff in every department of a customer's business, asking them to designate which needs were certain and which contingent, and when they were contingent on some event, what the event was so there could be follow-up. Dell fed this valuable information back to its customers, who extended the value of what Dell provided. The customer now had a better understanding of what its IT costs would be.

A technology adviser—Dell was evolving into a technology selector, or navigator. It talked to customers about "relevant technology" rather than the most powerful. It ran forums to ensure the free flow of information with customers on a constant basis.

Dell's core competence in mass customization (low-cost, personalized products and services) was based on these constituent capabilities. Alone, none of these capabilities was sufficient to reach Dell's goals in PCs or other IT-related equipment; it was the ability to merge, align, harmonize, and forge these capabilities that created Dell's success. Together, the capabilities were larger than the sum of their separate parts. Dell developed and refined the capabilities in historical accretions subject to time-consuming and tacit processes that rivals could not master unless they went through the same experience. There were no shortcuts. This unique configuration was the basis for Dell's discipline, a discipline focused on opportunity after opportunity.

14

TURNAROUNDS

What can you do to become a big winner if you are not one? If you are a winner, what can you do to prevent being a big loser? In this chapter, I argue that to become a big winner, you should start with focus and work your way to discipline and agility. Focus will bring you to a sweet spot, discipline will allow you to protect it, and agility will enable you to extend it. Similarly, to avoid being a big loser, guard against diffuseness as it brings you to a sour spot and leads to ineptness and rigidity.

To be a big winner rather than a big loser, you must begin by cultivating focus and avoiding diffuseness. This lesson emerges from the two turnaround stories I tell in this chapter, that of Safeco and SPX. From 1999-2004, Safeco and SPX transformed themselves.

From November 1999 to November 2004, few of the big winners did better than the big losers. Shifts, fluctuations, and about-faces were unusual. As of November 2004, 16 of the 18 companies analyzed in this book remained true to form. The only two firms that deviated from the performance they previously exhibited were Safeco and SPX.

I use a five-year window that partially overlaps with the 1992-2002 period previously analyzed. If you use shorter or different time frames, there are other reversals you might be able to find. Starting in 2001, Safeco beat the Dow Jones Industrial Average, and thereafter it made nice, steady progress. SPX did not fall behind Snap-On, but it came close, and it barely beat the Dow Jones Industrial Average. These trends meant that by the end of 2002, Safeco was outperforming SPX.

What accounts for this reversal? Why do some overachievers fall into the category of underachievers and some underachievers go in the other direction? As a practicing manager (and especially an investor), these questions are critical. As this chapter shows, Safeco went from diffuseness, ineptitude, and rigidity to focus, discipline, and agility, while SPX went from focus, discipline, and agility to diffuseness, ineptitude, and rigidity. This chapter traces the paths of these companies and derives lessons from their stories. The power of this book is that the insights about a sweet spot, agility, discipline, and focus apply to turnarounds. Winners can discover the secrets of turning it around in these principles, and losers can understand how to avoid a descent into failure.

Safeco

The main lessons to derive from the Safeco story is to rediscover your sweet spot, go from focus to discipline to agility.

Focus

Safeco started its turnaround with focus. It had become diffuse by way of acquisition and it had to cut back. It had to rediscover its identity. What kind of company was it? What kind did it want to be? It could not do everything well.

FOCUS ON YOUR CORE STRENGTHS—STICK TO YOUR MISSION
In 1997, Safeco acquired American States Financial Corporation to enhance its geographic presence and product offerings. This acquisition enabled the company to double its independent agent task force, increase its presence east of the Rockies, and make it the leading underwriter of corporate insurance for small- to medium-sized businesses. In the same year, the company acquired WM Life Insurance, a subsidiary of Washington Mutual Inc. This acquisition added a multistate banking network for the distribution of annuities.

Integrating American States into Safeco accounted for huge losses in 1999, however. Earnings during the first quarter of 2000 plunged 88 percent, to $9.5 million, and the company finished the year with just $115 million in net income, down by more than half from the previous year. Safeco had to write off $900 million in goodwill in the same year. The company's CEO Roger Eigsti and most of his top lieutenants were forced to resign under pressure.

In 2001, Mike McGavick, a corporate turnaround specialist, was brought in as president and CEO from CNA Financial Corp., where he had successfully resuscitated its ailing commercial insurance division. McGavick set in motion the revamping of Safeco's strategy. He refocused the firm on what it had historically done best. The company rediscovered its roots. McGavick put a clear emphasis on property and casualty insurance. He decided to sell its life and investments business unit.

McGavick articulated the rationale for the company's refocusing on property and casualty insurance as follows:

> We got out of lines of business where we think it's about big bets—in those lines of business, Safeco has failed. We really concentrated on lines of business where it's about lots of little things done repeatedly well. In those lines of business, Safeco has excelled historically.[1]

The CEO expressed five main ideas that were behind the new focus and that were the driving forces of the firm's turnaround:

- Focus on what makes the organization different from any other in the market.
- Don't be afraid to perform radical surgery.
- Take the pain sooner rather than later.
- Reinforce what is working properly in the organization, and change or add what is missing.
- Communicate, communicate, communicate.

The company had to have a well-defined niche. McGavick maintained that the company had to have the credibility to back up his words. Refocusing was not enough; Safeco needed discipline and agility.

Discipline

In addition to focus, McGavick introduced elements of discipline that had been lost or were missing. He recreated a special culture that got his employees involved and introduced ongoing, effective programs to reduce costs and raise quality. Focus without discipline would not have been enough to bring about the turnaround.

CREATE A SPECIAL CULTURE TO GET YOUR EMPLOYEES INVOLVED

McGavick tried to make Safeco distinctive through the experience customers had with the company. He was convinced that this distinctive experience depended on the people Safeco had and how they treated customers. Safeco had to have a special culture to get its employees involved in treating customers in a special way. The people and the services had to be distinctive because property and casualty insurance business was such a commodity business. Safeco was involved in selling a product that had no special or distinctive features.

Fighting against the tendency toward commoditization is what all big losers have to do. It is one of their main challenges. Big winners successfully oppose this tendency, while big losers do not effectively meet this challenge.

McGavick was acutely aware of this issue. He said, "If you have a product people don't want to buy, it's viewed as heavily regulated and therefore interchangeable, and the product itself gives you no satisfaction; the only thing that truly [is] distinctive between one experience with an insurance company and another *is* the experience of the company—the service and the people."

For the people and services to be distinctive, McGavick believed that the culture had to be very special. He understood that a special culture was a blend of qualities that were hard to put together.

He tried to instill eight traits into Safeco's culture:

1. Integrity
2. Compassion
3. Discipline
4. Delivery of excellent results
5. Accountability
6. Wise frugality
7. Competitive aggression
8. Diversity or inclusion

McGavick believed that the first four traits had been a part of the Safeco organization for a long time, and he was not interested in losing them. Under the pressure of the turnaround, Safeco's employers had responded quickly and powerfully, and they continued to adhere to the first four of these traits. Traits 5 and 6 McGavick felt used to be present at Safeco, but he had to restore them. He believed traits 7 and 8 were missing. He said that the company lacked "a heightened sense of competitive aggression."[2] It did not have "the will to win in the marketplace."[3] In addition, McGavick believed that new ideas were infrequently introduced, but were not "robustly discussed" or given a good going over, and this lackadaisical attitude had to be changed.[4] This type of discipline that was centered around accountability, wise frugality, competitive aggression, and diversity or inclusion were the contributions that McGavick made to Safeco's culture.

MAINTAIN ONGOING, EFFECTIVE PROGRAMS TO REDUCE COSTS AND RAISE QUALITY
Besides a will to win and new ideas, the new CEO took other steps to reduce costs and raise service quality. He addressed the fundamental issue of revamping underwriting procedures, which had resulted in heavy losses from low rates and high claim payouts. By 2002, Safeco was able to accomplish higher positive cash flows from its operating activities. It had an increase of almost 50 percent due to lower property and casualty claim payouts. Safeco achieved these results because the company changed underwriting criteria and actuarial techniques. It better assessed the variables that affected the loss experience in several of its insurance lines and applied new actuarial methods to those lines that had the greatest volatility. By doing this, the company reduced its risk exposure and managers had a more accurate estimate of reserves.

The amount of worker's compensation claims against Safeco's commercial insurance line went down. The company also had some luck because of fewer natural catastrophes and homeowner's insurance claims. McGavick was not content to rely on luck, however. He believed in the use of technology to increase Safeco's revenues and lower its costs. He gave the chief information officer, Yom Senegor, the charge to move Safeco toward a new revenue and leaner cost model. The new business model ultimately saved the company $100 million in annual expenses.

Senegor implemented a "virtual agent" Web-based interface that put customers in touch with agents and increased the timeliness and ease-of-use of quoting and selling the company's product lines. The information officer introduced a new suite of online products and services that relied on the Internet to deliver advice and expertise to independent agents and financial advisors. The new systems made it easier to browse the Web site, contract an agent, and buy a policy in a short time. In addition, Sengor had the company take advantage of real-time chat rooms, e-mail correspondence, and an immediate "call me" feature for those who needed quick answers and for those who wanted direct contact to licensed specialists.

Another innovation was Surety Online, a self-service system that helped agents process bonds on the Internet. The fully integrated Surety Online system produced a complete and printable bond package, including a bond form, a bond-specific power-of-attorney, a transaction receipt, and other ancillary documents. It expedited process completion.

Still another innovation was the New Business Automation Manager, a Web-based technology platform that made it faster and easier for distributors to quote and sell the company's commercial and personal insurance product lines.

A final move was a Web-based system that cut days off the traditional insurance industry underwriting process. The system gave customers quick price quotes and eliminated the manual approval that an underwriter needed before a policy could be issued formally.

These technology initiatives saved the company's 5,400 agents, who processed hundreds of thousands of policies every year, significant amounts of time and money.

McGavick believed that technology was the essence of operational effectiveness, and operational effectiveness was critical to the turnaround. The company's technology initiatives had streamlined operations and provided the firm with the capability to protect its position in the marketplace.

Agility

With the refocusing done and the additional discipline in place, Safeco was ready once again to be agile. It was a smaller-sized company, and with that smaller size came agility. It could take new initiatives. It could make new moves backed by the focus and additional discipline that had been put in place.

The turnaround was predicated on becoming smaller. As Safeco slimmed down, it started to recover from its losses. It went from being $1 billion in the red in 2001 to $300 million in profits in 2002. But this achievement was not without its price. Within 11 months of becoming CEO, McGavick had laid off 10 percent of the workforce.

McGavick, however, did not just reduce the number of workers. The company exited roughly half of its $270 million select markets business of specialty insurance products. It shut down offices in Chicago, Cincinnati, Denver, Hartford, Pleasant Hill (California), Portland (Oregon), Spokane, and St. Louis and consolidated operations in five locations—Atlanta, Dallas, Indianapolis, Seattle, and Fountain Valley (California). These offices were exclusively focused on aiding the sales efforts of insurance agents and on managing customer claims. The technology initiatives replaced services that Safeco used to do manually.

Safeco also completed the sales of Safeco Trust Company in April 2004 and Talbot Financial Corporation in July 2004. It completed the sale of Life & Investments operation to an investor group led by White Mountains Insurance Group, Ltd., and Berkshire Hathaway Inc. on August 2, 2004.[5] Proceeds from the sales of the trust company, the financial corporation, and the life insurance unit totaled $1.51 billion. Approximately $710 million was used to retire $620 million of debt, improving the company's debt-to-capital ratio. The company also expected to realize tax benefits in 2004 of $23 million related to the sales. Estimated net after-tax loss was $260 million, but with sales of these properties completed, the energy and focus of the company could be fully directed to its core property and casualty business.

McGavick and his executives were betting on a smaller and leaner business model to ensure the company's success. With smaller size came greater agility. Unburdened by non-essential operations, the company could take advantage of opportunities.

SPX

The main lessons of the SPX story complement those of the Safeco story. To prevent a meltdown, you must remain focused. Disintegration starts with diffuseness. Your diffuseness spreads. It extends to ineptness and rigidity. You land in a sour spot and lack the capabilities to dig yourself out of it

Diffuseness

SPX's decline started with diffuseness. It lost a clear strategic direction and began to spread itself too thin.

MAINTAIN A CLEAR STRATEGIC DIRECTION—DO NOT SPREAD YOURSELF TOO THIN
SPX had transformed itself from an auto-parts manufacturer to a multinational conglomerate that had diversified its operations into technical products and services, industrial products and services, flow technology, and service solutions. Former GE executive, John B. Blystone, SPX's chairman, president, and CEO, orchestrated this growth and shift in the strategic direction.

The core of SPX's problems came from a near myopic focus on acquisitions, without placing significant attention to how the company could bring the different pieces together in a long-term model for organic growth. The company did not fully achieve the goal of bundling different types of engineering products and technologies into integrated solutions for customers. Products and services remained disparate. They did not fit into neat and recognizable packages that attracted customers. It was unclear what the fit was between such diverse holdings as valves, controls, filtration, hydration, power cooling, fluid technologies, compacting, security, building safety, electrical testing and measurement, labs, and life sciences. General Signal and United Dominion had been the largest acquisitions. These companies had different cultures and traditions that were hard to amalgamate.

There was little overlap in who SPX's customers were and what they did for these customers. Customers ranged from the power industry to motor vehicle dealers. Products were all over the map, from industrial construction to storage networks to TV and radio broadcast antennas and towers to automated fare collection systems and high-integrity die casting. The risks of the firm's broad diversification were proving to be greater than the rewards.

Ineptitude

The lack of focus was bad enough, but by itself it would not have pulled SPX from the ranks of big winners. What also happened was that SPX lost its discipline. Its ineptitude was revealed in its inability to uphold high ethical standards and its failure to recognize and react to changes in customers' tastes. Its unraveling proceeded step-by-step from diffuseness to incompetence.

UPHOLD HIGH ETHICAL STANDARDS

The turnaround from Wall Street darling to a firm searching for a new direction and renewed investor confidence can be blamed on aggressive practices that were meant to increase market value while concealing increases in executive and director compensation. The basis of SPX's growth from a $1 billion company in 1995 to a $5 billion company in less than ten years was aggressive acquisitions.[6] Since 2000, the firm had made approximately 60 acquisitions. Such an active acquisition policy allowed SPX to benefit from nonrecurring expenses, goodwill, and special items in its financial statements, while concealing declining margins, overestimated cash flows, limited organic growth, and inadequate capital expenditure. Many of the moves were made to satisfy market analysts who were eager to see continued increases in earnings per share.

Of equal concern was CEO John Blystone's decision, with the board's support, to alter the bonus plan in 2003 to provide an unjustified increase in compensation to the board and management team. A 2002 rumor that Blystone was being courted by Tyco International to replace the disgraced Dennis Kozlowski prompted the SPX board to offer Blystone the fifth-largest grant of stock ever offered to an American corporate executive, with a market value of $48.85 million. Bonuses at SPX were significantly increased in 2003, with Blystone receiving $10.2 million and each director getting close to $100,000 in bonuses.

Less than two years later, Blystone faced significant criticism for corporate malfeasance and tastelessly altering the compensation schemes for himself and the six-person board. The investment firm Relational Investors LLC, a 5.7-percent shareholder of SPX, launched a proxy fight to alter the composition of the board of directors to resolve what it claimed to be "obvious conflicts of interest and overtones of self-dealing."[7]

Concerns with the firms accounting, long-term competitive position, and greedy executive team angered major shareholders and prompted media controversy that resulted in halving the share price in less than a year. In early December 2004, Blystone stepped down as CEO of SPX amid criticism of the manner in which he had altered the executive and director bonus system.

Don't Lag in Recognition and Reaction to Changes in Your Customers' Tastes

For years, Wall Street analysts were impressed with SPX's ability to diversify through acquisition, but concern developed about the company's weak organic growth. The firm propped up its earnings with a nonrecurring gain from a suit settled with Microsoft, a favorable tax settlement, and a favorable gain from an interest rate swap, but income from operating activities was not advancing. As a result, many analysts discounted SPX's results, claiming that the firm was out of touch with customers and that SPX was concealing its inability to maintain organic growth by means of its acquisitions.

Accounting tricks rather than closeness to customers gave SPX the appearance of a successful operation. In reality, it was languishing from an inability to recognize and react to changing customer wishes. The complexity of its financial statements was apparent in an odd balance sheet dominated by goodwill and intangible assets. Combined goodwill and intangible assets made up approximately $3.6 billion—five times more than net fixed assets. The firm's accountants argued that these allocations were due to the acquisition of troubled companies that were without significant physical assets, but they hid from view the company's inability to connect to the customers it obtained from its acquisitions.

What many analysts were starting to see was a steady decline in both gross and operating margins despite the firm's vaunted Value Improvement Process. In the second quarter of 2004, gross margins dropped from 30.5 percent to 27.5 percent, and operating margins decreased to 6.1 percent from 9.6 percent. The firm's explanations for these decreases were higher raw material prices, currency effects, restructuring charges, global competition, and supplier transition, but other conglomerates' margins grew during this time period while SPX was having trouble reaching its customers.

To keep the firm's customers in the fold, SPX was engaged in heavy discounting that did not bode well for the future.[8] Margins decreased, and the firm's cash position dropped. In 2003, organic revenue growth was down by 2 percent. SPX was losing touch with its customers.

Rigidity

Diffuseness and ineptitude were accompanied by bigness, which limited SPX's flexibility. Bloated with acquisitions, the company could not respond quickly. It could not take advantage of new opportunities.

BIGGER IS NOT NECESSARILY BETTER
SPX had reached saturation. Swollen from prior acquisitions and an inability to completely absorb and integrate what it had acquired, it was in transition from actively buying firms to divesting major elements of its portfolio. It replaced Blystone with its General Counsel Christopher Kearney and started a search to add independent directors in an attempt to satisfy the institutional investors that had claimed "self-dealing." In the month following Blystone's departure, the company sold off

three business units. In the first half of 2004, SPX sold two profitable units (Bomag and Edwards System Technology). The sale of these two business units brought in $1.8 billion.[9] The company's top management was forced to acknowledge that bigger was not necessarily better, that growth at any price concealed real weaknesses in the company's basic business modes.

The active acquisition policy had allowed the firm to claim benefits due to restructuring that if excluded would significantly cut the earnings it reported. Embedded within the firm's 2003 statements were special one-time charges due to employee terminations and restructuring charges that continued to appear year after year. But these one-time charges were just artifacts of acquisitions. They did not suggest a vibrant firm that was in close touch with its customers. It was expected that SPX would continue to rationalize the diversity of its operations and get smaller and smaller. Only if it was smaller and more mobile would it be able to regain its big winner status.

In Summary

The stories of Safeco and SPX reinforce the book's main message. Big winners base their success on being in sweet spots and having focus, discipline, and agility. Big losers fail because they are in sour spots. They have the traits of diffuseness, ineptitude, and rigidity. Turnarounds start with the cultivation of the same group of positive traits and the suppression of the same group of negative ones.

If you want to move from being a big loser to a big winner, take the route that Safeco followed. Regain your focus, rediscover your sweet spot, and reinforce it with discipline, and agility.

If you want to avoid the decline experienced by SPX, don't allow diffuseness to creep in. It will mean that you have migrated to a sour spot. If along with diffuseness you display ineptitude and rigidity, you will only become more entrenched in a sour spot.

Declines are a consequence of diffuseness, ineptness, and rigidity. Revivals are a consequence of focus, discipline, and agility.

The lessons in this chapter have special relevance if you are trying to manage yourself out of decline or trying to keep your company's strengths intact.

The key to being a big winner is to find a sweet spot. Focus on it. Have the discipline to protect it. Have the agility to move it.

The key to being a big loser is the opposite. Be diffuse, inept, and rigid, and you will find yourself in a sour position.

Appendix A

BEST SELLERS COMPARED

Starting with Tom Peters and Robert Waterman's *In Search of Excellence*, there has been a spate of books that purport to provide managers with the secrets to sustained competitive advantage (SCA).[1] Jim Collins' and Jerry Porras' best-selling *Built to Last* is another work in this genre.

The problem with these books is that the prescriptions they make often are contradictory and one sided. On the one hand, they urge you to take bold steps and explore entirely new markets, technologies, and business models, or risk becoming extinct (Peters and Waterman). On the other hand, you are admonished not to divert your attention to things you know nothing about, and to take small, gradual steps to get better at what you currently do (Collins). Most best-selling business books divide into these camps—those that put their primary emphasis on agility (see Tables A.1 and A.2) and those that put their primary emphasis on discipline and focus.[2]

Many books have been advocates for the dynamic elements in strategy. Others have been advocates for the more static elements. Some have argued for technological discontinuity, entrepreneurship, adaptability to unstable and fast-changing circumstances, and adroit management of fluid assets and capabilities. Others have argued for stable structures, long-term competencies, and fixed configurations of business-specific resources. Few have combined such traits into a powerful, integrative approach.[3] They have often missed the importance of managing the tension.

Because of the disparate advice managers have received—either be mobile or focused and disciplined—they have to be confused. The advice does not completely add up. For practicing managers who are trying to figure out what to do, this advice is not that useful. No one has combined the two sides and said that all of these elements are needed to be truly successful.

These books that have claimed to provide the secrets of sustained competitive advantage also base their conclusions on limited evidence, anecdotal in nature, which often comes from the consulting or other practical experience of the authors. *Execution* by Bossidy and Charan, for instance, is derived from the experiences of the authors, who happen to be a CEO and consultant. They refer to a few well-known companies like Dell, Johnson & Johnson, and Xerox. Slywotzky, Wise, and Weber refer to a number of well-known examples like Wal-Mart, Dell, Southwest Airlines, and Nucor. Similarly, Christensen and Raynor rely on firms like Wal-Mart, Southwest Airlines, Nucor, Schwab, Canon, Sony, Honda, Apple Computer, IBM, and Xerox. Godin's examples are unusual and include such stalwarts as Krispy Kreme, Logitech, and Curad.

Except for Finkelstein and Sull, none of the authors pay much attention to losers. Comparisons of companies that have done well with those that have not also are rare. *What Really Works* by Nohria and Joyce does compare firms that realized a return of 945 percent over a 10-year period with firms that yielded a 62 percent return. And *Good to Great* by Collins is a comparison of 10 firms with superior 15-year performance and 10 firms that did not do as well. Collins reports that the cumulative stock returns of the winners beat the general stock market by an average of seven times in 15 years. However, these gains were ephemeral. From 1992 to 2002, the *Good to Great* companies did not fare particularly well, as shown in Table A.3.

Given these limitations, is it a huge surprise that the companies selected as examples by the authors of these books often collapsed? Peters and Waterman's "excellent" companies included such giants of perpetual high performance as Digital Equipment, Westinghouse, Kodak, Wang Laboratories, Polaroid, and Kmart. Did Collins and Porras do any better with McDonnell Douglas, Ford Motor, Disney, and again Westinghouse? Collins is not the only author who has had to deal with the problem of firms' changing fortunes. Foster and Kaplan heaped abundant praise on Enron and Corning, whose good runs dissipated because of scandal and the telecom bust. Is it like the curse of being on the cover of *Sports Illustrated*? After receiving so much favorable attention, a company is bound to fail? Most writers on high-performing companies pick well-known firms, whose ultimate success is questionable. This book, in contrast, picks less well-known firms whose success in the period studied was more enduring.

Table A.1 Business Books That Primarily Emphasize Agility*

Book	Main Argument About Agility
Clayton Christensen and Michael Raynor, *The Innovator's Solution: Creating and Sustaining Successful Growth*	Large companies lack agility; they almost exclusively make bets on incremental improvements.
	They fail to enter markets perceived as undesirable, leaving this space uncontested because of what their executives believe to be the small profit margins.
	They are too concerned about the core competencies that have served them well in the past.
	Rapidly improving value requires breakthrough improvements; smaller, fringe companies tend to understand this better than large companies.
	The small, fringe companies often are able to provide simple, convenient, low-cost products that appeal to less-demanding customers; therefore, they are able to gain entry and to challenge dominant firms.
	Ultimately, the fringe companies move these innovations to the mainstream and pose formidable challenges to the established firms.
Sydney Finkelstein, *Why Smart Executives Fail and What You Can Learn from Their Mistakes*	Managers doggedly pursue the wrong goals based on their past successes.
	Their failure comes from a lack of agility—an inability to see and pursue new opportunities.
	This is reinforced by a reliance on the wrong type of metrics, which they use in evaluation.
	Managers' lack of clear or realistic understanding of themselves and their companies hold them back.

Table A.1 Business Books That Primarily Emphasize Agility*

Book	Main Argument About Agility
Richard Foster and Sarah Kaplan, *Creative Destruction: Why Companies That Are Built to Last Underperform the Market and How to Successfully Transform Them*	Success depends on the ability to cast aside the value propositions of the past for the value propositions of the future.
	Too many managers ignore important changes that are taking place in the external market; they focus on operational excellence to the exclusion of almost anything else.
	Too many managers fail to make the rapid strategic adjustments that are needed for their firms' growth and survival.
	Most are culturally locked in to their established routines.
	They have a comfort zone that makes them unwilling to recognize that business models mature and become outmoded.
	Survival depends on an understanding of this type of discontinuity—the regular creation and destruction of whole industries.
	Most growth comes from the emergence of fast-moving new entrants in the new industries.
Seth Godin, *Transform Your Business by Being Remarkable*	Rapid movement to new markets is needed to set a company's products apart.
	The main challenge that managers must meet is to create remarkable products; these products should be either "horrible" or "amazing."
	The products should be absolutely unique and different.
	The main task of management is to strive continuously to maintain the uniqueness of their products.
	Managers must keep innovating; standing still is a sure-fired route to failure.
	Managers have to keep shifting their business models for sake of rapid product development.
	"Every purple cow fades unless it figures out how to be remarkable again."
Mary Kwak and David Yoffie, *Turning Your Competitor's Strength to Your Advantage* [4]	Masters of movement continuously have shown that they have the ability to outmaneuver their opponents.
	Small corporate "Davids" often have been able to defeat much larger corporate "Goliaths" because they are faster moving and more agile than their opponents.

Table A.1 Business Books That Primarily Emphasize Agility*

Book	Main Argument About Agility
	To succeed, the upstarts manage to throw their competitors off balance, which neutralizes the competitors' initial advantage.
	The upstarts also must maintain their own balance to survive the inevitable counterattacks that the competitors they have attacked will launch.
	They have to go for the kill when they have the leverage to pin their opponents.
Adrian Slywotzky, *Value Migration*	The firms that succeed make the right moves; by making the right moves, they create value.
	"Business chess is a game… (of) constant shuttling between a focus on the current move and imagining the next several moves out."
	Managers must make these moves to avoid value loss and preempt the next growth cycle.
	They must move from obsolete to new business designs; at least seven patterns of value migration exist.
	Each pattern rests on an understanding of the customer and of innovative business designs.
	Managers must understand market value, customer priorities, and future industry positions to make the right moves.
Adrian Slywotzky, Richard Wise, and Karl Weber, *How to Grow Markets When Markets Don't* [5]	Corporate mindset, culture, history, leadership, and commitments reduce the ability that managers have to recognize and pursue new opportunities.
	To succeed, managers should follow a sequence of moves to differentiate their company's offerings.
	The aim should be to help customers make better decisions about their lives.
	Companies better serve customers through innovations that address the hassles and issues surrounding a product, rather than making improvements in the product.
	Managers should start by working on customers' most urgent problems, the issues customers constantly wrestle with, and the headaches they have.
	They should not rely on classic product-focused strategies that involve simple product extensions, enhancements, and even product breakthroughs, because even these can be easily copied.

Table A.1 Business Books That Primarily Emphasize Agility*

	Winning moves come from having maverick ideas about product use.
	Managers should focus on the customer value chain—how the customer spends time on and off the job.
	Managers should look for bottlenecks, repetition, information gaps, and missed opportunities in the customer's value chain.
	They should try to improve the customer's cost structure and reduce complexity in using products.
	They also should speed products to the market and reduce risk and volatility in their use.
	Donald Sull, Revival of the Fittest: *Why Good*
Companies Go Bad and How Great Managers Remake Them	Inflexible commitments create inertia that prevents adjustments in business formulas that at one time were successful but are no longer so when competitive situations change.
	Managers should not respond to the future by doing more of what worked well for them in the past.
	They must make creative adjustments to the new situation.
	The essence of these readjustments is to move away from old commitments and to create new ones.
* The list is alphabetical by the authors' last name.	

Table A.2 Business Books That Primarily Emphasize Discipline and Focus*

Book	Main Argument About Discipline	Main Argument About Focus
Larry Bossidy and Ram Charan, *Execution: The Discipline of Getting Things Done*	Discipline is integral to strategy execution.	Stay close to customers.
	Getting the job done is critical.	
	Make sure operations people understand the plans.	
	Link people, strategy, and operations in a systematic process.	
	Tenaciously follow through.	
	Hold people accountable.	
	Reward performers.	
	Get rid of or help nonperformers.	
	Continuously close the gap between results promised and delivered.	

Table A.2 Business Books That Primarily Emphasize Discipline and Focus

Book	Main Argument About Discipline	Main Argument About Focus
James Collins, *Good to Great*	Develop a culture of discipline. Show a fanatical dedication and passion to be the best in the world. Core ideology (principles) should never be jettisoned in the interests of expediency or in times of stress. Straightforward economic metrics like revenue per employee or cost per store should be used. Self-effacing leaders outperform flamboyant ones.	Focus on what drives the economic engine. Do not permit wavering or wandering. Be a hedgehog—go for depth rather than breadth. Do what you can do best, not what you want to do. Make continuous improvements that are evolutionary and not revolutionary in nature. Those who launch radical change programs and wrenching restructurings almost certainly fail.
Robert Kaplan and David Norton, *The Balanced Scorecard: Translating Strategy into Action*	Communicate clearly and consistently. Tie strategy to implementation. Link performance and incentives to outcomes. Execute by connecting goals to resources. Motivate employees to follow company plans. "If you can't measure it, you can't manage it."	"To develop advantage, deepen a firm's ties with its current customers.
Donald Mitchell, *The Ultimate Competitive Advantage: Secrets of Continually Developing a More Profitable Business Model*	Never let up. Create a stronghold that prevents entry by competitors.	Outsource to be more focused on profitable endeavors. Increase customer intimacy to understand customer needs and wants. Customize offerings to make them more closely match customer needs. Minimize or eliminate unnecessary costs that burden the customer. Modify pricing or pricing perceptions to increase profitability. Add benefits to the customer's to whom your customers sell. Add benefits by working with your customer's partners and suppliers. Continually refine and reinvent your firm's business model.

Table A.2 Business Books That Primarily Emphasize Discipline and Focus

Book	Main Argument About Discipline	Main Argument About Focus
Nitin Nohria, William Joyce, and Bruce Roberson, *What Really Works: The 4+2 Formula for Sustained Business Success*	Clearly communicate the firm's strategy. Develop and maintain flawless execution. Support high performance metrics. Simplify the work to reduce unnecessary bureaucracy. Deliver precisely what customers want. Continually improve the firm's productivity. Keep leaders and directors highly committed to the firm and its goals.	Devise and maintain a focused strategy. Keep growing the core business. Build business around a clear value proposition for customers. Base strategy upon what customers, partners, and investors want. Fine-tune the strategy to changes in the marketplace. Only innovate if you're absolutely certain of industry disruption. In general, beware of the unfamiliar; stick to the knitting.
C.K. Prahalad and Venkat Ramaswany, *The Future of Capitalism: Co-Creating Unique Value with Customers*		Allow customers to design their own individualized products. Facilitate shift to experience environments. Deliver value to customers through personalized interaction (cocreation). Dialogue with customers to get insights into their mindset about product risks and benefits. Make customers part of the corporate competence base. Build customer satisfaction and trust. Endeavor to create a unique customer experience across multiple channels and transactions.
Michael Treacy and Fred Wiersman, *The Discipline of Market Leaders: Choose Your Customers, Narrow Your Focus, Dominate Your Market*	Pursue three value disciplines—operational excellence, product leadership, and customer intimacy. Obsolete your own products before competitors.	Do not cater to a wide market. Cater to specific customers whose desires you know well and with whom you have a trusting relationship. Be intimate with a select group of customers. Focus on no-frills products when demand is huge and customers care more about price than choice. Focus on best-performing

Table A.2 Business Books That Primarily Emphasize Discipline and Focus

Book	Main Argument About Discipline	Main Argument About Focus
		products when you have ideas for highly desirable, previously unknown products.
Michael Treacy, *Double Digit Growth: How Great Companies Achieve It No Matter What*	Commit to a conscious, managed set of strategies. Commit to superior value. Use gross profits as the measure of value creation for customers.	Leverage existing advantage. Take small bites. Spread your risk with a portfolio of small initiatives. Derive growth from steady, one-step-at-a-time progress rather than high-risk, bet-the-company transformation. Retain your existing customer base; sell more to that base because it's harder to acquire a new base. Don't drift too far outside your area of expertise; expand mainly in adjacent markets.
Chris Zook, *Profit from the Core*	Build market power in a well-defined core. Don't leave your core unprotected. Do not make errors. Systematically block competitors. Keep costs low for the benefit of customers.	From focus comes growth. By narrowing your scope, create expansion. A well-defined core business is key to competitive advantage. Realize the full potential of your core by moving with caution to businesses that are only adjacent to your core. Avoid misadventures of growth. Only expand or redefine your core when you're forced to in times of extreme turbulence.
Chris Zook, *Beyond the Core*	Employ methods to tilt odds in your company's favor and control the cost of failure. Identify "adjacencies" in which you're already participating and assess how you're doing (market share, profitability, investment).	Identify adjacencies close by that you are considering or that you might have rejected. Identify other adjacencies that might seem promising because competitors or new entrants are moving to these spaces or because technology or other factors have opened them up.

Table A.2 Business Books That Primarily Emphasize Discipline and Focus

Book	Main Argument About Discipline	Main Argument About Focus
		Put together combinations of "adjacency moves" into areas related to your core, such as new product lines or new channels of distribution.
		Keeps risk down; by moving in well-trod paths close to your core business, there is less risk than by expanding using other growth methods.
		Competitive advantage comes from what the firm already knows and does best.
		Push boundaries, but just of your core business.
		Make small improvements in these dimensions.
* The list is alphabetical by the authors' last name.		

Table A.3 Collins' Good to Great Companies: 1992 to 2002

Company	Industry	Number of Companies in Industry	One-Year Surplus/Deficit Relative to Industry (%)	Three-Year Surplus/Deficit Relative to Industry (%)	Five-Year Surplus/Deficit Relative to Industry (%)	Ten-Year Surplus/Deficit Relative to Industry (%)
Abbott Laboratories	Medical supplies	15	–3.2	–6.1	1.2	1.4
Circuit City	Specialty retailers	25	61.2	–10.1	–11.2	–1.9
Fannie Mae	Diversified financial	24	–6.7	–15.6	–8.1	–5.5
Gillette (bought by P&G in 2004)	Cosmetics	5	2.0	–12.5	–12.0	–4.3
Kimberly Clark	Nondurable household products	6	–27.0	8.2	–3.7	–2.7
Kroger	Food retailers and wholesalers	9	–43.7	–12.4	–2.7	3.3
Nucor	Mining and metals	7	23.3	7.0	7.6	5.7
Pitney Bowes	Office equipment	3	–155.3	.2	18.5	7.4
Walgreens	Drug-based retailers	8	–29.0	2.8	19.9	10.5
Wells Fargo	Banks	60	–30.6	1.0	3.1	–0.1

Appendix B

USING THE STOCK MARKET AS AN INDICATOR OF PERFORMANCE

Recent analysts of sustained competitive advantage (SCA) in the strategic management literature increasingly rely on the stock market as a measure.[1] Geoffrey Moore goes so far as to say that the stock market is nothing more than an "information system about competitive advantage." He holds that investments in companies are based on the extent to which they are able to achieve competitive advantage, and that capital flows to firms that have competitive advantage and moves from firms that do not have it.[2]

But how good is the stock market as a measure? It is only one of two main indicators that typically are used to analyze corporate performance. Though companies have economic, legal, and ethical obligations to stakeholders including customers, suppliers, employees, and communities, shareholders own the firm and are burdened with the risk if the firm should fail. Legally, a firm's main obligation is to its shareholders. Stock market data is supposed to project what your company is likely to do in the future. It represents the present value of forecastable future earnings discounted for risk. The other regularly used measure of corporate performance comes from accounting data. Unlike stock market data, accounting data is based on the firm's past performance. Shareholders use accounting measures to determine if companies can achieve earnings objectives. Managers use it to evaluate strategic plans, assess product lines, appraise business units, and examine prospective acquisitions. But accounting data has its limits. Despite the best efforts of the accounting profession and legal authorities to prevent fraud, accounting data can be skewed. The regularity with which firms restate their earnings is astonishing. More than 10 percent of firms restate them every five years because of accounting irregularities. Firms can manipulate accounting results by engaging in such practices as recording revenue too soon or too late, recording revenue of questionable quality or of a bogus nature, boosting income with one-time gains, shifting current expenses to later or earlier periods, and failing to record liabilities or improperly reducing them.

Nor is the stock market a perfect indicator of firm performance. Without adequate accounting data, investors can be fooled. Investors do not always have the analytical capability to accurately assess a company's performance. Stock prices therefore can be inaccurate. Stock market data depends on investor psychology. After the stock market meltdown of the past few years, it should be obvious that investors are not entirely rational. They get caught in fads. They are swayed by irrational fears and enthusiasms. In the short term, the market is likely to be skewed by such factors, and a meaningful signal of what is happening might not emerge. In the long-term, however, distorting effects tend to cancel themselves out, and a more reliable signal begins to emerge. This difference between the short and long term is important because the analysis in this book is based on ten years of stock market results. If short-term stock market returns are not entirely good indicators of firm performance, a firm's long-term valuation relative to its competitors is more likely to be so. The rank of a company in its industry says something fundamental about how well it is doing against its main competitors.

Appendix C

ADDITIONAL DATA ON THE COMPANIES

Table C.1   Number of Companies and Average Returns: Industries With and Without Winning and Losing Firms

Industries with Big Winners or Big Losers	Number of Companies	Five-Year Average Return	Industries without Big Winners or Big Losers	Number of Companies	Five-Year Average Return
Aerospace: WINNING firms 2, LOSING firms 2	12	10.7	Advanced industrial equipment	12	14.8
Airlines: WINNING firms 2, LOSING firms 2	6	10.9	Advanced medical devices	9	24.6
Auto and parts: WINNING firms 2, LOSING firms 3	13	4.7	Advertising	7	25.1
Banks: WINNING firms 1, LOSING firms 3	60	14.1	Air freight	3	28.3
Biotech: WINNING firms 1, LOSING firms 2	38	77.1	Building material	6	11.5
Broadcasting: LOSING firms 1	18	32.3	Chemical commodities	3	2
Casinos: WINNING firms 1, LOSING firms 1	6	10.5	Clothing	3	8
Chemical specialty: WINNING firms 1, LOSING firms 1	17	6.3	Communication wireless	9	19.2
Communication technology: WINNING firms 1	31	14	Consumer services	11	7.6
Communication fixed line: LOSING firms 1	12	8.9	Cosmetics	5	10.4
Computers: LOSING firms 1	20	16.6	Consumer electronics	1	10.6
Containers and packaging: WINNING firms 2	8	3.7	Diversified technology services	6	11.5
Diversified financials: LOSING firms 2	24	26.2	Distillers and breweries	4	19.5
Electric components: WINNING firms 1, LOSING firms 1	14	14.2	Entertainment	3	22.6
Food products: WINNING firms 1, LOSING firms 4	18	8.8	Footwear	3	7.4
Food retail: LOSING firms 1	9	15.1	Furnishings and appliances	9	16.4
Forest products: LOSING firms 1	4	7.2	Heavy construction	2	22.8
Healthcare: LOSING firms 2	26	13.1	Heavy machinery	2	6.6
House products durables: WINNING firms 1, LOSING firms 2	5	5.9	Home construction	8	30.5
Industrial services: WINNING firms 2	36	14.3	House products nondurable	6	10.4
Industrial diversified: LOSING firms 3	19	10.2	Insurance full	6	13.7
Insurance, life: WINNING firms 1, LOSING firms 1	12	6.1	Internet services	3	65

Table C.1 Number of Companies and Average Returns: Industries With and Without Winning and Losing Firms

Industries with Big Winners or Big Losers	Number of Companies	Five-Year Average Return	Industries without Big Winners or Big Losers	Number of Companies	Five-Year Average Return
Insurance property and casualty: WINNING firms 3, LOSING firms 3	32	14.7	Land transportation	3	17.5
Medical supplies: LOSING firms 1	15	17.8	Lodging	4	-4.4
Oil secondary: WINNING firms 1, LOSING firms 4	21	5.8	Mining and metals	7	-5.6
Oil drilling: LOSING firms 1	22	4.8	Office equipment	3	-8.9
Pharmaceuticals: WINNING firms 1, LOSING firms 2	20	27.9	Oil company major	6	7.9
Pollution control: WINNING firms 1, LOSING firms 1	4	9.5	Paper products	5	3.7
Publishing: LOSING firms 2	14	11.5	Pipelines	3	14.4
Recreational: WINNING firms 1, LOSING firms 1	9	7.9	Railroads	4	-1.2
Restaurants: LOSING firms 2	11	20.1	Real estate	35	9.8
Retail apparel: LOSING firms 3	12	23.7	Retail drug	8	8.1
Retail broad: WINNING firms 1, LOSING firms 1	12	12.1	Savings and loan	13	14.6
Retail special: WINNING firms 1	25	23	Tobacco	3	8.7
Securities: LOSING firms 1	20	26.3	Trucking	3	12.7
Soft drinks: LOSING firms 1	5	4.3	Utilities, water	2	20.7
Software: LOSING firms 2	43	18.4			
Toys: WINNING firms 1, LOSING firms 2	4	12.2			
Semiconductors: WINNING firms 1, LOSING firms 1	41	25.4			
Utilities, electric: WINNING firms 1, LOSING firms 2	55	10.4			
Utilities, gas: WINNING firms 1	7	10.4			
Average	19.4	15.1	Average	5.7	12.7
Standard Deviation	13.4	12.3	Standard Deviation	6.2	13.7

Table C.2 Revenue and Employees of Winners: 2002

Winner	2002 Revenues ($ Billions)	2002 Number of Employees	Winner	2002 Revenues ($ Billions)	2002 Number of Employees
1. Titan	1.57	9,974	17. Concord EFS	2.17	2,640
2. Alliant Tech	1.8	11,600	18. Fiserv	2.28	19,400
3. Skywest	0.88	4,952	19. Lincoln National	4.64	5,830
4. Southwest	5.52	33,705	20. Brown & Brown	0.57	3,517
5. Gentex	1.14	8,600	21. Gallagher	1.35	7,359
6. Johnson Controls	20.1	111,000	22. White Mountain	3.86	5,055
7. Commerce Banc	1.26	1,600	23. Murphy Oil	3.98	2,995
8. IDEC (now Biogen IDEC)	1.1	3,727	24. Forest Labs	1.6	3,731
9. International Game Technology	1.94	6,200	25. Donaldson	1.29	9,409
10. Cabot	1.56	4,500	26. Harley-Davidson	4.09	9,100
11. Amphenol	1.32	13,900	27. Family Dollar	4.16	31,100
12. Ball	3.86	12,635	28. Best Buy	19.6	72,000
13. Bemis	2.37	12,000	29. Activision	0.95	1,214
14. SPX	5.05	23,738	30. Semtech	0.19	587
15. Dreyer's	1.34	4,600	31. RGS Energy (now Energy East)	4.5	6,288
16. Stanley Works	2.59	15,000	32. Equitable Resources	1.11	1,400
			Average	**3.49**	**14,496**
			Standard Deviation	4.61	22,697

Table C.3 Revenue and Employees of Losers: 2002

Loser	2002 Revenues ($ Billions)	2002 Number of Employees	Loser	2002 Revenues ($ Billions)	2002 Number of Employees
1. Goodrich	4.2	22,900	33. FMC	1.85	5,500
2. Raytheon	16.96	76,400	34. Conseco	6.15	14,300
3. AMR	17.3	105,500	35. Safeco	7.01	11,000
4. Delta	13.31	75,100	36. CNA Financial	12.2	12,100
5. TRW	10.6	60,000	37. American Financial Group	3.75	9,000
6. Goodyear	14	92,000	38. Bausch & Lomb	1.82	11,500
7. Dana	10	63,100	39. Amerada Hess	11.93	11,662
8. Old National	1	3,019	40. Kerr-McGee	3.74	4,407
9. Bank One	22	73,685	41. Forest Oil	1.36	458
10. KeyCorp	6.14	20,437	42. Burlington Resources	2.96	2,003
11. Alkermes	.0	436	43. Halliburton	12.58	83,000
12. VerTex	1	720	44. Merck	51.79	77,300
13. Disney	25.33	112,000	45. Pharmacia	16.93	43,000
14. Mandalay Resort	2.43	33,000	46. Waste Management	11.14	53,000
15. IMC Global	2.31	5,276	47. Belo	1.42	7,700
16. Broadwing	2.24	5,400	48. Reader's Digest	2.37	5,000
17. Compaq (acquired by HP)	56.59	141,000	49. Eastman Kodak	12.84	70,000
18. Franklin Resources	2.52	6,700	50. Wendy's	2.73	26,200
19. Country Wide	8.88	25,355	51. McDonald's	15.41	413,000
20. Cooper Industries	3.33	23,024	52. Gap	14.46	165,000
21. Conagra	27.63	89,000	53. Nordstrom	5.98	44,000
22. ADM	23.45	24,746	54. Saks	5.91	55,000
23. Campbell Soup	6.13	25,000	55. Kmart	32.77	212,000
24. Tyson	23.67	120,000	56. T. Rowe Price	6.03	3,783
25. Winn-Dixie	12.943	76,700	57. Coca-Cola Co.	19.56	56,000
26. Georgia Pacific	23.27	61,000	58. Novell	1.13	6,233
27. HealthSouth	4.31	38,577	59. Parametric	0.742	3,500
28. Humana	11.26	13,500	60. Hasbro	2.81	7,200
29. Snap-On	2.11	12,900	61. Mattel	4.89	25,000
30. Newell Rubber	7.45	47,000	62. LSI Logic	1.82	5,534
31. Honeywell	22.27	108,000	63. Constellation Energy	4.7	8,700

Table C.3 Revenue and Employees of Losers: 2002

Loser	2002 Revenues ($ Billions)	2002 Number of Employees	Loser	2002 Revenues ($ Billions)	2002 Number of Employees
32. Textron	10.66	49,000	64. CMS Energy	6.68	11,510
			Average	**10.66**	**48,032**
			Standard Deviation	**11.3**	**64,158**

Table C.4 Winning Companies: Using the Fortune 1000 Industry Classification. April 14, 2003

Firm	Ten-Year Average Annual Return (%)	Industry	Median Return (%)	Firm	Ten-Year Average Annual Return (%)	Industry	Me Re (
Titan	13	Computer and data services	15	Concord EFS	28	Computer and data services	I
Alliant Tech	22	Aerospace and defense	12	Fiserv	21	Computer and data services	I
Southwest	14	Airlines	−8.0	Lincoln National	9	Insurance, life and health	9
Johnson Controls	16	Motor vehicles and parts	3	Murphy Oil	14	Petroleum refining	8
Cabot	17	Chemicals	6	Forest Labs	26	Pharmaceutical	I
Ball	15	Packaging, containers	4	Harley-Davidson	26	Transportation equipment	4
Bemis	10	Containers and packaging	4	Family Dollar	17	General merchandisers	
SPX	16	Electronic components	10	Best Buy	27	Specialty retailers	9
Dreyer's	20	Food products	7	Stanley Works	20	Household and personal products	

Table C.5 Losing Companies: Using the Fortune 1000 Industry Classification. April 14, 2003

Firm	Ten-Year Average Annual Return (%)	Industry	Median Return (%)	Firm	Ten-Year Average Annual Return (%)	Industry	Median Return (%)
Goodrich	1	Aerospace and defense	12	FMC	0	Chemicals	6
Raytheon	4	Aerospace and defense	12	Conseco	-43	Insurance life and health	9
AMR	-8	Airlines	-8	Safeco	6	Insurance, property and casualty	12
Delta	-7	Airlines	-8	American Financial Group	2	Insurance, property and casualty	12
Goodyear	-13	Motor vehicles and parts	3	Bausch & Lomb	-2	Medical products	11
Dana	-4	Motor vehicles and parts	3	Amerada Hess	3	Petroleum refining	8
				Kerr-McGee	3	Oil secondary	4
Bank One	5	Commercial banks	15	Burlington Resources	2	Mining, crude oil production	4
KeyCorp	9	Commercial banks	15	Halliburton	5	Oil and gas equipment services	13
Disney	2	Entertainment	7	Merck	13	Pharmaceutical	15
Mandalay Resort	-2	Hotels, casinos, resorts	12	Pharmacia	17	Pharmaceutical	15
IMC Global	-6	Chemicals	6	Waste Management	5	Waste management	6.5
Broadwing	1	Telecommunications	7	Belo	9	Publishing, printing	8
Franklin Resources	12	Securities	19	Reader's Digest	-10	Publishing	8
Country Wide	14	Diversified financials	15	Eastman Kodak	4	Scientific, photographic	5
Cooper Industries	11	Motor vehicles and parts	16	Wendy's	9	Food services	6
Conagra	7	Food consumer products	7	McDonald's	4	Food services	6
ADM	2	Food production	3	Gap	13	Specialty retailers	9
Campbell Soup	4	Food product	7	Nordstrom	1	General merchandisers	3

Table C.5 Losing Companies: Using the Fortune 1000 Industry Classification. April 14, 2003

Firm	Ten-Year Average Annual Return (%)	Industry	Median Return (%)	Firm	Ten-Year Average Annual Return (%)	Industry	Median Return (%)
Tyson	-3	Food production	3	Saks	0	General merchandisers	3
Winn-Dixie	-6	Food and drug stores	5	Kmart	-37	General merchandisers	3
Georgia Pacific	-1	Forest and paper products	4	Coca-Cola Co.	9	Beverages	16
HealthSouth	-4	Healthcare	9	Novell	-19	Computer software	13
Humana	4	Healthcare	9	Hasbro	-1	Toys, sporting goods	2
Snap-On	6	Industrial and farm equipment	10	Mattel	5	Toys, sporting goods	2
Newell Rubber	6	Home equipment furnishings	8	LSI Logic	8	Semiconductors	13
Honeywell	7	Aerospace and defense	12	Constellation Energy	7	Utilities, gas and electric	8
Textron	0.6	Industrial diversified	10.2	CMS Energy	-2	Utilities, gas and electric	8

Appendix D

PATTERNS OF WINNING AND LOSING COMPANIES

AGILITY
- Keeps working closely with customers
- Moves toward specialty markets
- Has become a consolidator
- Has diversified into new market

DISCIPLINE
- Use of systems such as advanced computer aided design & manufacturing, statistical process control, and just-in-time inventory
- Reliance on globalization and long-term supply agreements
- Expertise at selecting acquistion targets and giving them autonomy

FOCUS
- Extending collaborative solution providing activities into new domains
- Capitalizing on overseas market growth

SWEET SPOT
CODESIGN
- Niche marketing
- Leverage with suppliers and customers
- Full integration

Figure D.1 Amphenol's pattern of success.

AGILITY
- Collaborates with customers
- Finds new industries
- Purchases diverse firms
- Acquires varied products

DISCIPLINE
- Relies on value improvement process (VIP) with the goal being to increase economic value added (EVA)
- Has a formal process for consolidating acquired businesses

FOCUS
- Derives advantage from solutions, not patented technologies
- Makes acquisitions to extend global presence

SWEET SPOT
CODESIGN
- High potential niches
- Multiple growth platforms

Figure D.2 SPX's pattern of success.

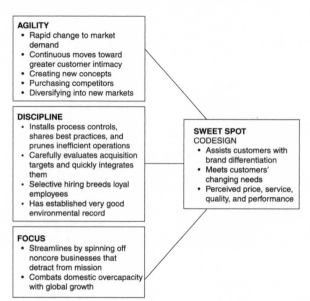

Figure D.3 Ball's pattern of success.

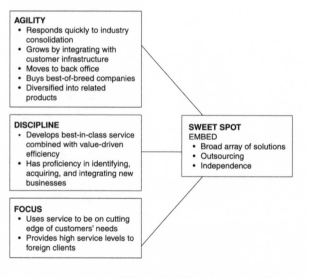

Figure D.4 Fiserv's pattern of success.

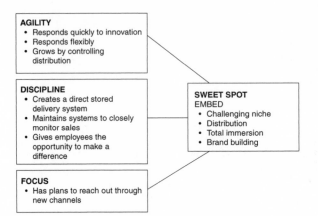

AGILITY
- Responds quickly to innovation
- Responds flexibly
- Grows by controlling distribution

DISCIPLINE
- Creates a direct stored delivery system
- Maintains systems to closely monitor sales
- Gives employees the opportunity to make a difference

FOCUS
- Has plans to reach out through new channels

SWEET SPOT
EMBED
- Challenging niche
- Distribution
- Total immersion
- Brand building

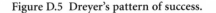

Figure D.5 Dreyer's pattern of success.

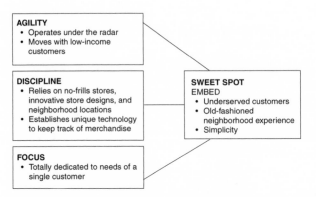

AGILITY
- Operates under the radar
- Moves with low-income customers

DISCIPLINE
- Relies on no-frills stores, innovative store designs, and neighborhood locations
- Establishes unique technology to keep track of merchandise

FOCUS
- Totally dedicated to needs of a single customer

SWEET SPOT
EMBED
- Underserved customers
- Old-fashioned neighborhood experience
- Simplicity

Figure D.6 Family Dollar's pattern of success.

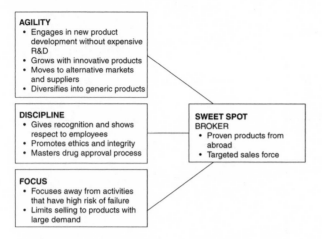

Figure D.7 Forest Lab's pattern of success.

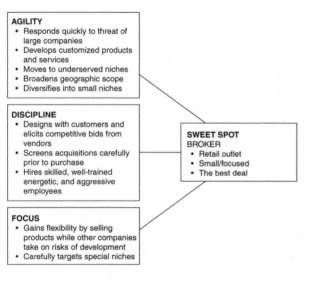

Figure D.8 Brown & Brown's pattern of success.

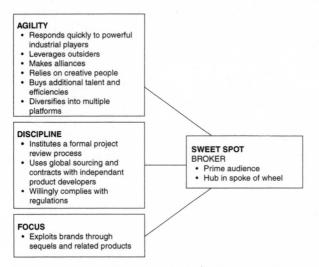

AGILITY
- Responds quickly to powerful industrial players
- Leverages outsiders
- Makes alliances
- Relies on creative people
- Buys additional talent and efficiencies
- Diversifies into multiple platforms

DISCIPLINE
- Institutes a formal project review process
- Uses global sourcing and contracts with independant product developers
- Willingly complies with regulations

FOCUS
- Exploits brands through sequels and related products

SWEET SPOT
BROKER
- Prime audience
- Hub in spoke of wheel

Figure D.9 Activision's pattern of success.

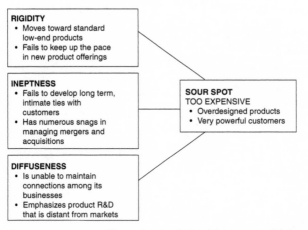

RIGIDITY
- Moves toward standard low-end products
- Fails to keep up the pace in new product offerings

INEPTNESS
- Fails to develop long term, intimate ties with customers
- Has numerous snags in managing mergers and acquisitions

DIFFUSENESS
- Is unable to maintain connections among its businesses
- Emphasizes product R&D that is distant from markets

SOUR SPOT
TOO EXPENSIVE
- Overdesigned products
- Very powerful customers

Figure D.10 LSI Logic's pattern of failure.

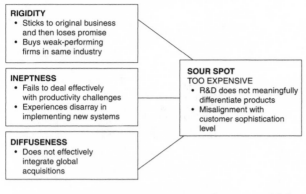

Figure D.11 Snap-On's pattern of failure.

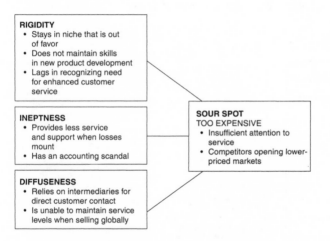

Figure D.12 Parametric's pattern of failure.

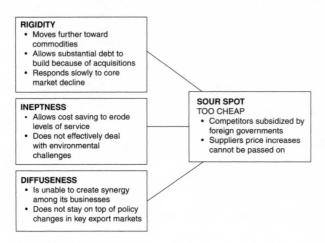

Figure D.13 IMC's pattern of failure.

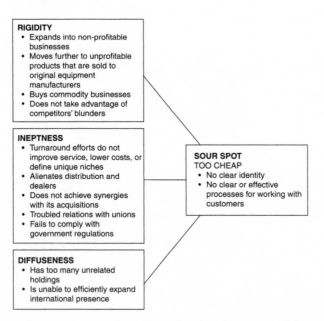

Figure D.14 Goodyear's pattern of failure.

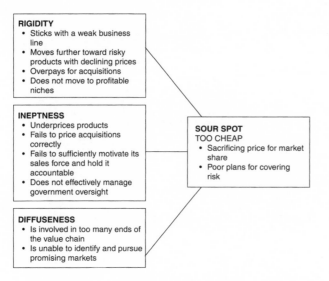

Figure D.15 Safeco's pattern of failure.

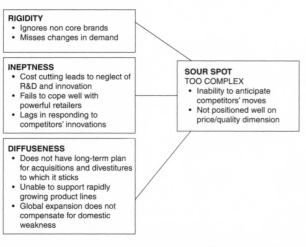

Figure D.16 Campbell's pattern of failure.

RIGIDITY
- Keeps expansion in line with growth in sales
- Too far removed from core customers
- Does not anticipate demand

INEPTNESS
- Loses touch with fashion
- Loses touch with core customers

DIFFUSENESS
- Broadens scope of operations rather than simplifies
- Deals with complications of managing many diverse brands

SOUR SPOT
TOO COMPLEX
- Quality and prices not in customer's comfort zone
- Too complex business model

Figure D.17 The Gap's pattern of failure.

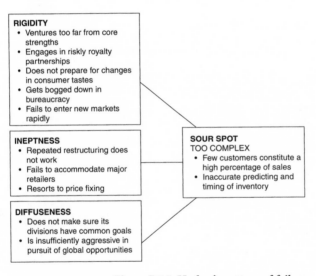

RIGIDITY
- Ventures too far from core strengths
- Engages in riskly royalty partnerships
- Does not prepare for changes in consumer tastes
- Gets bogged down in bureaucracy
- Fails to enter new markets rapidly

INEPTNESS
- Repeated restructuring does not work
- Fails to accommodate major retailers
- Resorts to price fixing

DIFFUSENESS
- Does not make sure its divisions have common goals
- Is insufficiently aggressive in pursuit of global opportunities

SOUR SPOT
TOO COMPLEX
- Few customers constitute a high percentage of sales
- Inaccurate predicting and timing of inventory

Figure D.18 Hasbro's pattern of failure.

ACKNOWLEDGMENTS

Adam Fremeth, a Ph.D. student at Carlson School of Management, helped with the last chapter comparing Safeco and SPX. I would also like to acknowledge the assistance of the three fine reviewers for the publisher: Scott Shane, Russ Hall, and Louis Columbus. I would like to thank Jim Boyd for sticking with me on this project—he was terrific in many ways—and Jerry Wind from Wharton for his excellent comments and suggestions for making improvements and for sharpening the argument. I would also like to acknowledge some of the people who made helpful comments when I presented this material: Jay Barney from Ohio State University; Joseph Mahoney from the University of Illinois; Myles Shaver and Isaac Fox from the Carlson School of Management; Gerald Keim and William Glick from Arizona State; Niron Hishai, Avi Meschulach, and Dror Zuckerman from Hebrew University; Blian N. Sullivan and Jaepil Choi from Hong Kong Technical University; Avi Fiegenbaum, Eitan Naveh, and Ella Miron from the Technion; Shmuel Ellis from Tel Aviv University; and Rob Zenilman from the Target Corporation. I learned a great deal from Richard Pula and other members of the management team of Power Electric Company with whom I discussed the ideas in this book. Will Mitchell of Duke University was very encouraging when he read an early draft. Joseph Goldman of the Carlson School of Management wrote very interesting comments upon reading a draft. Of course, I would like to acknowledge my family, who support and continue to tolerate me: my patient wife, Judy; my son David, who is a creative writer; and my son Ariel, who will be a University of Chicago student.

The managers who assisted me with the analysis of company pairs, and with Appendix A, and with the validation study are listed here.

Amphenol and LSI Logic

Dave Abbruzzese, Brooks Beaudoin, Gautam Bhatia, James Butler, Maria Cordova, Fritz Sabine, Pam Gaik, Marissa Gautsch, Anne Gustin, Shaan Hamilton, Jennifer Harrison, Dave Hoag, Ryan Jenner, Ryan Kuhn, Aaron Literski, Jennifer Mathiowetz, Chris Morgan, Casey Nelson, Thusuong Nguyen, Daniel Nylin, Michael Pederson, Mike Penake, Ganesh Ram, Melanie Savage, Andy Schleiger, Douglas Shepard, Cliff Smith, Jenny Sopousek, Craig Sprowls, Jolene Stephens, Catherine Stier, Brian Waelti, Jessica Welsch, Sandy Wraley

SPX and Snap-On

Eric Anderson, Tanya Anderson, Pam Aufderhar, Kristine Bettermann, Kingsuk Chakrabarty, Rachelle Clinard, Susan Einess, Michael Fehl, Jingfeng Feng, Nitin Gandhi, Heidi Gottschalk, Dave Gunderson, Christine Gwynn, James Hamilton, Melissa Hermanson, Adam Jacobson, Carmen Johnson, Jeanne Krull, Katy Lintner, Vinita Mahadevan, Kevin McCormack, Jason Micks, David Nathan, Chad Olsen, Steve Panciocco, Julie Parina, Allan Reding, Melissa Robeck, Brian Shepard, Gregg Steiger, Robert Strand, Andre Ziegler

Fiserv and Parametric

Stacy Anderson, Brian Berge, John Berge, Stephanie Dwinal, Chris Enstrom, Dion Evans, Peter Fjellman, Tadiwos Gebeyehu, Michael Groneberg, Amy Haberman, Justin Hanley, Lisa Hedden, Elizabeth Hermsen, Brandon Jackson, Karla Jackson, Matt Jones, Josh Kaiser, Mike Knoihuizen, Julia Kravchenko, Nathan Kreps, Jeff Kurland, Brian Lammers, Stephen Lemmons, Jana Mauck, Brandon Michael, Thor Mickelson, Sjur Midness, Brent Murray, Nathan Ostertag, Janet Pool, Deborah Schreiner, Aric Schroeder, Tony Schuler, Krishna Sridharan, Jim Taller, Dan Wyatt

Campbell and Dreyer's

Ana Aguilar, Kent Ashley, Dave Behrens, Paula Castellanos, Mike Chandler, Alraune Chowdhury, Stephanie Deckas, Irina Fucsalla, Mimi Fung, Kristin Geisler, Laura Grabski, Amy Gruye, Suzanne Haverkamp, Wayne Helm, Dave Hutton, Michael Jung, Khaliun Lkhagvadorj, Cortney Madden, Bryan Maser, Magnus McDowell, Steve Miller, Mark Muckerheide, Jeremy Olson, Ankur Patel, Fred Rio, Kim Sapetta, Christina Schwie, Joe Stoeffler, Kelly Tallaksen, Gary Willenbring

Forest Laboratories and IMC Global

Matt Bentley, Ann Cahoy, Brian Carlson, Kevin Cook, Heather Davis, Rod Dorschner, Claudia Drayton, Edric Funk, Dena Gabrielson, Charlie Gehring, Scott Gilbert, Mathew Greeson, Zachary Herness, Rene Hoogmoed, Josh Howard, Amy Johnson, Sarah Larson, Kimberly Leistikow, Sara Lind, Vanessa Linder, Peter Martin, Jonathan Mooney, Perry Parendo, Amanda Parker, Jason Peterson, Kate Piva, David Sayers, Derek Siebert, Sue Simonett, Tonia Stoffregen, Kris Stouffer, Matthew Thell, Cheryl Trahms, Valerie Vos, Elizabeth Wefel, Jeremy Witikko, Ryan Wilson

Ball and Goodyear

Sarah Adrian, Eric Anderson, Jacob Bjorstrom, Mike Blahnik, Jason Callan, Weng Chan, Caleb Cross, Matt Dickinson, Jeff Dreher, Deborah Erstad, Jodi Gowan, Jacque Graham, Keith Halasy, Lisa Han, Sean Hayward, Liz Hojan-Figge, Nicholas Jejel, Scott Krusemark, Kara McGuire, Matt Myers, Juliette Najjar, Kelly Oertli, Michael Olson, Jolene Panciocco, Brian Peterson, Brad Quello, John Rothering, Michael Schick, Julie Thedens, David Toole, Anthony Welter

Brown & Brown and Safeco

Dyna Boen, Kevin Boren, Jeremy Crawford, Sarah Cumming, Darrell DeMello, John DuBois, Deborah Ekeren, Gretchen Freeman, Matthew Fries, Randall Gambill, Jennifer Gariano, Sanjay Gunasekaran, Amy Halford, Leah Hoeschen, Mandar Khiste, Tim Landro, Pummy Laul, Jeremy Maniak, Rebekka Meyers, Philip Michaelson, Wael Mohammed, Chris Moore, Pohleng Oh, Bill Oswald, Kevin Reiners, Allison Rubow-Seeber, Stephen Thambian, Tim Tripp, Jeremy Wedel

Family Dollar, Inc. and Gap

Jeffrey Arendt, Jon Berg, Brenda Bijnagte, Bridgette Bruce, Richard Cawood, Mark Devore, Jason Dick, Philippe Duliere, Michelle Else, Brooke Evinger, Nate Geske, Joe Goodhart, Scott Grawe, Kirstin Grev, Wilson Hendrawan, Erika Henk, Eric Hoag, Erin Irmiter, Abha Jain, Steve Lacke, Angela Leitz, Angela Miller, Jael North, Wendy Perry, Peter Quimby, Alex Ramirez, Pat Sheahan, Stacey Sventek, Travis Tschepen, Jeremy Voigts, Dave Waddell

Hasbro and Activision

Quinn Arnold, Robbie Burkhart, Henry Chang, Darcey Cremer, Andrew Deming, Sabrina Drigout, Craig Fellman, Troy Fliegel, Marsha Hopwood-Jones, Sarah Keller, Taesung Kim, Tami Koosmann, Rich Macke, Patrick Magnusson, Carissa Otte, Matt Stockhaus, Julian Suwandi, Holly Thomas, Scott Vuong, Eric Wenschlag

Best Sellers (Appendix A)

Edward Anderson, Haider Atwah, Rose Dunn, Brian Dye, Daniel Flaig, Tim Floyd, Ben Hoxie, Brandon Khieu, Christine Krizan, Scott Lafortune, David Lerner, Mark Levdahl, Lori Lorenz, Keith McLaughlin, David Mitchell, Barmack Rassi, Ven Reddy, Beatrize Rivera-Mercado, Angie Roach, Tom Scheppat, Steve Siegel, Steve Smith, David Urke, Myra Urness, Andy Vander Woulde

Validation Study

Steve Aaron, Piyash Agrawal, Joe Allen, Josh Anderson, Karl Anderson, Kirk Anderson, Laura Anderson, Sheldon Anderson, Rebecca Armitage, Eric Aska, David Auerbach, Nadine Babu, Benjamin Balto-Bongard, Brian Bade, Aaron Bangasser, Dan Beenken, Daniel Berg, Scott Berg, Steve Berg, Hiral Bhavani, Greg Blenkush, Megan Boie, Heather Boschke, Jamie Bown, Scott Bradley, Matt Branson, Greg Brinkmeyer, Elliot Brody, Melodie Carlson, James Casey, James Center, Debbie Christenson, Yee Sian Chua, Karen Conway, Leah Cress, Alissa Cunningham, Mark Czarniecki, Kim Dahlquist, Josh Daniels, David DeAzevedo, Stephanie Dobson, Chad Dolly, Brandon Doyle, Jeff Dubois, Rebecca Eddy, James Elasky, Tom Evers, Amy Falls, Cliff Fan, Scott Farwig, Jamie Fontaine, Dave Francis, Lindsay Frank, Ryan French, Clayton Fresk, Jenny Fritz, Yi Fu, Justin Furst, Sarah Galaswyk, Colin Gan, Kristine Gerard, Billy Gibbs, John Green, Tony Grosso, Thomas Gualdoni, Amy Gustafson, Brian Gustafson, Pat Halverson, Kristin Hand, Adam Hankins, Pete Hanson, Beth Heinz, Josh Helmich, Rashi Hemnani, Michael Hoagberg, David Hoffman, Jason Holeman, Lynn Houghtling, Matthew Johnson, Greg Janey, Nick Johnson, Kathryn Jones, Sarah Jones, Nathan Jorgensen, Ed Just, Ben Kanz, Reena Kanodia, Jeff Keller, Gary King, Tom Kluis, Neil Koepke, Kerri Kotsmith, Jason Kraft, Blaine Kriesel, Richard Kronstad, Matthew Krull, Peter Kuechle, Venod Kurpad, Michael Lang, Dale Larson, Ted Lazarkis, Robert Lee, Joseph Lettween, Tim Lieser, Matthew Linabery, Carrie Lindon, Peter Littlewood, Chris Lodermeier, Kevin Lyons, Amy Maciasek, Lee Mackendaz, Erin Magee, Brian Mallari, Ashmin Mansingh, Elisabeth Marvin, Jamie Mattson, Scott Matzke, Ketan Mehta, Rushik Mehta, Melissa Meinke, David Melberg, Ken Merdan, Steve Mickelson, Jason Micks, Brian Mielke, Rob Miriglia, Todd Miron, James Misialek, Nathaniel Mollison, Christina Morgan, Rica Morris, Rut Muglai, Brian Nicholson, Matt Neis, Thong Nguyen, Khurram Nizami, Eric Noren, Kevin O'Brien, Stacia O'Connell, Greg Ogdahl, Andrew Olson, Michael Olson, Paul Olson, Jeff Otos, Anuracha Pal, Sumit Pal, Steve Palks, Janet Paulson, Michael Percic, Matt Picchetti, Brad Pogalz, Nick Pontikos, Jihong Qu, Phil Raines, Matthew Rennerfeldt, Gaston Ray, Tamara Redmond, Tony Riter, Bruce Robb, Erika Roberts, Tricia Roberts, David Ruhland, David Rynders, Martina

Sailer, Marc Salmon, Manoj Samgarshannan, Lowell Sandell, Ted Scearcy, Nicholas Schultz, David Semersky, Brian Shoemaker, Robert Sicora, Barry Sneeden, Kristi Solberg, Kristin Spargo, Tara Spieker, Marion Stein, John Stutzman, Dana Sullivan, Andrea Swinehart, Mark Tabor, Siddharth Tambe, Michael Tamte, Michael Taylor, Ramish Tehnnadil, Eric Tennessen, Jeff Thompson, Keith Tran, Ka May Tsang, Stella Tseng, Phuong Ton, April Ueland, Ed Valencia, Daniel Van Dyk, Tim Varecka, Angela Wagner, Becky Waller, Kevin Walters, Holly Waters, Tony Watson, Theresa Weimerskirch, Matt Westlund, Dan Whalen, Matt Whaley, Melissa Wiley, Shawn Williams, Joseph Winkels, Mark Woell, Chee Wong, Ryan York, Kim Zabel, Linda Zahrt, Lauren Zeller, Tony Zich, Doug Ziegler

SOURCES

Amphenol and LSI Logic Sources

10Ks, Amphenol 1993–2002.

10Ks, LSI Logic 1993–2002.

"1998 ASIC Market Share: The Photo Finish." Gartner Group's *Dataquest*, 7 June 1999. ASIC-WW-DP-9906.

"2002 Third Quarter Earnings Call." Amphenol Corporation.

Amphenol Corporation, 8K 1997-1-23.

"Amphenol TFC Business Thrives Overseas." *Electronic Buyers' News*, 28 Aug. 1995: 970: 70.

"Amphenol to Disappoint." *Electronic News*, 1 July 1996: 42 (2123): 14.

Annual Reports, Amphenol 1996–2002.

Annual Reports, LSI Logic 1994–2002.

Baljko, Jennifer L. "Another Buy for Amphenol." *Electronics Buyers' News*, 17 Aug. 1998: 1122: 8.

Bubbeo, Daniel. "Feeding an Acquired Taste for Expansion." *Electronic Buyers' News*, 19 Aug. 1996: 1020: E16+.

Clarke, Peter. "LSI Logic Takes to Platform-Based Design with RapidChip." *Semiconductor Business News*, 4 Sept. 2002.

Commscope Inc. 10K 1998-12-31.

Commscope Inc. 10K 1999-12-31.

Commscope Inc. 10K 2001-12-31.

Dunn, D. "LSI Logic Engineers Evolution." *Electronic Buyers' News*, 26 March 2001: 1255: 1.

Dunn, D. "LSI Steps Up Communication Efforts as Q1 Revenue Falls Sharply." *Electronic Buyers' News*, 19 March 2001: 1254: 3.

Fleck, Ken. "A Look at Amphenol." *Electronic News*, 5 May 2001: 44.

Fuhs, Clark, and Chris Ko. "LSI: Accelerated Restructuring Brings in Profitability Window; 'Adjusting' Estimates—Neutral," Fulcrum Global Partners, 24 July 2003.

Gain, Bruce, and Crista Souza. "IBM Gains Share as ASIC Market Shrinks." www.ebnews.com. www.ebnews.com/story/OEG20020403S0023.

Gibson, P. "Liverpudlian Logic." Sept. 1999. *Electronic Business*, 25, 9, pp. 78-84.

Haber, C. "Tough Times Toughen LSI Logic." *Electronic News*, 1999: 45 (2260): 36.

http://bigcharts.marketwatch.com/.

http://busref.lib.umn.edu.

http://busref.lib.umn.edu/tools/compdata.com.

http://edgarscan.pwcglobal.com/servlets/edgarscan.

http://finance.yahoo.com/?u.

http://www.amphenol.com/index.cfm.

http://www.amphenol.com/index.cfm/fuseaction/financial.go/default.cfm.

http://www.amphenol.com/index.cfm/fuseaction/financial.dspReports-/index.cfm.

http://www.bigcharts.com.

http://www.datamonitor.com.

http://www.investors.com.

http://www.kkr.com/about/about.html.

http://www.lsilogic.com.

http://www.lsilogic.com/investors/index.html.

http://www.yahoo.com/Business.

Investext Select Merrill Lynch Capital Markets, 15 Aug. 2003.

Investors Business Daily—Investext Select Analyst Reports—
http://80web6.infotrac.galegroup.com.floyd.lib.umn.ued/itw/info-
mark/0/1/1/purl=rc6_INV?sw_aep=umn_twincities.

Jorgensen, Barbara. "Amphenol RF to Bolster Channel Services."
Electronic Buyers' News, 27 Sept. 1999: 48.

"KKR Officially Buys Amphenol for Nearly $1.5 Billion." *Electronic
Buyers' News*, 26 May 1997: 1059: 18.

Kressler, Alvin, and Carter Driscoll. "LSI: Unveils a New Process
Technology." Freidman Billings Ramsey. 5 Sept. 2002.

Levine, Bernard, and Fred Guinther. "KKR to Buy Most of Amphenol."
Electronic News, 27 Jan. 1997: 43: 2152, pp. 1-2.

Liotta, Bettyann. "Amphenol Executives Jump Ship." *Electronic Buyers'
News*. 7 Oct. 1996: 1027: 6.

"LSI Logic Completes $760 Million Symbios Acquisition." 7 Aug. 1998.
www.lsilogic.com.
www.lsilogic.com/news/financial_news/fr1998007.html.

"LSI Logic Corporation to Outsource Gresham Manufacturing Facility
Ion Implantation to Implant Center, Inc." 20 June 2000.
www.lsilogic.com/news/corporate_news/cr20000620.html.

"LSI Logic Cuts 600 Jobs, Transfers R&D to Oregon from Silicon
Valley." *Semiconductor Business News*. 19 Sept. 2001.

"Molecular Electronics Corp. Launches Joint Product Evaluation with
Amphenol Corporation." 19 Feb. 2003. Article on PR Newswire.

Molex Inc. 10K 1998-12-31.

Molex Inc. 10K 1999-12-31.

Molex Inc. 10K 2001-12-31.

Norman, Diane. "Amphenol to Buy Sine Companies." *Electronic
Buyers' News*, 1 June 1996: 1000: 4.

Reuters.multexinvestor.com; company ranks—size (semiconductor
industry).

Richtmyer, Richard. "Amphenol Corp." *Electronic Buyers' News*, 19 Oct. 1998: 1131: 12.

Scheck, Susan and Waurzyniak, Patrick. "Connectors." *Electronic Buyers' News*, 3 Nov. 1997: 1082: 3C.

Scouras, Ismini. "Amphenol Scouting Acquisitions." *Electronic Buyers' News*, 22 May 2000: 1212.

"Unit Wins 6-Year Contract to Supply Cable for Network." *Wall Street Journal—Eastern Edition*, 24 May 1995: 225 (101): B8.

Vallipuram, Nimal, and Gregory Wowkun. "United States Semiconductors; LSI Logic Corp. Good Cost Control," Dresdner Kleinwort Wasserstein Research. 24 July 2003.

Waurzyniak, Patrick. "Amphenol Posts Record Income." *Electronic Buyers' News*, 21 April 1997: 1054: 12.

Will, Wade. "LSI, Motorola Execs: It's Worse Than We Thought." *Electronic Engineering Times*, 2001: 1155: 1.

Zhao, Zhiping, and Daniel Kranson. "LSI: Will RapidChip Technology Change the Balance of the Competition Away from PLDs?" Bernstein Research Call. 5 Sept. 2002.

SPX and Snap-On Sources

10Ks, Snap-On Incorporated 1994–2002.

10Ks, SPX Corporation 1994–2002.

"Aftermarket Business." 12 Feb. 2000. 110 (2).

Annual Reports, Snap-On Incorporated 1996, 1999–2002.

Annual Reports, SPX Corporation 1996, 1999–2002.

"Bringing Collaboration to Bear." *Infoworld*: 23 (17).

"Case Study of a CEO 'Thinking Quantum.'" *Directors & Boards*, Fall 1998: 23 i1: 37 (6).

Daniels, Eric L. "Snap-On: Still Turning It Around (analyst report)." JP Morgan Securities Inc. 17 Sept. 2002.

"Deals & Deal Makers—Back to the Basics—New Deal Era: Old Economy Wins the Favor of the M&A Crowd." *Wall Street Journal Eastern Edition*, 27 Nov. 2000: C1.

Forbes. 17 July 2000: 85.

http://busref.lib.umn.edu.

http://www.finance.yahoo.com.

http://www.sec.gov.

http://www.snap-on.com.

http://www.spx.com.

Inch, John G., and Elana S. Hordon. "SPX Corp: Focus 1: Premier Company (analyst report)." Merrill Lynch Global Securities Research & Economics Group. 14 June 2002.

"Industrial Machinery & Equipment Manufacturing Profile." Yahoo Finance.com. 16 Oct. 2003.

"Information Week Magazine Recognizes Snap-On Incorporated for Innovation Technology and Organizational Innovation." Yahoo Finance.com. 6 Oct. 2003.

Kahn, Jeremy. "Is Their Screw Loose at Snap-On?" *Fortune*, 24 July 2000: 142 (3).

Kimball, Darren S., and Roger A. Freeman. "Snap-On Incorporated: Despite Problems, Strong Franchise Is Undervalued (analyst report)." Merrill Lynch & Co. 26 Feb. 1999.

Kimball, Darren S., and Roger A. Freeman. "Snap-On Incorporated: Recovery Timetable Stretched Out (analyst report)." Merrill Lynch & Co. 23 Oct. 1998.

Lucas, James C., and Aaron H. Ravenscroft. "Snap-On Incorporated (analyst report)." *Janney Montgomery Scott*, 11 Feb. 2002.

Lucas, James C., and Sally H. Sulcove. "Snap-On Incorporated (analyst report)." *Janney Montgomery Scott*, 23 March 1999.

Martin, Justin. "Another GE Veteran Rides to the Rescue." *Fortune*, 29 Dec. 1997: 136 (12): 282.

Merrill Lynch Analysis. 29 June 2001.

"Moody's Cuts Snap-On Inc. Unsecured Debt." Yahoo Finance.com. 16 Oct. 2003.

Morgan Stanley Snap-On Inc. Analysis, 24 July 2003.

Mullins, R. "Keeping Growth Simple at Snap-On Inc." *The Business Journal Serving Greater Milwaukee*, 3 July 1998.

Olofson, C. "Change Is a Snap." *Fast Company Magazine*, June 2000.

Salamon Brothers Research. 2003.

Salomon Smith Barney Analysis. 18 June 2001.

Snap-On Inc. (ticker: SNA, exchange: New York Stock Exchange). News Release, 28 Dec. 2001.

Standard & Poor's Industrial Surveys. March 2003: 42, 44–45.

Young, Pua K., and Michael Gardiner. "SPX Corp: Outlook Solid; Shares Look Undervalued (analyst report)." Merrill Lynch & Co. 29 Sept. 1999.

Young, Pua K., and Michael Gardiner. "SPX Corp: Solid Start to 2002 on the Way with Healthy March Quarter Gain (analyst report)." Merrill Lynch & Co. 17 April 2002.

Fiserv and Parametric Sources

10Ks, Fiserv 1993, 1995, 1996, 1997, 1998, 1999, 2001, 2002.

10Ks, Parametric 1995, 1996, 1998, 1999, 2001, 2002.

10Q, Fiserv June 2002.

Annual Reports, Fiserv 1999–2002.

Annual Reports, Parametric 2001, 2002.

Christman, Alan. "CIMdata Ranks CAM Software Vendors." CIMdata Inc. http://www.mmsonline.com/articles/0802cad.html.

Day, Martin. "PTC Settlement and Other Issues." CADServer. 31 Jan. 2002.

"The Decline of Parametric Technology." CAD/CAM Publishing. Computer Aided Design Report. 16 Jan. 2002. http://www.tenlinks.com/NEWS/ARTICLES/cad_report/011602–Parametric.htm.

"Fed Vice-Chairman Speaks of Technology Impact in Retail Banking." BankTech. Oct. 2003. http://www.banktech.com/story/BSTeNews/BNK20031014S0003.

Fiserv Company Profile. http://www.cbs.marketwatch.com/tools/quotes/profile.asp?sid=2019-&symb=fisv&siteid=mktw.

"For First Time, Fiserv Stock Finishes Year Down." *Milwaukee Journal Sentinel*, 1 Jan. 2003.

Fung, Amanda. "Fiserv, Bisys, and Jack Henry More Than Weathering Storm." *American Banker*, 16 July 2001: 21.

Gillis, M. Arthur. "Too Many Tech Companies Merge for Wrong Reasons." *American Banker*, 25 Jan. 2002: 16.

"Gloves Off Between PTC & Rand." *CADServer*, 10 Dec. 2002.

Hintze, John. "Fiserv Finds New Business as Consolidation Ends." *Securities Industry News*, 3 Sept. 2001: 7.

http://www.bigcharts.com.

http://www.caddigest.com/subjects/research/select/cadspaghetti_reseller.htm.

http://www.fiserv.com.

http://www.fiservais.com/Services/supdesc.htm.

http://www.ptc.com.

http://www.quicken.com.

http://www.yahoo.com/finance.

Hoover's Inc. Feb. 2003.

Huxley, Mark. "Pro/E Wildfire: Intuitive, Scalable, Parametric Pioneer Adopts Windows-Style Interface." *Cadalyst*, Feb. 2003. http://www.cadalyst.com/reviews/software/cad/0203proe/.

Munster, C. Eugene. "Parametric Technology Corp." Piper Jaffray US Bancorp. 14 Aug. 2002.

"The Net Threat to Banking: Convergence of Services Force Banking Industry to Think About the Box." BankTech. Oct. 2003. http://www.banktech.com/story/BNK20030122S0001.

"Parametric Sales Restatement Tanks Stock." *Boston Business Journal*, 2 Jan. 2003.

"Parametric Technology Corp." International Directory of Company Histories. Vol. 16, St. James Press, 1997. Reproduced in Business and Company Resource Center. http://www.galenet.com.

"Parametric Technology Corp." Notable Corporate Chronologies 3rd Ed. Gale Group, 2001. Reproduced in Business and Company Resource Center. http://www.galenet.com.

Parametric Technology (NASD)–Business Description (http://yahoo.multexinvestor.com).

"PTC Faces Possible Delisting for Filing Delay." *Boston Business Journal*, 17 Jan. 2003.

"PTC Receives 'NDES Show Stopper' Award from CADENCE Magazine." PRNewswire-Comtex. 5 March 2003. http://money.excite.com/jsp/nw/newsheadlinebysymbol.jsp.

"PTC's Pro/Engineer Wildfire Delivers Highest Functionality at Lower Cost Than Competition." PRNewswire-Comtex. 4 Feb. 2003. http://money.excite.com/jsp/nw/newsheadlinebysymbol.jsp.

"Rand Sues PTC." *CAD Digest*, June 2003. http://www.caddigest.com/subjects/pro_engineer/select/grabow-ski_rand_sues.htm.

Reuters. "Update—PTC Posts Narrower 4th Quarter Loss by Cutting Costs." Yahoo Finance. Oct. 2003. http://biz.yahoo.com/rc/031022/tech_ptc_earns_1.html.

Rojas, P. "Banking on More Automation." *The NASDAQ International Magazine*, March/April 2003: 41.

Roth, Andrew. "Fiserv Finds a Low-Tech Edge in Handling Currency." *American Banker*, 4 June 2001: 23.

"Sector Watch: Three Dimensions of the Markets." *USA Today*, 6 Oct. 2003: 12B.

Sidel, Robin and Randell Smith. "Perishing Deal Marks a Trend–Credit Suisse First Boston Sells Stock-Trading Unit to Bank of New York." *The Asian Wall Street Journal*, 9 Jan. 2003.

Standard & Poor's Stock Reports. 22 Feb. 2003.

US Bancorp. 30 July 2002 report.

Vleeschhouwer, Jay. "Merrill Lynch Technical and Design Software." 9 July 2002.

Vleeschhouwer, Jay. "Merrill Lynch Technical and Design Software." 25 Sept. 2002.

Vleeschhouwer, Jay. "Parametric Technology Corp." 16 July 2002.

Weinberger, Joshua. "Parametric Technology: Designed to Lead?" Baseline, The Project Management Center. 17 Jan. 2003.

Campbell's and Dreyer's Sources

10Ks, Campbell's 1994–2002.

10Ks, Dreyer's 1994–2002.

10Ks, General Mills 2002.

10Ks, Kraft Foods, Inc. 2002.

Annual Reports, Campbell's 1993–2003.

Annual Reports, Dreyer's 1993–2003.

"Are Slotting Allowances Legal Under the Antitrust Laws?" *Journal of Public Policy and Marketing*, Spring 1991: 1: 169.

Balakrishnan, S., and B. Wernerfelt. "Technical Change, Competition and Vertical Integration." *Strategic Management Journal*, 7 (186): 347–358.

Ball, Deborah, and Shelly Branch. "Nestlé to Increase Stake in Dreyer's, Take on Unilever in Ice Cream War." *The Wall Street Journal*, 18 June 2002.

Bennett, Elizabeth. "Campbell to Spend $300M to Transform Company." *Business Journal*, 27 July 2001.

"Bowl Game—Inside Campbell's Big Bet: Heating Up Condensed Soup; Battling Progresso; Company Tinkers with an Icon; Nicer Approach to Veggies; Keeping Smiles on Goldfish." *Wall Street Journal*, 31 July 2002: A1.

Branch, Shelly. "Campbell Tries to Stir Its Innovation Pot with Convenience Meals: Hot or Not." *Wall Street Journal*, 16 May 2001: B9.

Business Week. Online company research.

Caltagirone, Stephanie. "Cott Foresees New Clients in Consolidation: U.S. Grocery Retailers." The America's Intelligence Wire. 10 Feb. 2003.

"Campbell Soup Sales Fail to Sizzle." *Foodservice News*, 14 Feb. 2003.

"Campbell's Cooks Up New Strategy." *The Cincinnati Enquirer*, 21 Aug. 2001.

"Campbell's Warns on '02." *CNN Money*, 27 July 2001.

"CEO Conant's Announcement of the 3-Year Strategic Transformation Plan." 23 July 2001. http://philadelphia.bizjournals.com.

"Consolidation Melts Competition." *Frozen Food Age*, Aug. 2002: 1: 44.

"CoolBrands Big Winner in Nestlé/Dreyer's Deal." *Ice Cream Reporter*, 20 July 2003: 16 (8): 1.

"Delivering in the Store." *Frozen Food Age*, July 2002. Supplement, 26.

"Delivering the Goods: Global Consolidation in the Grocery Industry."
Europe, June 2001: 20.

"Dinner Call." *American Demographics*, March 1998: 20 (3): 37.

"Done Deal: Nestlé Acquires Dreyer's." *Refrigerated and Frozen Foods*,
July 2003: 14 (7): 8(1).

"Dreyer's Reports Loss, Cuts Jobs." *Dairy Foods*, 10 Sept. 2003: 104 (9).

"Girl Scouts Benefit from Colossal Cookie Order." http://www.drey-
ers.com.

"The Grocery Supply Chain Freshens Up." *Modern Materials Handling*,
Sept. 2002: 10: 7.

Harrison, J.S. *Strategic Management of Resources and Relationships:
Concepts*. New York: John Wiley & Sons, Inc., 2003

Harvard Business Review. Dreyer's Grand Ice Cream.

Harvard Business Review. Transformation at Campbell Soup
Company.

Hoover's Company Profile Database (American Public Companies.
2003. Hoover's Inc. Austin, TX).

http://finance.yahoo.com.

http://splenda.com/index.jhtml.

http://sweetpoison.com/aspartame-case-histories.html.

http://www.bigcharts.com.

http://www.campbellsoup.com.

http://www.datamonitor.com.

http://www.dreyers.com.

http://www.edgarscan.pwcglobal.com/servlets/edgarscan.

http://www.progressosoup.com.

http://www.quicken.com.

http://www.yahoo.com/business.

Jones, Simon. "The Cold Stuff's Still Cool." *Dairy Industry International*, Aug. 2001: 66 (8): 27.

"Keeping Frozen Is Hard to Do." *Food Logistics*, 15 Nov. 2001: 46: 39.

Kuhn, Mary Ellen. "Coping with Consolidation." *Food Processing*, Aug. 1999: 60 (8): 29.

Labetti, Kristi Sue. "Consolidation Melts Competition." *Frozen Food Age*. Aug. 2002: 51 (1): 44.

"Nestlé… Wraps Up Dreyer's Acquisition." *Dairy Foods*, Aug. 2003: 104 (8) 1.

"Progresso Soup Gets Direct vs. Campbell's in New Ads." *Advertising Age*, Oct. 1998: 69 (42): 8.

"Sales Flat, Prices Up for Top 12 Ice Cream Brands." *Dairy Foods*, Sep. 2001: 102 (9): 20.

Schiffman, Betsy. "Campbell Soup: Nostalgia and Stars." *Business Week*, 11 March 2003.

"Shelf Determination." *Forbes*, 15 April 2002: 9: 131.

"What Campbell's New Chief Needs to Do Now." *Business Week*, 25 June 2001: 3738: 60.

Wherry, Rob. "Ice Cream Wars." *Forbes*, 28 May 2001: 167 (13): 160.

"Who's Minding the Shelves?" *Consumer Report*, Aug. 2000: 8: 8.

Forest Laboratories and IMC Global Sources

10Ks, Forest Laboratories 1992–2004.

10Ks, IMC Global 1993–2004.

"2002 World Agriculture and Fertilizer Situation." IMC Global, Inc. August 2002. http://www.imcglobal.com/general/agoutlook/Review.pdf.

Annual Reports, Forest Laboratories 1992, 1996–2002.

Annual Reports, IMC Global 1996–2002.

Baca, Aaron. "Carlsbad Mine Is Laying Off 74." Bell & Howell Information and Learning Company. 6 Sept. 2003.

"Banking and Insurance, 'Bank Credit and Financial Markets'." China in Brief. 13 July 2000. http://www.china.org.cn/e-china/banking/banking.htm.

Barnhart, Bill. "Investor Concern Fuels Broad Local Sell-Off." *Chicago Tribune*, 26 Oct. 2003.

Berfield, Susan. "A CEO and His Son." *Business Week*, 27 May 2002.

"The Business Week Fifty." *Business Week*, Spring 2002.

Cargill Crop Nutrition. "Applications." Spring 2003: 18. http://www.cargillfertilizer.com.

Dow Jones & Company. "Lexapro Gets FDA Approval Letter." 29 Sept. 2003.

"Drug for Late Stages of Alzheimer's Is Approved." *New York Times* National Desk, 18 Oct. 2003.

Fleming, Jonathan. "The Wall Street Transcript: Questioning Market Leaders for Long-Term Investors." Oxford Bioscience Partners. 26 May 2003.

"Forest Labs Cuts W-L Tie." CNN Money, 12 May 2000. http://money.cnn.com/2000/05/12/companies/celexa.

"Forest Labs Profits More Than Double on Celexa." The Industry Standard. Reuters. 17 July 2001. http://www.thestandard.com/wire/0%2C2231%2C5908%2C00.html.

"Forest Labs' Quarterly Profit Jumps on Celexa Sales." Forbes.com. Reuters. 17 July 2001. http://www.forbes.com/newswire/2002/07/17/rtr664268.html.

Gallagher, Kathleen. "Forest Labs Given Good Bill of Health." JSOnline, 2 June 2001. http://www.jsonline.com/bym/invest/jun01/gallcol03060201a.asp.

Galliard Capital Management. Proprietary Research.

Harrington, Jeff. "Mining for New Markets." *St. Petersburg Times Online*, 24 July 2002.

Hoover's Online. Forest Laboratories, Inc. Quarterly Financials. 2002.

Hoover's Online. IMC Global and Forest Laboratories. 14 Oct. 2003.

http://80-www.mergentonline.com.floyd.lib.umn.edu.

http://www.andrx.com.

http://www.bigcharts.com.

http://www.edgaronline.com.

http://www.fax.com.

http://www.forestlaboratories.com.

http://www.frx.com.

http://www.hoovers.com.

http://www.imcglobal.com.

http://www.lib.umn.edu/cgi-bin/bsp.cgi. Datamonitor Business Reference Center.

http://www.sec.gov.

IMC Global, Inc: Company Profile. Datamonitor. http://www.data-monitor.com.

"IMC Global Reports Reduced 2002 Fourth Quarter Loss from Continuing Operations." PR Newswire. 30 Jan. 2003.

Industry Surveys. 1 Standard and Poor's Corporation. Dec. 2001: 169 (52).

International Directory of Company Histories. "Forest Laboratories, Inc." Vol. 52. St. James Press. 2003.

Joshi, Pradnya. "Success Story Had a Depressing Start for CEO, Son." Newsday.com. 24 June 2002. http://www.newsday.com/business/ny-bzsol242761810jun24.story.

Juvekar, P.J., et. al. Citigroup Smith Barney: *Monthly Chemical Cracker*, 19 May 2003.

King Pharmaceuticals, Inc. Web site. http://www.kingpharm.com.

"Lake Forest, Ill.–Based Phosphate Producer's Net to Grow with Fertilizer." Knight-Ridder Open. 30 Jan. 2003.

Morgan Stanley Stock Reports: Forest Labs. July 16, 2003–Nov. 21, 2003.

"New Hands/Old Head at the Helm of IMC Global." Fertilizer Focus. Sept. 2002. http://www.imcglobal.com/investor/press_releases/2002/pdf/FergusonInterview.pdf: 31–34.

One Source. US Business Browser, Forest Laboratories. 7 Feb. 2003.

One Source. US Business Browser, IMC Global, Inc. 7 Feb. 2003.

OneStop Report. US Business Browser, Forest Laboratories. 7 Feb. 2003.

OneStop Report. US Business Browser, IMC Global Inc. 7 Feb. 2003

"Parent of Mulberry, Fla-Based IMC Phosphates Posts $8.4 Million Loss." Knight-Ridder Open. 7 Feb. 2003.

Prichard, David A. Personal Interview. Vice President of Investor and Corporate Relations. IMC Global. Oct. 7–8, 2003.

Rudnitsky, Howard. "Sardines, Not Whales." *Forbes*, 5 Dec. 1994.

Shook, David. "Forest Labs: No Need for a Mood Enhancer." *Business Week Online*, 29 March 2001.

Shook, David. "Online Extra: Forest Labs: Feeling No Pain." *Business Week Online*, 25 March 2003.

Standard & Poor's Stock Reports: IMC Global and Forest Labs. 13 Sept. 2003.

Stein, Lisa. "New Alzheimer's Drug." *U.S. News and World Report*, 27 Oct. 2003.

"What Went Right 2002." *Fortune*, 18 Dec. 2002.

Goodyear and Ball Sources

10Ks, Ball 1993–2003.

10Ks, Bridgestone 2002.

10Ks, Continental 2002.

10Ks, Goodyear 1995, 1997, 2000, 2001, 2002, 2003.

Aeppel, Timothy. "How Goodyear Blew Its Chance to Capitalize on a Rival's Woes." *Wall Street Journal*, 19 Feb. 2003.

Annual Reports, Ball 2001.

Annual Reports, Goodyear 1996–2001.

"Ball Completed Acquisition, Forms Ball Packaging Europe; Acquisition Expected to Boost Ball's 2003 Results." Financial Times Information. Global News Wire. 19 Dec. 2002.

Ball Corp. 3rd Quarter 2003 press release.

"Ball Reports Sharp 2002 Earnings Improvement; Expects Further Growth in 2003." PRNewswire-FirstCall. www.ball.com. Investor relations site. 29 Jan. 2003.

"Ball to Relocate Atlanta-Area Plastics Office, R&D Operations to Colorado." PRNewswire-FirstCall. www.ball.com. Investor relations site. 9 Dec. 2002.

Big Charts.com's Tire Industry Overview. http://bigcharts.market-watch.com/industry/bigchartscom/focus.asp?bcind_ind=tir&bcind_sid=171604.

CEO Interview: Hoover, David R., Ball Corporation. Wall Street Transcript Corporation. 28 Nov. 2000.

Dawson, Brad. "Alliance Returns Goodyear to No. 1 Spot." *Automotive News*, 8 Feb. 1999: 4.

Davis, Bruce. "China Factor." *Tire Business*, 1 Sept. 2003: 9.

Davis, Bruce. *Tire Business*, 1 April 2002.

Fahey, Jonathan. "Blowout!" *Forbes*, 3 Feb. 2003.

"Fitch Downgrades Goodyear's Unsecured Debt Ratings to B+."
Business Wire, 10 Feb. 2003.

Fung, Jenny. "Ball Still Rolling Along—Ball Corporation." Credit
Suisse First Boston Analyst Report. 12 July 2002.

Gerdel, T.W. "Goodyear Needs Major Repairs." Cleveland.com Web site
Business Section. 23 Feb. 2003: 1–6.

Hodel, Michael, Goodyear Morningstar Analyst Report; Morningstar
Services. 6 Feb. 2003.

http://biz.yahoo.com/fin/l/b/bll.html.

http://biz.yahoo.com/prnews/030306/lath012_1.html.

http://biz.yahoo.com/prnews/030312/law004_1.html.

http://finance.yahoo.com.

http://moneycentral.msn.com.

http://quickstart.clari.net/qs_se/webnews/wed/ct/Agoodyear-job-
cuts.Rgyk_DJG.html.

http://www.ball.com.

http://www.bigcharts.com.

http://www.enterasys.com/solutions/success/trust/goodyear.html.

http://www.goodyear.com.

http://www.marketwatch.com.

"In a Native Tongue, Ball Says 'Can' Do with Commitment to East
Europe." Gale Group, Inc. Business News Publishing. 31 Jan. 2002:
21 (1).

Investor Presentation to Credit Suisse First Boston for Ball
Corporation. Feb. 2003.

Luzadder, Dan. "On the Ball." eWeek. 1 June 2003. Baseline: The
Project Management Center. EBSCOhost.

Maxwell, John C. Beverage Digest Fact Book and The Maxwell Consumer Report, quoted by David B. Yoffie in *Cola Wars Continue: Coke and Pepsi in the Twenty-First Century*. Boston: Harvard Business School Publishing, 2002. 16.

Miller, James P. "Ball Is Preparing to Clean Out Its Corporate Cupboard." *Wall Street Journal*, 24 Feb. 1993.

Miller, James P. "Ball to Acquire Aluminum Can Line from Reynolds in $820 Million Deal." *The Wall Street Journal*, 24 April 1998.

Moore, Miles. "Changing Times; Global Economic Conditions Forge Transformations in Tire Industry." *Rubber and Plastics News*, 30 April 2001.

"Much Ado About Containers." Business News Publishing. *Beverage World*, Jan. 2002: 120: 1.

"On-the-Ball Sourcing at Coors Brewing." Business News Publishing. *Food Engineering*, 74: 1. 15 Jan. 2001.

Scott, Ann. Ball Corp. Investor Relations.

"Tire Business Market Data Book." *Tire Business*, 4 Feb. 2002: 22.

Welch, David. "What Goodyear Got from Its Union." *Business Week*, 20 Oct. 2003: 148.

White, Joseph B. "Goodyear Moves to Cut Capacity, Jobs—U.S. Tire-Making Factory Will Close as Alliance with Sumitomo Is Set." *The Wall Street Journal*, 4 Feb. 1999.

Zielasko, Dave. *Tire Business*, 1 April 2002.

Zielasko, Dave. *Tire Business*, 10 Sept. 2001.

Brown & Brown and Safeco Sources

10Ks, Brown & Brown 1993–2002.

10Ks, Safeco 1993–2002.

Annual Reports, Brown & Brown 1999–2002.

Annual Reports, Safeco 1999–2002.

Banham, Russ. "Safeco's Alignment Strategy." *CIO Insight Magazine*, 1 July 2002.

Benacci, N.C., et. al. "Property and Casualty Industry 2003 Preview." McDonald Investments Inc. 9 July 2003.

Bradford, Michael. "B&B Inc." *Business Insurance*, 22 July 2002: 36 (29).

Carini, Nancy E. "Conning: Agencies on Shaky Ground." National Underwriter Property & Casualty Risk & Benefits Management. 14 Aug. 1995.

Employee Benefit News. 1 Jan. 2003.

Farinella, Michael A. "Squeeze on Independent Agents Tightens, with No End in Sight." Best's Review—Property Casualty Insurance Edition. Aug. 1995.

Hillman, John. "SAFECO Reorganizes, Plans Sale of Life Company." BestWire. 29 Sept. 2003.

http://80-web5.infotrac.galegroup.com.floyd.lib.umn.edu/itw/info-mark/143/214/40483382w5/purl=rc1_INV_0_J4358891&dyn=4!xrn-_6_0_J4358891?sw_aep=umn_twincities.

http://bigcharts.marketwatch.com/intchart.

http://biz.yahoo.com/e/l/b/bro.html.

http://brown-n-brown.com/pages/welcome.asp.

http://finance.yahoo.com.

http://finance.yahoo.com/q/pr?s=SAFC.

http://galenet.galegroup.com/servlet/BCRC?c=2&ste=74&docNum=I2-501300601&ccmp=SAFECO.

http://money.cnn.com.

http://quicken.com/investments/comparison/?symbol=AJG.

http://www.bbinsurance.com.

http://www.bigcharts.com.

http://www.brown-n-brown.com.

http://www.charter-ins.com/industry.htm.

http://www.corporate-ir.net/ireye/ir_site.zhtml?ticker=-
safc&script=2100.

http://www.insurancejournal.com/magazines/west/.

http://www.morningstar.com.

http://www.safeco.com.

http://www.safeco.com/safeco/about/companies.asp.

http://www.safeco.com/safeco/about/employment/ataglance.asp.

http://www.safeco.com/safeco/about/history.asp.

http://www.senate.gov/~banking/conf/grmleach.htm.

http://yahoo.multexinvestor.com/FullDesc.aspx?target=/stocks/quick-
info/companyprofile/fulldescription&ticker=BRO.

Insurance and Technology, May 2002.

Investors' Business Daily—Online.

Niedzielski, Joe. "American States Deal Gives SAFECO Bigger Reach."
National Underwriter/Property Risk & Benefits, 16 June 1997: 1010
(24).

Ruquet, Mark E. "B&B Builds Via M&As After Going Public." *National
Underwriter/Property & Casualty Risk & Benefits*, 1 April 2002: 106
(13).

Shinkle, Kirk. "Buyouts, Efficiency Ensure Steady Gains Here."
Investor's Business Daily. 11 June 2003.

Taleb, Nassim Nicholas. *Fooled by Randomness: The Hidden Role of
Chance in the Markets and in Life*. London; Texere, 2001.

Family Dollar Inc. and Gap Inc. Sources

8K, Gap Inc. 2003.

10Ks, Family Dollar Inc. 1995, 1997–2002.

10Ks, Gap Inc. 1996–2002.

Annual Reports, Family Dollar Inc. 2000, 2001, 2002.

Annual Reports, Gap Inc. 2001.

Baker, Michael, and David Weiner. "Family Dollar Stores Inc." Deutsche Bank. 3 Oct. 2002.

"Bargain Hunters Lift Family Dollar Profit." Reuters. 10 March 2003.

Blumenthal, R. "Dressed for Success: Gap's Got the Goods Again, and a New CEO. Can a Higher Share Price Be Far Behind." *Barron's*.

Carter, Adrienne. "Down But Not Out." *Money*, Sept. 2002: 31 (9): 43.

"Credit Suisse First Boston Equity Research Report." 19 Aug. 2003.

"Credit Suisse First Boston Equity Research Report." 10 Oct. 2003.

Creswell, Julie. "Gap Got Junked, Now What?" *Fortune*, 3 March 2002.

Cuneo, A., and Linnett, R. "Gap Calls on Burnett for Strategic Advice." *Advertising Age*, Dec. 2002: 73: 1

D'Innocenzio, Anne. "Retailers Report Dismal February." Associated Press. *Fortune*, 6 March 2003.

"Family Dollar Eyes Even Faster Openings." *Home Textiles Today*, 18 June 2000: 21 (41): 4.

"Family Dollar Propels 3Q Profits." *Home Textiles Today*, 8 July 2002.

"Family Dollar Value Line." 15 Aug. 2003.

"Gap Bear Stearns Report." 10 Oct. 2003.

"Gap Bear Stearns Report." 23 Oct. 2003.

"Gap February Same Stores Sales Up 8 Percent." Reuters. 6 March 2003.

"Gap Inc. Value Line." 15 Sept. 2003.

"How Competitive Forces Shape Strategy." Harvard Business School, referenced in *Sustaining Competitive Advantage*, Marcus, Alfred. Ch. 2: 4.

http://finance.yahoo.com.

http://www.bananarepublic.com.

http://www.bigcharts.com.

http://www.cbsmarketwatch.com.

http://www.familydollar.com.

http://www.gapinc.com.

http://www.multexinvestor.com.

http://www.oldnavy.com.

http://www.onesource.com.

http://www.onlinepressroom.net/gappr/.

http://www.onlinepressroom.net/gappr/bananarepublic.asp.

http://www.onlinepressroom.net/gappr/oldnavy.asp.

http://www.quicken.com.

http://yahoo.multexinvestor.com/FDO.

Kruger, R.M. "Family Dollar on More Than Store Per Day Opening Pace." Retail Merchandiser. Jan. 2001: 41(1): 13.

Lee, Louise. "Gap Starts Patching Its Holes." *Business Week Online*, 24 Feb. 2003.

Levitan, Lauren. "Gap Appoints Pressler as President, CEO." SG Cowen. 26 Sept. 2002.

Merrick, Amy. "Gap CEO Seeks Holiday Strategy Reversing Slide." *Wall Street Journal*, 24 Sept. 2002.

Merrick, Amy. "Target, Gap, and Kohl's Most Improved 3rd Quarter Earnings." *Wall Street Journal*, 15 Nov. 2002.

Ohmes, Robert F., and Marc Irizarry. "Family Dollar Stores." Morgan & Stanley. 3 Oct. 2002.

Patsuris, P. "Gap's Good Looks Can Be Deceiving." *Forbes*, 6 Feb. 2003.

Peterson, Anne Marie. "Specialty Apparel Retail September Sales Preview; Dockworkers Strike Update." Thomas Weisel Partners. 2 Oct. 2002.

Schlosser, J. "Don't Discount Those Retailers." *Fortune*, 14 Oct. 2002: 146 (7): 254.

Schneidnes, J. "Spring Fashion Awaits Warm Reception at U.S. Stores." Reuters. 14 March 2003.

Stankevich, D. "Dollar Stores Finally Getting Their Due." *Retail Merchandiser*, June 2002: 42 (6): 6.

Stankevich, D. "Family Dollar Makes an Empire Statement. *Retail Merchandiser*, July 2002: 42 (7): 15.

Wee, Heesun. "The Challenge in Store for Gap." *Business Week*, Oct. 2002.

Weinswing, Deborah. "FDO: Fourth Quarter Earnings Review." Salomon Smith Barney. 2 Oct. 2002.

Weinswing, Deborah. "Retailing—Broadlines." Salomon Smith Barney. 12 Sept. 2002.

Wolverton, Troy. "Sears on the Wrong Side of Gap." 7 Feb. 2003. www.thestreet.com.

Yamamoto, D.T. et. al. "Family Dollar Stores, Inc." Wedbush Morgan Securities, Inc. 15 Jan. 2003.

Hasbro and Activision Sources

10Ks, Activision, Inc. 1999, 2002.

10Ks, Hasbro, Inc. 1999, 2001, 2002.

Annual Reports, Activision, Inc. 1996, 1999, 2002, 2003.

Annual Reports, Hasbro, Inc. 2002.

Arner, Faith. "Pass Go and Collect the Job of CEO." *Business Week*, 14 Aug. 2003: 3844: 85, 1c.

Cheng, Andria, Chandra Shobhana, and Greg Wiles. "Retailers Having Worst Holiday Gains in Decades." 24 Dec. 2002. Retrieved from Bloomberg Professional Services.

Ferro, Mario. "Value Line." Hasbro, Inc. 22 Aug. 2003: 1.

Finnigan, David. "A Knock-Down Drag-Out Fight." *Brandweek*, 12 Feb. 2001: 42 (7).

Fortune, 4 March 2002: 145 (5): 149.

http://80-galenet.galegroup.com.

http://bigcharts.com.

http://bloomberg.com.

http://finance.yahoo.com.

http://www.activision.com/en_US/news_article_cc/cc_companyback-ground.html.

http://www.datamonitor.com.

http://www.hasbro.com.

http://www.hoovers.com/activision/—ID__12007—/free-co-fact-sheet.xhtml.

http://www.hoovers.com/activision/—ID__42465—/free-co-fact-sheet.xhtml.

http://www.motleyfool.com.

Jensen, Bill. "Bored Games No More." *Playthings*, July 2000: 98 (7).

Mehta, Stephanie N. "Activision's Novel Restructuring Pays Off in Sales Rise—Debt-for-Equity Swap, Seldom Used by Small Businesses, Keeps Focus on Operations." *Wall Street Journal Eastern Edition*, 15 Nov. 1994: B2.

News Release. Hasbro, Inc. 21 July 2003.

Prior, Molly. "Spinning Tops and Retro Toys Create a Buzz at Toy Fair 2002." *Retailing Today*, 25 Feb. 2002: 41 (4).

"Pushing the Right Buttons at Activision." *Business Week Online*, 13 Dec. 2001. Retrieved from Business Source Premier Database.

"S&P Revises Hasbro's Outlook to Stable from Negative." Reuters. 21 Oct. 2003. Retrieved from CBS Market Watch Web site.

Salkever, Alex. "Playing the Gaming Giants on Wall Street." *Business Week Online*. 13 Dec. 2001. Retrieved from Business Source Premier Database.

Smith, Rebecca. "Activision Plans Charge, Retooling of Its Operations." *Wall Street Journal Easter Edition*, 10 April 2000: 1.

"X-Treme Profits." *Fortune*, 4 March 2004: 145 (n5): 149.

ENDNOTES

Preface

1 The managers were enrolled in programs at the University of Minnesota—either the part-time MBA program at the Carlson School of Management or the part-time Master's of Technology (MOT) program at the Center for Technology Development and Leadership. They were taking a course in strategic management, where I introduced them to classical analytical techniques used in strategy, such as five-force analysis and product positioning. See Alfred A. Marcus, *Management Strategy: Achieving Sustained Competitive Advantage* (New York: McGraw Hill-Irwin, 2005). The managers applied the techniques to pairs of companies prior to analyzing the big winners and losers. The companies they analyzed were: Intel and AMD, Barnes and Noble and Amazon.com, Dell and Gateway, Best Buy and Circuit City, Morgan Stanley and Charles Schwab, Time Warner and Disney, Coke and Pepsi, Monsanto and Dupont, and Wal-Mart and Spartan Foods. See Alfred A. Marcus, *Winning Moves: A Casebook* (Lombard, IL: Marsh Publications, 2005).

I also asked for a review and comparison of other books that claimed to have found the secrets of winning and losing companies. (See Appendix A.)

I used the reports as the jumping-off point for my observations. I looked for recurring themes and coded and grouped common elements.

In the fall of 2004, I validated my findings by having a fresh group of managers analyze 10 new company pairs.

Sector	Winner	Loser
Aerospace/defense	United Tech	Raytheon
Chemicals	Cytec	International Flavors
Computer software	Veritas	Compuware
Food production	Pilgrim's Pride	Tyson
Food and drug	Whole Foods	Winn-Dixie
General merchandisers	Dollar General	Saks
Health care	Omnicare	Magellan
Home equipment	Fortune Brands	Newell Rubbermaid
Motor vehicles and parts	Thor	Exide
Wholesalers diversified	Watsco	Audiovox

These winners were dominant from 1993 to 2003 but not 1992 to 2002. I used a slightly different methodology in choosing the companies. I had 30 reports of about 25 pages on each of these company pairs. The findings were consistent with those of the earlier reports and corroborated the importance of being in a sweet spot and having agility, discipline, and focus.

Chapter 1

1 T. Powell, "Varieties of Competitive Parity," *Strategic Management Journal*, 24, 1 (2003), pp. 61–87. Over a long period, performance converges toward the mean. According to Hawawini, Subramanian, and Verdin, only about 5 percent of firms were able to achieve sustained competitive advantage with respect to an indicator of profitability (return on assets), and only about 2 percent were able to do so with respect to an indicator of stock market performance

(the firm's market value divided by the replacement costs of its assets, or Tobin's q) during the time they did their investigation. See G. Hawawini, V. Subramanian, and P. Verdin, "Is Performance Driven by Industry or Firm-Specific Factors?" Strategic Management Journal, 24, 1 (2003), pp. 1–17.

2   M. Porter, *Competitive Advantage: Creating and Sustaining Superior Performance* (New York: Free Press, 1985), p. 1. Also see R. Wiggins and T. Ruefli, "Sustained Competitive Advantage: Temporal Dynamics and the Incidence and Persistence of Superior Economic Performance," *Organization Science*, 13, 1 (2002), pp. 82–107.

3   A sweet spot is the place on a bat, club, racket, or paddle where a person obtains maximum leverage in hitting a ball. Firms achieve superior performance by creating monopoly or near-monopoly power in such a spot. They strive to be in the right segment or niche in an industry to neutralize pressure from competitors. They counter the behavior of rivals through the erection of barriers to entry via scale and scope economies, experience and learning-curve effects, product differentiation, capital requirements, and so on. See M. Porter, *Competitive Strategy: Techniques for Analyzing Industries and Competitors* (New York: Free Press, 1980); M. Porter, *Competitive Advantage: Creating and Sustaining Superior Performance* (New York: Free Press, 1985).

4   According to Porter, industry structure and market power determine performance.

5   The idea that a firm achieves sustained competitive advantage by possessing rare, hard-to-imitate, valuable, and nonsubstitutable capabilities derives from the resource-based view of the firm. As the name implies, the resource-based view (RBV) is a view rather than a theory, which some have criticized for being tautological and not rigorous in its reasoning. In explaining why some firms consistently outperform others, it offers an "evocative description" rather than a series of logically deduced and tightly related falsifiable propositions. RBV has had nearly 40 years of development, starting with Edith Penrose's 1955 classic, *Theory of the Growth of the Firm*, and culminating in a flurry of attention in the past 15 years. It has been developed to the point where it is close to being the dominant paradigm in strategic management. RBV sees the organization as a combination of resources, capabilities, and competencies. Some of the RBV literature includes the following: E. Penrose, *The Theory of the Growth of the Firm* (Oxford, Basil Blackwell, 1959); R. Amit and P. Schoemaker, "Strategic Assets and Organizational Rent," *Strategic Management Journal*, 14 (1993), pp. 333–346; J.Barney, "Strategic Factor Markets: Expectations, Luck, and Business Strategy," *Management Science*, 32, 10 (1986a), pp. 1231–1241; J. Barney, "Organization Culture: Can It Be a Source of Sustained Competitive Advantage?" *Academy of Management Review*, 11, 3 (1986b), pp. 656–665; J. Barney, *Gaining and Sustaining Competitive Advantage* (Reading, MA. Addison-Wesley; 1997); A. Brumagin, "A Hierarchy of Corporate Resources," *Advances in Strategic Management*, 10A (1994), pp. 81–112; I. Dierickx and K. Cool, "Asset Stock Accumulation and Sustainability of Competitive Advantage," *Management Science*, 35, 12 (1989), pp. 1504–1513. G. McGrath, R. MacMillan, and S. Venkatraman, "Defining and Developing Competence," *Strategic Management Journal*, 16 (1995), pp. 251–275; R. Hall, "A Framework Linking Intangible Resources and Capabilities to Sustainable Competitive Advantage," *Strategic Management Journal*, 14 (1993), pp. 607–618; A. Lado, A. Boyd, and P. Wright, "A Competency-Based Model of Sustainable Competitive Advantage: Toward a Conceptual Integration," *Journal of Management*, 18, 1 (1992), pp. 77–91; R. Nelson and S. Winter, An Evolutionary Theory of Economic Change (Cambridge, MA: Harvard University Press, 1982). R. Reed and R. DeFillippi, "Causal Ambiguity, Barriers to Imitation, and Sustainable Competitive Advantage," *Academy of Management Review*, 5, 1 (1990), pp. 88–102; B. Wernerfelt, "Resource-Based View of the Firm," *Strategic Management Journal*, 5 (1989), pp. 171–180.

6   The criteria used to choose the winning firms which will be the subject of further analysis in this book were as follows: (1) as of January 1, 2002, the winning companies' 10-year, 5-year, 3-year, and 1-year average market return exceeded that of their industry; (2) their 5-year

average market return was double or more than double their industry average; and (3) their 6-month average return, January 1 to June 1 of 2002, also was greater than that of their industry. Nine opposite cases involving losing firms with reverse characteristics are also shown in the table. Excluded from the analysis, but also showing sustained competitive advantage, were Alliant Tech, Southwest, Donaldson, RGS Energy, and Equitable Resources. Chapter 2 details more about how these companies were chosen. See the Wall Street Journal, Feb. 25, 2002, pp. B10–B12.

7 "Taking Risks at Intel: Andy Grove, CEO, Intel Corp." Video, Hedrick Smith, *The View from the Top: Managing Change in the Global Marketplace*, 1994.

8 D. Yoffie and M. Cusumano, "Judo Strategy," *Harvard Business Review*, January–February 1999, p. 74.

9 M. Porter, "How Competitive Forces Shape Strategy," *Harvard Business School Press*, March–April, 1979, p. 137.

10 The organization has to hit the mark between extremes. This is a classic idea that may be derived from the philosophy of Aristotle's Ethics, which emphasized harmony and proportionality among competing inclinations.. Or for a more contemporary example, see Charles O'Reilly and Michael Tushman, "The Ambidextrous Organization, *Harvard Business Review*, April 2004.

11 Although on the whole an unabashed proponent of corporate change, Gary Hamel has it right when he writes that managers should "embrace paradox:" He writes:
"Embrace paradox. The modern corporation is a shrine to a 100-year-old idea: optimization. But… companies must embrace a creed that extends beyond operational excellence and flawless execution. The value of diligence, focus, and exactitude are reinforced every day, in a hundred ways. But where is the reinforcement for strategic variety, widespread experimentation, and rapid resource redeployment? …a company must master the paradox of penny-pinching efficiency on one hand and break-the-rules innovation on the other." See Gary Hamel and Lisa Valikangas, "Zero Trauma—The Essence of Resilience," *Wall Street Journal*, Sept. 16, 2003, p. B2.

12 D. Smith, R. Alexander, and D. Robinson, *Fumbling the Future* (New York: William Morrow, 1988). Its management made a conscious choice to stay out of the PC market, reasoning that PCs were not the company's main competence. Factions in the firm that favored entering the PC market lost out to factions that favored sticking to the company's existing business. Xerox's managers missed an unprecedented opportunity and let other firms carry the ball.

13 J. March, "Exploration and Exploitation in Organizational Learning," *Organization Science* 2 (1991), pp. 71–87.

14 R. Miles and C. Snow, *Organizational Strategy Structure and Process* (New York: McGraw Hill, 1978).

15 M. Baghai, S. Coley, and D. White, *The Alchemy of Growth* (New York: Perseus, 1999).

Chapter 2

1 Every February, the Wall Street Journal publishes a scorecard of 1,000 major U.S. firms whose average compound annual total returns to investors are compared to their peers in 78 industry groups. See http://online.wsj.com/page/0,,2_0812,00.html. The average compound annual total returns include price changes and reinvestments from any dividends or other cash or noncash distributions.

2 See http://online.wsj.com/page/0,,2_0812,00.html.

3 These industries are: aerospace, airlines, auto and parts, banks, biotech, food products, house products durables, insurance property and casualty, oil secondary, pharmaceuticals, toys, and utilities electric. The largest of these industries includes banks with 60 firms and the smallest industries are toys with 4 firms. These industries average 23.7 firms, with an average return of 16.0 percent. The industries that have the most big losers were food products (4 firms out of 18 in the industry) and oil secondary (4 firms out of 21 in the industry). The industry with the most big winners was insurance property and casualty (3 firms out of 32 in the industry).

4 They are broadcasting, computers, communication fixed line, diversified financials, food retail, forest products, healthcare, industrial diversified, medical supplies, oil drilling, publishing, restaurants, retail apparel, securities, soft drinks, and software. The largest of the industries with just big losers is software with 43 firms, and the smallest is forest products with 4. The average number of firms in these industries is 16.9, and the average return is 14.9 percent.

5 These industries are communications technology, containers and packaging, industrial services, retail special, and utilities, gas. The largest of these industries is industrial services with 36 firms, and the smallest is utilities, gas with 7. These industries average 21.4 firms. Their average return is 13.8 percent.

6 These industries are casinos, chemical specialty, electric components, insurance life, pollution control, recreational, retail broad, and semiconductors. The largest of these industries with one big loser and one big winner is semiconductors with 41 firms, and the smallest is pollution control with 4. These industries average 14.4 firms, and their average return is 11.8 percent.

7 Some writers, however, argue that time should not be a factor. Rather, competitive advantage is profit that persists after the efforts of competitors to take it away have been exhausted. Although elegant theoretically, this definition is hard to operationalize. Therefore, big winning is defined in this book as above-average performance over a long-term period in an industry. See J. Barney, 1991 "Firm Resources and Sustained Competitive Advantage," *Journal of Management*, 17, pp. 99–120. Powell points out that performance explanations are "latent" in dependent variables: "5-year profits correspond to executives' tenures and planning horizons, and are conducive to firm-specific, managerial explanations…; longer-term profit rates randomize shorter-term fluctuations, bringing market structures into account[el]; long-term mortality rates yield ecological and institutional theories[el]; and research on long-term change yields theories of cycles, path dependency, and punctuated equilibrium." pp. 62–63.

8 Many researchers rely on outdated SIC codes to determine the industry to which a firm belongs. SIC codes were designed for the manufacturing era and do not adequately take into account the services sector that has taken off. They have an abundance of categories for industrial firms, many of which are no longer relevant. They are not very good at capturing the differences among service firms.

9 It is worth looking further at these exceptions. *Fortune* categorizes Titan as being in the computer and data services industry and competing with such companies as Concord EFS and Fiserv, whereas the *Wall Street Journal* classifies it as being in aerospace and competing with such companies as Boeing and United Technologies. If Titan is considered as part of the aerospace industry as opposed to being in the computer and data service industry, it continues to outperform its industry. *Fortune* categorizes Stanley Works as being in the household and personal products industry and competing with such companies as Procter & Gamble and Estee Lauder, whereas the *Wall Street Journal* classifies it as being in durable household products and competing with such companies as Black & Decker and Snap-On. Even if Stanley Works is put in the Fortune industrial and farm equipment category with Black & Decker and Snap-On, it does not outperform the industry. Fortune has nine airlines, including US Airways Group (officially bankrupt). The airlines saw average declines of 33 percent per year in returns. The *Wall Street Journal* has just five airlines on its list, and US Airways Group is not listed. US Airway Group's presence on the *Fortune* list lowers the hurdle rate for Delta and AMR to outperform the industry. It makes their performance seem better than it

otherwise would be. Fortune has 19 pharmaceuticals on its list, and the *Wall Street Journal* has 20, but just 13 firms overlap on the two lists. The overlapping firms are Merck, Johnson & Johnson, Pfizer, Bristol-Myers Squibb, Pharmacia, Lilly, Schering-Plough, Allergan, Forest Labs, Watson, Barr, King, and Ivax. The *Wall Street Journal* has a separate category for biotech firms, which Fortune does not have. Four of *Fortune's* pharmaceuticals can be found in the biotech category in the *Wall Street Journal* list (Amgen, Genzyme, Chiron, and Biogen). These differences may account for Pharmacia's better performance when compared to the *Fortune* pharmaceutical industry list. *Fortune* has 18 firms in publishing and printing, whereas the *Wall Street Journal* has just 14 firms in a category it calls publishing. The two agree about 10 firms. However, by combining printing with publishing, *Fortune* has a lower hurdle rate for a firm to beat the industry standard. Belo's 2003 performance also is very good. It looks like a 2003 turnaround story. A 15-percent return to investors also helps explain why it exceeded the industry standard. *Fortune* has 12 firms in restaurants, whereas the *Wall Street Journal* has 11companies. Yet they overlap on just six firms. By adding companies like CBRL Group, Jack in the Box, and CKE Restaurants and subtracting the Cheesecake Factory and Ruby Tuesday, *Fortune* has a lower hurdle rate for a firm to surpass to beat the industry standard. Wendy's also does very well in 2003, with an 8-percent return to investors, which helps explain why it outperforms the industry. *Fortune* only includes Hasbro and Mattel under toys, whereas the *Wall Street Journal* adds the gaming companies Electronic Arts and Activision. By excluding these firms, Fortune has a lower hurdle rate for firms to exceed to beat the industry. But it is also true that Mattel does well in 2003, with a 12-percent return to investors, which helps explain why it beats the industry standard. *Fortune* includes the Gap under specialty retailers with 62 other firms, whereas the *Wall Street Journal* puts it in the retail apparel category with 12 other companies. By putting the Gap in this category, *Fortune* has established a lower hurdle for the company to surpass to beat the industry standard. The Gap's good year in 2003, a 12-percent return to investors, also is a factor. Gap will be discussed as a turnaround.

10 In larger industries, there are more subsectors and more opportunities for specialization and segmentation. More new niches can be carved out. In the strategy literature, these subsectors are called industry groups, and there is a great deal of discussion about them.

11 Wall Street responds to your ability to set expectations and meet them. It wants a good account of how your company is going to improve earnings and hold onto them against the inroads of competitors. It reacts to what you reveal about your current and future prospects. Indeed, Geoffrey Moore, the consultant, writes that market cap is nothing more than "a grade on your company's competitive advantage strategy." He goes on to say that "the most straightforward way to raise stock price... is to communicate a... strategy... and follow... (it) up with financial results that demonstrate you are executing... successfully." See G. Moore, *Living on the Faultline: Managing for Shareholder Value in Any Economy* (New York: Harper Business, 2002).

Chapter 4

1   Andrew has written a best-selling book about his ordeal: *The Noonday Demon* (New York: Touchstone, 2001).

2   Forest Labs spent $205 mill on research in 2003, equal to 9.2 percent of revenues, but most of it was used to help identify high potential drugs developed by other companies and to pay for the clinical and pre-clinical studies needed for approval of new products by FDA.

Chapter 6

1   For example, as part of the General Signal acquisition, SPX obtained the Best Power
     Company (BPC), which manufactured uninterrupted power supplies. SPX reduced head-
     count by 25 percent, outsourcing commodity products and revamping 70 percent of the
     product line. These steps improved operating margins and income, but BPC only had the
     fifth best market share in its industry, so SPX sold it for $240 million, double what it previ-
     ously was worth. Other underperforming units that SPX sold were GS Electric, a division of
     its industrial products and systems segment, and Marley Pump, a business acquired with the
     United Dominion acquisition. From 2000 to 2002, it divested nine companies.

2   Fiserv had to be disciplined about the acquisition process. The market for information tech-
     nology products and services within the financial industry was highly competitive.
     Competitors included internal data processing departments, data processing affiliates of
     large companies or large computer hardware manufacturers, independent computer service
     firms, and processing centers owned and operated as user cooperatives. The competition
     intensified because computer hardware vendors encouraged the growth of internal data cen-
     ters. Many of Fiserv's competitors had far greater financial, sales, and marketing resources
     than the company.

3   For example, Fiserv attempted to expand into the human resources arena but deemed the
     business model too different from its core skills and quickly got of this business. Although
     divesture was a costly way to learn a lesson, Fiserv's willingness to experiment and cut back
     on an acquisition it made worked in its favor.

4   Government regulations also affected the company's aerospace unit. A congressional ruling in
     2000 severely restricted what aerospace companies could contract and sell overseas. This rul-
     ing was designed to prevent sensitive technology from falling into the wrong hands.

5   Forest also had a talented marketing and sales force, strong relationships with physicians, and
     key industry contacts to effectively promote the product in the U.S. market after it was
     approved. Forest's ability to market drugs through an established network of sales representa-
     tives and distributors was a plus. Its appeal was based on its sales and marketing strength in
     addition to its proven record of success with the FDA. These qualities made it a preferred
     partner among foreign drug companies seeking to enter the United States.

Chapter 8

1   The three primary nutrients required for plant growth are nitrogen (N); phosphorus (P),
     contained in phosphate rock; and potassium (K), contained in potash. Phosphorus (P2O5)
     plays a key role in the photosynthesis process. Potassium is an important regulator of a
     plant's physiological functions. All these nutrients occur naturally in the soil; however, they
     need to be replaced after crops drain them, and no viable substitutes exist. P and K are also
     mineral supplements used for animal feeds.

Chapter 10

1   In 1992, Snap-On acquired Sun Electric Corporation, which had a leading position in the
     auto analyzer market. In 1994, it bought J.H. Williams Co., which was in the hand tool busi-
     ness. In 1994, it purchased a piece of Alldata Corporation, a vendor of computerized auto
     repair databases. In 1997, Snap-On acquired a 50-percent interest in Thomson Corporation's
     Mitchell Repair Information Division, a provider of car-repair information in print and elec-
     tronic form. In the same year, it bought Brewco Collision Repair System, a manufacturer of
     mechanical collision repair equipment. In 1998, it purchased Hein-Werner Corporation,

another manufacturer of auto collision repair equipment. Snap-On bought firms that made products that competed with its own and firms in its value chain, such as Penske Auto Centers, for which it supplied equipment. There were some exceptions, however. The company also acquired Herramientas Eurotools, S.A., which gave it its first manufacturing presence in Europe. Herramientas was involved in heating, ventilation, and air conditioning; electrical; plumbing; agriculture; and construction. Snap-On also bought Bahco Group AB (Sandvik), one of the world's largest manufacturers of hand tools.

2　In early 1996, IMC merged with the Vigoro Corporation of Chicago. This merger doubled its potash capabilities with new mines in Saskatchewan and Michigan. In 1997, it bought Freeport McMoran's Ag-business.

3　By means of this acquisition, IMC became the world's third-largest producer of salt and soda ash, but it left the company with significant indebtedness.

Chapter 11

1　LSI Logic also had a troubled relationship with subcontractors. It was outsourcing a portion of a production and could not depend on suppliers to meet deadlines or achieve quality.

2　In 2001, less than 50 percent of LSI Logic's sales were in the United States. Twenty-eight percent were in Europe, and 23 percent were in the rest of the world. In 1995, LSI Logic had 12 facilities in the United States and 9 overseas, with a total of $1,148,524 invested in property and equipment. By 1998, it had 21 facilities in the United States and 11 overseas, with $1,480,113 invested in property and equipment.

Chapter 12

1　Safeco acknowledged these risks in its 2002 10K filing: "The process of estimating loss and... reserves involves significant judgment and is complex and imprecise due to the number of variables and assumptions inherent in the estimation process. These variables include the effects on ultimate loss payments of internal factors such as changes in claims handling practices and changes in business mix, as well as external factors such as trends in loss costs, economic inflation, judicial trends, and legislative changes. In addition, certain claims might be paid out over many years, for example, worker's compensation medical costs for severe injuries, and there might be significant lags between the occurrence of an insured event and the time it is actually reported to us, contributing to the variability in estimating ultimate loss payments. Variables such as these affect the reserve process in a variety of ways, and the impacts of many of these variables cannot be directly quantified, particularly on a prospective basis. "

Chapter 13

1　P. Kotler and G. Armstrong, Principles of Marketing (Prentice Hall; Englewood Cliffs, N.J., 1994 ed.) p. 258.

2　In the first chapter, I called this a best value strategy. Perhaps a better designation is a superior value strategy.

3　R. Grant, *Contemporary Strategy Analysis* (Oxford: Blackwell; 4th edition, 2002), p. 121.

4　B. Charkravarthy and V. Kasturi, "Best Buy," Harvard Business School/Strategic Management Research Center University of Minnesota case, 9-598-016, revised October 28, 1967.

5 "Michael Porter on Competitive Strategy," Harvard Business School video, 1988.

6 According to D'Aveni, "competitors... react and maneuver around... price-quality positions (and)... change their relative positions over time..." See R. D'Aveni, *Hypercompetition* (New York: Free Press, 1994), p. 14.

7 A. Slywotzky and D. Morrison, *The Profit Zone* (New York: Three Rivers Press, 2001).

8 See E. Miron, M. Erez, and E. Naveh, "Do Personal Characteristics and Cultural Values That Promote Innovation, Quality, and Efficiency Compete or Complement Each Other?" *Journal of Organizational Behavior*, 25, 2004, pp. 175–199.

9 A. Marcus, Winning Moves

Chapter 14

1 "Safeco CEO Mike McGavick on Leading a Turnaround," *Academy of Management Executive*, August 2004, p. 144.

2 Ibid.

3 Ibid.

4 Ibid.

5 In 2002, the Life & Investments had generated pretax operating earnings of $237 million on revenues of nearly $2 billion. Total assets of this unit were $23.2 billion, and mutual funds assets under management were $4 billion in 2003.

6 Revenue figures.

7 Joann S. Lublin, "SPX Proxy Fight Looms on Bonuses," The Wall Street Journal (Nov. 15, 2004), A6.

8 ibid.

9 Jonathan R. Laing, "Humble Pie," *Barrons*, Nov. 22, 2004, 14.

Appendix A

1 T. Peters and R. Waterman, *In Search of Excellence* (New York: Warner Books, 1982).

2 Students in the Strategic Management of Technology course in the Management of Technology program at the university helped compile these charts.

3 An exception is Derek Abell, who wrote a book about the need for this type of combination in 1992. See Derek F. Abell, *Managing with Dual Strategies: Mastering the Present, Preempting the Future* (New York: Simon & Schuster, 1993); also see Rosabeth Moss Kantor, *Confidence: How Winning and Losing Streaks Begin and End* (New York: Crown Publishing Group, 2004).

4 This book's insights are similar to those advanced here in that the authors advocate a form of discipline after movement to protect the new space occupied. They also advocate using the full leverage of the new position occupied to entirely dominate an opponent.

5 This book might be placed in the focus category because it calls on managers to deepen relations with customers and not to go off on radical new paths. However, it is critical of management lethargy and is based on Slywotzky's earlier work, which called for management movement and agility. Therefore, it has been categorized as belonging in this camp.

6 This book easily could be put in the agility category. It is placed in the discipline and focus category primarily because the authors are discussing how to deepen relationships with existing customers rather than developing relationships with whole new customer classes.

Appendix B

1 See Wiggins and Ruefli (Chapter 1, Footnote 2), who use both ROA and Tobin's q (a stock market indicator) for their analysis.

2 G. Moore, *Living on the Faultline: Managing for Shareholder Value in Any Economy* (New York: Harper Business, 2002).

INDEX

"Great schools have... endeavored to do more than keep up to the respectable standard of a recent past; they have labored to supply the needs of an advancing and exacting world..."

— **Joseph Wharton,** *Entrepreneur and Founder of the Wharton School*

The Wharton School is recognized around the world for its innovative leadership and broad academic strengths across every major discipline and at every level of business education. It is one of four undergraduate and 12 graduate and professional schools of the University of Pennsylvania. Founded in 1881 as the nation's first collegiate business school, Wharton is dedicated to creating the highest value and impact on the practice of business and management worldwide through intellectual leadership and innovation in teaching, research, publishing and service.

Wharton's tradition of innovation includes many firsts—the first business textbooks, the first research center, the MBA in health care management—and continues to innovate with new programs, new learning approaches, and new initiatives. Today Wharton is an interconnected community of students, faculty, and alumni who are shaping global business education, practice, and policy.

Wharton is located in the center of the University of Pennsylvania (Penn) in Philadelphia, the fifth-largest city in the United States. Students and faculty enjoy some of the world's most technologically advanced academic facilities. In the midst of Penn's tree-lined, 269-acre urban campus, Wharton students have access to the full resources of an Ivy League university, including libraries, museums, galleries, athletic facilities, and performance halls. In recent years, Wharton has expanded access to its management education with the addition of Wharton West, a San Francisco academic center, and The Alliance with INSEAD in France, creating a global network.

University of Pennsylvania

www.wharton.upenn.edu

Academic Programs:

Wharton continues to pioneer innovations in education across its leading undergraduate, MBA, executive MBA, doctoral, and executive education programs.

More information about Wharton's academic programs can be found at:
http://www.wharton.upenn.edu/academics

Executive Education:

Wharton Executive Education is committed to offering programs that equip executives with the tools and skills to compete, and meet the challenges inherent in today's corporate environment. With a mix of more than 200 programs, including both open enrollment and custom offerings, a world-class faculty, and educational facilities second to none, Wharton offers leading-edge solutions to close to 10,000 executives annually, worldwide.

For more information and a complete program listing:
execed@wharton.upenn.edu (sub 4033)
215.898.1776 or 800.255.3932 ext. 4033
http://execed.wharton.upenn.edu

Research and Analysis:

Knowledge@Wharton is a unique, free resource that offers the best of business—the latest trends; the latest research on a vast range of business issues; original insights of Wharton faculty; studies, paper and analyses of hundreds of topics and industries. *Knowledge@Wharton* has over 400,000 users from more than 189 countries.

For a free subscription:
http://knowledge.wharton.upenn.edu

For licensing and content information, please contact:
Jamie Hammond,
Associate Marketing Director,
hammondj@wharton.upenn.edu • 215.898.2388

Wharton School Publishing:

Wharton School Publishing is an innovative new player in global publishing, dedicated to providing thoughtful business readers access to practical knowledge and actionable ideas that add impact and value to their professional lives. All titles are approved by a Wharton senior faculty review board to ensure they are relevant, timely, important, empirically based and/or conceptually sound, and implementable.

For author inquiries or information about corporate education and affinity programs, please contact:
Barbara Gydé, Managing Director,
gydeb@wharton.upenn.edu • 215.898.4764

The Wharton School: http://www.wharton.upenn.edu
Executive Education: http://execed.wharton.upenn.edu
Wharton School Publishing: http://whartonsp.com
Knowledge@Wharton: http://knowledge.wharton.upenn.edu

The 86 Percent Solution
Eradicating Poverty Through Profits
BY VIJAY MAHAJAN AND KAMINI BANGA

Most global businesses focus nearly all their efforts on selling to the wealthiest 14% of the world's population. It's getting harder and harder to make a profit that way; these markets are oversaturated, overcompetitive, and declining. *The 86 Percent Solution* shows how you can unleash new growth and profitability by serving the other 86%. Drawing on his unsurpassed insights into marketing in emerging markets, Vijay Mahajan offers detailed strategies and implementation techniques for product design, pricing, packaging, distribution, advertising, and more. You'll discover radically different "rules of engagement" that make emerging markets tick, and how European and Asian companies are already driving billions of dollars in sales there. Mahajan previews the future of emerging markets, showing how to segment income strata, leverage price elasticity, and more. As traditional markets become increasingly unprofitable, emerging markets become your #1 opportunity for growth. With this book, you can act on this historic opportunity—before it's gone forever.

ISBN 0131489070, © 2006, 256 pp., $26.99

Capitalism at the Crossroads
The Unlimited Business Opportunities in Solving the World's Most Difficult Problems
BY STUART L. HART

"Professor Hart is on the leading edge of making sustainability an understandable and useful framework for building business value."
– CHAD HOLLIDAY, Chairman and CEO, DuPont

Capitalism is at a crossroads, facing international terrorism, worldwide environmental change, and an accelerating backlash against globalization. Your company is at a crossroads, too: finding new strategies for profitable growth is now more challenging than it has ever been. Both sets of problems are intimately linked: The best way to recharge growth is to pursue strategies that also solve today's most crucial social and environmental problems. In this book, you'll learn how to identify sustainable products and technologies that can drive new growth; how to market profitably to four billion people who have been bypassed or damaged by globalization; how to build effective new bridges with stakeholders; and much more.

ISBN 0131439871, © 2005, 288 pp., $27.95

An Invitation from the Editors:
Join the
Wharton School Publishing Membership Program

Dear Thoughtful Executive,

We hope that you've discovered valuable ideas in this book, which will help you affect real change in your professional life. Each of our titles is evaluated by the Wharton School Publishing editorial board and earns the Wharton Seal of Approval — ensuring that books are timely, important, conceptually sound and/or empirically based and — key for you — implementable.

We encourage you to join the Wharton School Publishing Membership Program. Registration is simple and free, and you will receive these and other valuable benefits:

- **Access to valuable content** — receive access to additional content, including audio summaries, articles, case studies, chapters of forthcoming books, updates, and appendices.
- **Online savings** — save up to 30% on books purchased everyday at Whartonsp. com by joining the site.
- **Exclusive discounts** — receive a special discount on the Financial Times and FT.com when you join today.
- **Up to the minute information** — subscribe to select Wharton School Publishing newsletters to be the first to learn about new releases, special promotions, author appearances, and events.

Becoming a member is easy; please visit Whartonsp.com and click "Join WSP" today.

Wharton School Publishing welcomes your comments and feedback. Please let us know what interests you, so that we can refer you to an appropriate resource or develop future learning in that area. Your suggestions will help us serve you better.

Sincerely,

Jerry Wind
windj@wharton.upenn.edu

Tim Moore
tim_moore@prenhall.com

Become a member today at Whartonsp.com